Psychology in Search of a Soul

Psychology

in Search of a Soul

Ψ

John W. Drakeford

BROADMAN PRESS • Nashville, Tennessee

DEWEY DECIMAL CLASSIFICATION: 201.6

Library of Congress catalog card number: 64—15096

Printed in the United States of America

To
Robina

who left the purple heather of Scotland
for the golden wattle of Australia and
was willing to follow to the bluebonnets of Texas

Contents

The Psychologist

He takes the saints to pieces,
  And labels all the parts,
He tabulates the secrets
  Of loyal loving hearts.
He probes their selfless passion,
  And shows exactly why
The martyr goes out singing,
  To suffer and to die.
The beatific vision
  That brings them to their knees
He smilingly reduces
  To infant phantasies.
The Freudian unconscious
  Quite easily explains
The splendour of their sorrows,
  The pageant of their pains.
The manifold temptations,
  Wherewith the flesh can vex
The saintly soul, are samples
  Of Oedipus complex
The subtle sex perversion,
  His eagle glance can tell,
That makes their joyous heaven
  The horror of their hell.
His reasoning is perfect,
  His proofs as plain as paint,
He has but one small weakness,
  He cannot make a saint.

G. A. STUDDERT-KENNEDY

And man became a living soul.—GENESIS 2:7

PART ONE

The History and Development of the Search

It has been said that if we don't know where we've been, we won't know where we're going. Psychology, as one of the youngest sciences, has a fascinating but often unrecognized past. In Part One a review is given of the past developments of psychology.

Of particular interest is the "psyche," or soul. Originally the center of attention in the early days of psychology, like a country cousin, it was gradually ignored as psychology entered upon its new sophisticated and scientific status. Psychology of religion is seen as a returning to the historic function and thus is "psychology in search of a soul." The story of the quest in the various avenues of religious experience forms the basis of this book.

The history of the search, personified in the study of psychology of religion, has been a sporadic one. From the unlikely source of the New England revivalist, Jonathan Edwards, came the insightful moment as a man of faith sought, not only for people's salvation, but also critically evaluated the experiences through which they passed.

Many voices were raised in the nineteenth century, but some spoke with such an uncertain sound that at times it seems their words sounded like the laments of Oriental mourners at the funeral bier of the soul. Nevertheless, through it all came gradual development with new gains in methodology and techniques.

The methods themselves show an infinite variety as they are marshaled in the search for cause-effect relationships in examining religious experience.

1

1

The Background of the Search

Damon Runyan (**109**, p. 102)* tells the story of two would-be kidnappers scheming to spirit away a victim known as Bookie Bob. The abductors plan to capitalize on Bookie Bob's concern about his status in the eyes of his "ever-loving" wife. Harry the Horse explains to his fellow conspirator that Bookie Bob will do anything to prevent his wife from learning that people have so little respect for him they will actually hold him for ransom. Harry concludes by saying, "It is what you call psychology." Harry the Horse's rather unacademic definition of psychology is typical of the loose usage of the word so frequently heard. Psychology is a magic word, and its use is not characterized by sharpness of definition.

Words are like children. They grow and in the process change, until at last in full development it is sometimes difficult to find any resemblance to their earlier meanings. Psychology is a good example. It is derived from two Greek words: *psyche,* meaning "soul," and *logos,* meaning "word." Thus, it literally means "the study of the soul." In their observations of personality the Greeks were concerned about the soul, often seen as the breath of life. Observers had noted that at death breathing stopped, and all communication with the individual was cut off. When the last breath was drawn it was felt that the essential element of man had fled from his body. Therefore, the study of the soul was the major task of these prescientific students of personality.

Passing time brought a change in the concept. Psychology had been a part of the over-all discipline of philosophy, but the two branches of study gradually diverged into separate pathways with psychology borrowing more of its methods and techniques from the

---

*Boldface number refers to an item in the numbered bibliography.

2

developing scientific fields. Experimental methods, statistical procedures, and laboratory techniques became increasingly important. Previously, sharply-drawn distinctions between body and soul were abandoned, and it was no longer thought necessary to give attention to the soul. The word "soul" lost its place in the psychologist's vocabulary, as he left to the theologian the task of clarifying the troublesome word.

In the process many psychologists jettisoned all religious concepts as unworthy of psychological consideration. In Gordon Allport's words (5, p. v), "Psychology without a soul became its badge of distinction and pride." Some present-day psychologists feel their fellow workers of an earlier day went too far in their rejection of the soul. Fromm (71, p. 6) states it:

Academic psychology, trying to imitate the natural sciences and laboratory methods of weighing and counting, dealt with everything except the soul. It tried to understand those aspects of man which can be examined in the laboratory and claimed that conscience, value judgments, the knowledge of good and evil are metaphysical concepts, outside the problems of psychology; it was more often concerned with insignificant problems which fitted an alleged scientific method than with devising new methods to study the significant problems of man. Psychology thus became a science lacking its main subject matter, the soul; it was concerned with mechanisms, reaction formations, instincts, but not with the most specifically human phenomena: love, reason, conscience, values. Because the word "soul" has associations which include these higher human powers I use it here.

It should be noted that the psychoanalytic school to which Fromm belongs is not necessarily sympathetic with religious concepts. In many instances practitioners of psychoanalysis are totally opposed to religion, but their protest is against a mechanistic view of man.

One branch of the now scientific psychology has retained its interest in religion. It is known as "psychology of religion." Seeking to apply the techniques of psychology to the study of religion, this branch of psychology might well be called "psychology in search of a soul."

The scientific study of religion has developed in a number of different directions. History of religion delves into the past and aims at a clear understanding of the forms of religion practiced in primitive cultures, tracing their evolution to modern times. Sociology of religion explores the place and influence of religion in society, concerning itself with the interaction of religion with social, economic, and political factors. Marxists have majored on the sociological aspects of religion. *Psychology* of religion more specifically examines the influence of religion on individuals and their adjustment to life. None of these areas is exclusive of the others; there is a constant borrowing from, and reference to, both history and sociology of religion in most writings on the psychology of religion.

The study of psychology of religion has not enjoyed a sustained popularity. After an awakening of interest in the mid-nineteenth century, there was a tapering off, and now has come a strange reluctance to discuss the subject. Allport (5, p. v) in a penetrating analysis of the present situation claims that during the past fifty years religion and sex have reversed their positions in public interest. During the Victorian age William James wrote *The Varieties of Religious Experience,* and his monumental book had only about two pages on the subject of sex. Sex was called "the instinct of love" and was dealt with in a very delicate manner. However, his voluminous work is evidence that he was willing to discuss religious experience in all its aspects. Today, by way of contrast, psychologists and sociologists write with the frankness of a Freud or a Kinsey and discuss the most intimate details of the sex life quite openly. But when they come to speak about religion, psychologists grow strangely silent, and there is comparatively little written about religious experiences from a psychological point of view.

The reluctance to examine religion is hard to understand when it is realized that fully two-thirds of the adults who live in our country regard themselves as religious people, and more people than ever align themselves with some institutionalized form of religion. Moreover, even though not belonging to churches, at least nine out of every ten in our population, by their own report, believe in God. The time is far overdue for attention to be turned to the examination of this vital factor in human experience.

Difficulties Involved in the Study

In an analysis of the status of psychology of religion Clark (34, p. 5) shows that it has never enjoyed the same academic standing as other areas of psychological study. Psychology of religion represents a shotgun wedding of two unlike disciplines. The groom, a bright, young, horn-rimmed science graduate, stands somewhat sheepishly beside a much older, homely spinster, clad in a traditional, old-fashioned wedding dress and smiling sentimentally at the onlookers, as if seeking their approval to bolster her sagging morale.

Psychology, newly aware of its scientific status, is the self-conscious bridegroom. To gain scientific status has not been easy, and there is a lurking suspicion that many members of the scientific fraternity are not altogether happy with this Johnny-come-lately. Consequently, the psychologist increasingly endeavors to use scientific methods in his work, devising experiments and utilizing statistical procedures to validate his conclusions. Coming to the examination of religion, he finds it complex, intangible, and often defying normal experimental procedures, causing him to have a tendency to leave it for more promising fields of investigation.

On the other hand, like a bashful bride, religion has traditions, sentimentality, and a certain naïvete towards life. Students of religion have generally not had a training geared to behavioral research. Most of their studies are carried on in the areas of language, literature, philosophy, and theology. With this background and with little or no training in behavioral research methods, the religious scholar frequently finds it difficult to undertake objective research in psychology of religion. He often finds himself bothered by the threats of irreverent and iconoclastic researchers who fail to appreciate the past and the traditional legacy of religion.

The father standing by, shotgun in hand, is the scientific spirit of the nineteenth century, which had entered upon a crusade to send scientists out to investigate all available phenomena. Motivated by an optimism that all of nature would yield up its secrets to scientific investigation, it deemed nothing sacred, sheltered, or beyond its fierce scrutiny. It was inevitable that religious institutions and experiences should become the focal point of scientific inquiry.

If we take the analogy of the shotgun wedding a little further, the young husband is seen constantly trying to remake his elderly spouse. Nothing about her pleases him. He points out to her that red flannel underwear doesn't really protect against disease which is caused by germs. Strait-laced corsets inhibit her movements and slow up her circulation. A bustle is a strange appendage to be protruding from behind and will not allow her to sit comfortably as she should. Button boots do not really strengthen the ankles, and long sweeping dresses are not hygienic. With his scientific training he considers it his solemn responsibility to give his uneducated wife the benefit of his training and presents reasoned and rational explanations for her sentimental old-fashioned ideas. Moreover, there are so many ways in which she could improve herself, and he floods her with suggestions of new attitudes she should have toward her work.

After examining the early writings in psychology of religion, Uren (**179**, pp. 263-64) concludes there is an unfortunate barrenness about the work done, as it is mainly critical rather than constructive:

READ Conversion has been shown to be an adolescent phenomenon, which is conditioned by training, environment, physical development, and social influences. Far from being unique, conversion is shown to be a perfectly natural psychological phenomenon which can be paralleled in departments of human life other than the religious. It is generally a process of the unification of a fractured self, and involves the sub-conscious factors of the mental life.

The phenomena of religious revivals are explicated in terms of crowd psychology. Psychology asserts that the methods of the revivalist are those of the hypnotist.

The Mystic is explained as a religious person who is an adept in the art of self-hypnosis. He takes into his mystic trance the ideas which he imagines he gets out of it; all these insights and ideas are explained as due to his theological prepossessions and his social education.

Prayer is considered as a genuine psychological method of relaxation and an invaluable means of gaining power and poise. Its subjective effects are many and valuable, but all these valuable effects are due to auto-suggestion. From the standpoint of the psychology of religion, prayer is self-communion which has tonic results.

These, then, are some of the loose generalizations of the American School. It is quite obvious that the general result of psychological investigations with regard to the religious life has been to reduce religion to mere subjectivism.

With the memories of these negative and naturalistic attitudes of psychology of religion in the past still vivid, it is small wonder that devout believers are apprehensive about its future activities.

Psychology and religion do not have to be antagonistic, and both disciplines have been oversensitive about the relationship. Religion, anxious to conserve the values of the past, has been defensive in its attitude towards psychology but really needs its probings and questionings. Ikin (**94**, p. 76) shows that dynamic religion and psychology have similar objectives.

Psychology makes a penetrating analysis and seeks to debunk cant and hypocrisy. Christ did the same as he denounced the hypocrisy of the leaders of his day and poured out his scorn upon their failure to discern the true issues facing men and women. Psychology is opposed to the type of religious fervor which diverts attention from the reality of everyday responsibilities. Christ had a similar attitude as he condemned religious practices such as corban, in which a religionist evaded his normal everyday responsibilities. Psychology is the enemy of rituals which bind people and prevent them from reaching their potential. So was Christ as he broke through such practices as sabbath laws to insist that the welfare of man was more important than mere religious observances.

Even in its theological formulations, psychology may render a service to religion. As far back as 1857 the Rev. Fredrick Temple, who afterwards became the Archbishop of Canterbury, stated the situation very succinctly:

Our theology has been cast in the scholastic mode, that is based on logic. We are in need of, and we are gradually being forced into, a theology based on psychology. The transition, I fear, will not be without much pain. But nothing can prevent it (**94**, p. 9)

In a large measure the transition has taken place, and some of the most incisive theologians of our day have presented the psychological aspects of theological formulations.

On the other hand, religion can make a contribution to psychology. Motivation is a fertile field for study and needs a much more careful investigation. Values and value systems are areas that also demand investigation. Both of these have a vital and peculiar association with religion.

According to Allport (**4**, p. 18), one of the criticisms of psychological investigation of the past is:

Some theories of becoming are based largely upon the behavior of sick and anxious people or upon the antics of captive and desperate rats. Fewer theories have derived from the study of healthy human beings, those who strive not so much to preserve life as to make it worth living. Thus we find today many studies of criminals, few of law-abiders; many of fear, few of courage; more on hostility than on affiliation; much on the blindness in man, little on his vision; much on his past, little on his outreach into the future.

People with religious connections present an opportunity for the study of just these very areas, and psychology cannot afford to ignore these people or the motivating forces in their lives.

Fromm (71, p. 26) feels that religion and psychology have similar goals. The theologian is concerned about the truth of his particular belief, while the psychologist is interested in religion discovering what its effect is upon man and whether it is good or bad for the development of man's powers. Fromm maintains that much psychological research goes into seeking the psychological roots of religion, whereas there should be a greater concern about what religion does to and for people.

It is the conviction of Uren that American psychological investigations have had very little apologetic value and do virtually nothing to confirm the validity of religious experience. The attitude of the past has too often been negative, with the underlying assumption that psychological explanations of religious behavior indicate that God had no part in the activity. The personality of the invesitgator is of primary importance. Uren (179, p. 269-70) does not overstate the situation.

The limitations which belong to the investigator ought to be considered first of all. Many psychologists who confidently treat of the religious life do not know what it is from experience. We are willing to concede to Pratt that the psychologist who is a total stranger to religious sentiments can know as much about religion as a blind man knows about colours, or a non-musical person about music, but, we would add, no more. It is a psychological commonplace that men may be so destitute of certain mental traits themselves, that they may be unable to understand their presence in others. . . . As a matter of fact, the non-religious psychologist does not really know what he is talking about. He certainly knows a number of things about religion, but he does not know what religion is.

Complete objectivity is a commendable goal for all writers, but it is not easy to attain. All too easily the author tips in one direction or the other. As the foregoing statement of Uren shows, the very objectivity can easily represent an attitude of antagonism, because involvement is at the heart of religious experience. The writer of this volume is also frail human flesh, and will have an inquiring but sympathetic attitude toward religion. To some this may represent bias, but it will simply be positive bias rather than the negative bias so frequently found in the past formulations in the field of psychology of religion.

Another difficulty in the study of psychology of religion is the objection of some individuals who feel a psychologist has no right to investigate such an intimate and personal area as an individual's religious experience. An outstanding young man in a seminary class on psychology of religion objected very strongly that the study of the subject was damaging to his faith. Incidentally, this particular young man's faith stood up to the experience remarkably well. However, if a well-educated person experienced qualms at the prospect of the study, it can readily be seen that an unsophisticated individual might easily feel threatened by the experience.

The Soil in Which the Study Grew

Although Americans are descendants of people who left Europe physically, there is a constant returning of Americans culturally to the land of their forebears. Herberg (**82**, p. 30) shows the strange phenomenon of the descendants of migrants from Europe constantly looking back to the land of their forebears. Studies show that while the second-generation migrants are anxious to throw off their older associations, there is a tendency for the next generation to be interested in the culture of their grandparents. Hansen's law expresses it in the statement, "What the son wishes to forget, the grandson wishes to remember." A visitor from abroad in the United States is amazed at the pride with which people recall that their ancestry is Scotch-Irish, English, or something of the sort. Just as interesting is the veneration with which many speak of European educational institutions.

In most of the areas of theological study there is a constant returning to European authorities. Many seminaries require their graduate students to study French and German. The implication is that the best source materials are available in these languages. Similarly, in the study of psychology there is a frequent reference to outstanding European authorities, and names like Freud, Jung, Adler, and Wundt are often encountered.

The situation is far otherwise in the study of psychology of religion, for while there have been occasional contributions from Europe, the United States has been the source of most of the outstanding work. It could be said that the study of psychology of religion is the distinctive American contribution to the total body of theological knowledge. There are a number of reasons why the study of psychology of religion came to birth on American soil. The English

scholar, Uren (**179**, p. 1), has formulated several of these which will
repay attention.

There is much religion in the United States of America.—Although
Uren's book was written in 1928, the passing of time has not in any
way changed the situation. In fact, there is more religion today than
there was in Uren's day. The *1963 Yearbook of American Churches*
shows that for 1961 there was an increase of membership, bringing
membership in churches of the United States to the all-time high of
116,109,929 in 258 bodies. Representing 63.4 per cent of the country's estimated population, this is the highest ratio of church members
in any period of American history.

*America has been, and still is, noted for the number of its religious
sects.*—The number of sizeable denominations in the United States
today has been variously estimated as anything from 236 to 267,
according to the way in which the figure has been arrived at, and
there are numerous peripheral groups that have not been included.
Taking just Baptists, it is noted that there are twenty-eight different
bodies listed in the *1963 Yearbook of American Churches.* These
are diverse and include such groups as the Southern Baptist Convention, the American Baptist Convention, the Christian Unity Baptist
Association, Duck River Association of Baptists, Freewill Baptist,
National Baptist Evangelical Life and Soul Saving Baptist Assembly
of U.S.A., National Primitive Baptist Convention of the U.S.A., Separate Baptists in Christ, Seventh Day Baptists, Two-Seed-in-the-Spirit
Predestinarian Baptists, and United Baptists. The very multiplicity of
types of religious expression offers much possibility for the investigator.

Religion has not become stereotyped in the United States.—In
many countries where there is a state church or a predominant denomination there has been a subtle tendency for this church's type of
government and theology to permeate the surrounding religious
groups. This is particularly so in Roman Catholic countries where
the church is an integral part of the government, inflicting its viewpoint on the total population with a resultant stereotyping of religious
expression. As every American schoolboy knows, one of the characteristics of the American scene has been freedom of religious expression. The early settlers in America came seeking freedom of
religion. It is true that in the early days many of these were unwilling
to grant to people who differed with them the very freedom which

they themselves sought. But freedom of religion became one of the significant foundational concepts of the American scene. Americans can give their allegiance to whatever form of religious expression they care to, and some of these are at times extreme and uninhibited. Even within denominational groupings there is a considerable diversity in church life.

Americans seem to be more willing to talk about their experiences than other people do.—A foreign visitor somewhat jocularly remarked, "Americans seem to be more willing to talk, period." The frank attitude is not confined to discussing religion. It is doubtful whether the interviews used in connection with the Kinsey report could have been carried out in any other part of the world; yet the process was relatively simple in America because of this frankness. Multitudinous surveys are periodically carried out on the population at large, and most people are very co-operative.

Here then are the elements making up the background for the study: First, the new nation, composed of people with an infinite variety of backgrounds and untrammeled by tradition, where religion is popular, diverse in expression, and frankly acknowledged. Second, the people, conditioned to the process of being surveyed and polled as well as very willing to express their opinions. The researcher has an open field before him, and it is certainly small wonder that the study of psychology of religion rapidly took root and matured in America.

Jonathan Edwards, the Great Pioneer

If any one person can be designated as the pioneer in the field of psychology of religion, many will agree with Uren in naming Jonathan Edwards. The role was not conscious, for psychology was not known as a separate discipline in Edwards' day, and he would probably have envisaged himself pre-eminently as a theologian and a preacher. Nevertheless, his systematic observation and analysis of the facts of religious experience give him the place of honor as the pioneer student of psychology of religion.

Jonathan Edwards was born in 1703 and educated at Yale University. At the time of his death in 1758, he was president of the College of New Jersey (now Princeton University). Most of his life was spent as a minister of the Congregational Church of America, from which perspective he witnessed several revivals of religion. The first was the movement known as the Great Awakening. Of it Herberg (**82**, p. 101) says:

It was initiated by a series of sermons which Jonathan Edwards, a profound scholar and theologian, preached at Northampton, Massachusetts, in December 1734. It is still difficult to understand the shattering effect of these sermons, so learned, so carefully prepared, so closely reasoned, so utterly theological. But as the sermons progressed the effects were sensational. Men and women were stirred into violent manifestations of repentance; hundreds were converted and gave fervent testimony of their conversion. The movement spread from New England and New Jersey, where sporadic revivals had already broken out, to New York and Pennsylvania and the other colonies.

The revival movement which was developing strongly caused conflict between the more conservative churches and those preaching the revival message. Much argumentation followed with Charles Chauncy championing the cause of respectability, sobriety, and reason in the Christian life and Jonathan Edwards defending revivalism. A movement of the people, the revival emphasis became the message of the frontier. Richard Niebuhr (**137**, pp. 151-68) states:

The heir of the movement, however, was the Baptist church. . . . Henceforth the Baptists became the exponents of the religion of the frontier in New England. . . . the Baptist church seemed to become the frontier branch of Congregationalism.

Carefully examining the events taking place around him, Edwards wrote about them in 1734 in his book called *A Faithful Narrative of the Surprising Work of God in the Conversion of Many Hundred Souls*. Watching the effects of another revival in 1740, he took up his pen and wrote on the subject under the title of *Some Thoughts Concerning the Present Revival of Religion in New England*.

Edwards is generally remembered because of his famous sermon, "Sinners in the Hands of an Angry God." Considering the circumstances under which the sermon was delivered and the violent reaction which followed, it presents a fascinating psychological study. We can reconstruct the picture and see Edwards, a tall, thin man with a deliberate manner and piercing eyes, as he walked very slowly to his high pulpit where he prepared to address his congregation. His complete sermon manuscript was before him on the pulpit, written out in a tiny booklet with pages three by four inches and stitched together by hand. His main assets were his piercing eyes and his voice, which was a little lanquid with a note of pathos but which he used very effectively with well-placed pauses and great distinctness of pronunciation.

Tradition says, he placed the tiny sermon booklet on the open pulpit Bible, keeping his finger on his place. The writing was so fine and the sermon page so crowded that he followed his own script with some difficulty, particularly on a dark day, for the church had no lighting except the sun. The setting was far removed from the generally accepted idea of a revival meeting with an enthusiastic, shouting preacher, and it is difficult to account for the response. Yet, response there was, as people cried and moaned and shrieked, causing the preacher to pause and fix his eyes upon the bell rope. Only an intimate knowledge of the times could give evidence for evaluating the tremendous results coming from such an unpromising setting.

Sermons are not made to be read; yet even upon reading Edwards' message one can sense the earnestness of the preacher as he "slowly, with implacable slowness, coils a monstrous accusation against mankind" (129, p. 145). The climactic image is of the spider.

The God that holds you over the pit of hell, much as one holds a spider, or some loathsome insect, over the fire, abhors you, and is dreadfully provoked: his wrath towards you burns like fire; he looks upon you as worthy of nothing else, but to be cast into the fire; he is of purer eyes than to bear to have you in his sight; you are ten thousand times more abominable in his eyes than the most hateful venomous serpent is in ours. You have offended him infinitely more than ever a stubborn rebel did his prince: and yet, it is nothing but his hand that holds you from falling into the fire every moment. It is to be ascribed to nothing else, that you did not go to hell the last night; that you was suffered to awake again in this world, after you closed your eyes to sleep. And there is no other reason to be given, why you have not dropped into hell since you arose in the morning, but that God's hand has held you up. There is no other reason to be given why you have not gone to hell, since you have sat here in the house of God, provoking his pure eyes by your sinful wicked manner of attending his solemn worship. Yea, there is nothing else that is to be given as a reason why you do not this very moment drop down into hell (157, II, 10).

Trying to make an evaluation of the utterance, some investigators have come up with strange conclusions. Coleman (37, p. 8) reaches the melancholy conclusion that a "vicious sadism" lay behind Edwards' "fantasy." Other critics are concerned about the image of the spider. As a boy of twelve Edwards had written a masterpiece of microscopic observation in an essay on "The Spider." Some have felt that Edwards was really a potential scientist forced into theology and thus expressing his frustrations. But Edwards used many metaphors, and it was natural that he should return to the figure which had occupied his mind for so long in earlier days.

Thinking of Edwards as the fervent evangelist, it is all too easy to envisage him as an extremist. In many ways he was the great moderate, able to take an objective position and evaluate what was taking place. Miller (**129**, p. 178) shows that in the early days Edwards was busily engaged in contending with Chauncy, the critic of the revival movement, and refuting his accusations. Later, he became concerned with his own followers as many of them were going to extremes and excesses, and he contended against his own people in rebuking unbridled enthusiasm.

Edwards was a man of rare intellectual gifts. Miller (**129**, p. 177) states he made "the most profound exploration of the religious psychology in all American literature." Fay (**60**, p. 46) claims that Edwards anticipated William James by making a psychological study of the varieties of religious experience. Examination of James's work, *The Varieties of Religious Experience,* shows that he was very familiar with the writings of Jonathan Edwards and drew freely from them to illustrate many of his points. Uren (**179**, p. 3) says of Edwards:

He moreover possessed marvellous introspective powers. One hundred and seventy-seven years before Freud, Edwards was seized with the significance of dreams for revealing a concealed inclination repressed from consciousness during the waking life.

Edwards' outstanding work came in 1746 with the publication of *A Treatise Concerning Religious Affections.* It was the first important work on experiential religion ever published in America. Edwards was eminently qualified to write on the subject, having deep religious convictions and being possessed of a discriminating and discerning intellect. In addition to being a minister engaged in church work, he was a careful observer, paying attention to the emotions and sentiments which are commonly associated with the religious life. With pitiless analysis he discriminated between spurious experiences and the genuine, between the incidental and the essential elements in religious experience. In many ways before his time, this great scholar showed a glimmering of what could possibly be done by examining religious experience.

Summary — Rea d

The word "psychology" has had a slow and often tortuous evolution. Originally meaning the study of the soul, developing scientific psychology was happy to forget the idea of the soul. It may be said that psychology of religion is a returning to the historic quest of psychology as it investigates man's experiences of religion and life. Interest has waxed and waned for, despite rising church membership figures, inquiring into religious experience is not welcomed.

Difficulties present themselves in the study. Being two unlike approaches to life, psychology, and religion are not easily united. Moreover, some of the early writings in psychology of religion have been almost invariably negative in their attitudes and findings concerning religion. But the two disciplines can be allied, and some psychologists have seen both psychology and religion as having similar aims. Despite the formulations of earlier writings, this book envisages the possibility of psychology of religion having a certain apologetic value.

Although much of the body of theological knowledge looks back to Europe, psychology of religion is a distinctively American phenomenon. Many features unite to make this so. The amount of religion, number of sects, and willingness to discuss—all make America pre-eminently a field for the study.

The great pioneer Jonathan Edwards is generally thought of as a revivalist preacher but was also a careful investigator of individual religious experience. In many ways before his time he anticipated some of the work done later.

2

Later Developments of the Search

There was a dearth of interest in the study of psychology of religion for over a hundred years. It seemed the pioneer efforts of Jonathan Edwards might have been in vain. Then came the stirrings of scientific interest in the nineteenth century. Karl Marx was formulating his revolutionary social theories, and Charles Darwin was stating his equally controversial concepts of organic evolution. Like a child come of age and leaving home to begin a new life, psychology was now entering upon its own separate existence and breaking from philosophy. Science and theology often found themselves in conflict during this period. But, of all the areas of science, psychology was most likely to conflict with religion as it began to focus its attention upon the mind and personality of man.

It has been said that psychology has a short history but a long past. Although most researchers trace the study back to the ancient Greeks, the founding of Wilhelm Wundt's psychological laboratory at Leipzig in 1879 marked a new era in psychological study. The scientific spirit of the age was making its impact upon the infant discipline, and the developing spirit of inquiry inevitably focused upon religious experience as a factor affecting personality. Psychology of religion entered its heyday, and voices were heard from many directions. Great personalities participated in the drama of its development. The chronology and sequence of their work is not always clear, and there is much overlapping. Acquaintance with some of the personalities helps the student of psychology of religion trace the pathway of its growth.

G. Stanley Hall

After graduating from Williams College, G. Stanley Hall attended Union Theological Seminary in New York City for one year. Following a trip to Germany to study philosophy, he returned to the seminary to take his divinity degree. Apparently Hall's theological views were not always orthodox. He tells us that while at Union Seminary he preached a sermon in the homiletics class and the professor, instead of commenting, knelt and prayed for his soul. His ministerial career was short-lived. After being the preacher in a country church for ten weeks, he answered the call to become professor of Philosophy and English at Antioch College.

The pioneer experimental work in psychology was being done in Germany. Wundt was the towering giant of that day. After the publication of one of Wundt's books, G. Stanley Hall was captivated by the possibilities of psychological study. Entering Harvard University, he worked as tutor, studying with the celebrated William James. In 1878 he completed the first American Ph.D. in psychology. Hall traveled to Germany for further study and lived next door to Fechner, the outstanding experimental psychologist. Hall became Wundt's first American student.

Returning to America, he ultimately assumed the presidency of Clark University and founded the American Psychological Association, being elected as its first president. Kemp (108, p. 74) credits Hall with the establishment of the first genuine psychological laboratory in America in 1883. Throughout his career Hall worked vigorously in a variety of fields. He was one of the first to introduce psychoanalysis to American psychologists by inviting Freud and Jung to lecture at Clark University in 1909. It should be noted that Freud was not impressed with America. He commented, "America is a bad experiment conducted by Providence. At least, I think it must have been Providence. I at least should hate to be held responsible for it."

William James attended those pioneer lectures at Clark University in 1909. Being intrigued both by Freud and his ideas, James invited him up to his summer camp in the Adirondacks. To entertain the distinguished guest, they all went out in the woods and cooked a beefsteak dinner, picnic fashion, over an open fire. That dinner was the awful beginning of Freud's indigestion, according to Barnays, and of his anti-Americanism. "Why they're still savages over there," he grumbled, "they cook their food on heated stones out in the woods!"

On February 5, 1881, in the second of a series of twelve public Harvard lectures, G. Stanley Hall first reported his empirical studies of religion and conversion. Walter Houston Clark (34, p. 207) comments:

The first great student of the psychology of adolescence, G. Stanley Hall, was much ridiculed in 1881 when in a public lecture in Boston he pointed out that this was the most characteristic age for conversions.

The climax of G. Stanley Hall's work came in 1904 with the publication of his book, *Adolescence,* in which he dealt with adolescence and its relationship to other experiences of life. Among these he included religion and education.

In the realm of methodology, the historian Pillsbury credits G. Stanley Hall with the development of the questionnaire as a technique of research. From this start the questionnaire became one of the most widely used instruments in the investigation of psychology of religion. G. Stanley Hall stands as one of the great figures in the field. Of him Kemp (**108,** p. 100) says:

No one can rightfully be called the founder of the psychology of religion, but as much credit is due to G. Stanley Hall as to any one individual, not only for his own efforts, but also for the fact that he was the type of personality that inspired others to take an interest in the field.

Moreover, much of the credit for having emphasized the study of the child in general, and the adolescent period of life in particular, must go to G. Stanley Hall and the school which he created.

Edwin Diller Starbuck — *1899 Psychology of Religion*

Starbuck, who lived from 1866 to 1947, was the writer of the first full-length book on the study of psychology of religion. He studied at Harvard under William James and, while studying with him, tried to interest James in a project calling for the investigation of religious experience. In the preface of Starbuck's book (**168,** p. vii), James tells of his reactions:

Dr. Starbuck, then a student in Harvard University tried to enlist my sympathies in his statistical inquiry into the religious ideas and experiences of the circumambient population. I fear that to his mind I rather damned the whole project with my words of faint praise. . . .

I must say the results amply justify his own confidence in his methods, and that I feel somewhat ashamed at present of the littleness of my own faith.

Starbuck's (**168,** p. 3) basic premise was that "there is no event in the spiritual life which does not occur in accordance with immutable laws." Attempting to discover the laws, he conducted an investigation, using open-ended questionnaires which he called question lists. The questions sought information about the age of conversion, the forces and motives leading to conversion, experiences preceding conversion, the mental and bodily affections accompanying conversion, the feelings following conversion, the character of the new life, and the experiences of those whose religious awakening took the form of a gradual development.

The number of cases used for the study of the conversion age was 1,265 with 192 followed up for a more intensive study of the factors in religious experience. For studying the lines of religious growth, 272 cases were used. In each instance Starbuck made a careful analysis of the response of the subjects. He then painstakingly classified the material before making his generalizations.

Starbuck concluded that the average age of conversion for men was 16.4 years and for women was 14.8 years. The important finding of his writing was that "the spiritual and physical aspects of development in individual instances tend to supplement each other" (168, p. 43). This statement has led some writers to speak of Starbuck's "psychophysical approach." In the introduction to his book, endeavoring to assess the value of his investigation, Starbuck expresses the opinion that psychology will contribute to religion by leading to greater wisdom in religious education.

Expanding his generalizations, Starbuck almost becomes a preacher on some topics. An example is his conclusion that there are three important precepts for the developing individual (168, p. 415):

1. *In childhood, conform.*—The child learns by accepting and learning obedience to the cultural patterns of its society.

2. *In youth, be thyself.*—The youth must learn to develop his own individuality and to discover himself as a person.

3. *In maturity, lose thyself.*—Here Starbuck claims the only successful way to live is to lose one's self in a great enterprise of helpfulness and service to one's fellows.

Starbuck's work represented a magnificent contribution to the field of the study of psychology of religion, but there are many criticisms. One is that he tried to cover too much. Strangely enough, there are other critics who dislike his preoccupation with the phenomenon of conversion. Another criticism is his small number of cases which were not representative enough of the various religious backgrounds and stations of life. A shortcoming seen by some is that Starbuck accepted statements uncritically. Among his cases six people said they were perfect. Apparently Starbuck accepted this somewhat overvalued estimate of their lives. A final criticism by some is that Starbuck seems to imply adolescence is the cause of conversion.

George Albert Coe

George Albert Coe spent a lifetime investigating the psychology of religion and wrote the book, *The Spiritual Life*. Starbuck had said, "Much depends on temperament." Coe set about to discover just how much.

Coe made an intensive study of seventy-seven persons who were healthy in mind and body and who had positive moral and religious training. He constructed a list of questions, much like the modern projective techniques, aimed at revealing personality patterns as well as facts about the respondents. Following the answering of the questions, he cross-examined the subjects, then interviewed their friends and acquaintances to verify the answers. He rounded out his methodology by using hypnotism, in an effort to discover the subject's suggestibility, and concluded suggestibility was high in people expecting and experiencing striking conversions. However, as Johnson points out, Coe did not try to indicate that this either explained conversion or proved that the experiences in conversion were mere mechanical events.

Coe's work is of value for several reasons. While investigations of later men like Jung have given us better classifications of temperament, Coe was responsible for making an early emphasis on its importance. He also refined the use of the questionnaire, supplementing it with personal interviews and discussing the answers with subjects' friends and acquaintances. He further emphasized experimentation by using hypnosis as a tool in research. However, most authorities feel that Coe's sample was not representative enough for valid conclusions.

William James

Just one year after the appearance of Coe's book, Professor William James of Harvard delivered the Gifford Lectures at Edinburgh University. William James was one of the great figures on the American scene. He had been invited to go to Edinburgh in 1901 but the previous summer, while on vacation, lost his way in the woods. The strain and exposure damaged his heart, and he was forced to postpone his lectures for a year. During this period William James had time to reflect on the subject, and the enforced retirement may have contributed to the quality of the lectures he ultimately delivered. The lectures were published in 1902 under the title of *The Varieties of Religious Experience*. It is one of the most fascinating books ever written on the subject.

Although Uren says James was not a professing Christian, Kaltenborn speaks of him as a man of great spiritual insight. He had an excellent preparation for his work, being a keen student of philosophy and psychology, with a remarkable understanding of human beings and having a fine literary style. William James' brother, Henry, was a novelist, and it has been said that James wrote psychology like a novelist, while his brother wrote novels like a psychologist. The material James used was in a large measure derived from recorded cases. Many of the cases were of extreme religious belief and behavior. James (**97**, p. 6) says:

We must make search rather for the original experiences which were the pattern-setters to all this mass of suggested feeling and imitated conduct. These experiences we can only find in individuals for whom religion exists not as a dull habit, but as an acute fever rather.

Two suggestive chapters on conversion drew heavily on the store of data and knowledge collected by his former pupil, Starbuck. James's apathy toward Starbuck's investigation of psychology of religion has been previously noted. In this case the student inspired his teacher, who then became the outstanding figure in the field.

James used many concrete illustrations in his book, and some were of the intense types of religious behavior. The following extract from *The Varieties of Religious Experience* is not typical but shows the somewhat unorthodox religious motivation that attracted James (**97**, p. 471):

Robert Lyde, an English sailor, along with an English boy, being prisoners on a French ship in 1689, set upon the crew, of seven Frenchmen, killed two, made the other five prisoners, and brought home the ship. Lyde thus describes how in this feat he found his God a very present help in time of trouble:—

"With the assistance of God I kept my feet when the three and one more did strive to throw me down. Feeling the Frenchman which hung about my middle hang very heavy, I said to the boy, 'Go round the binnacle, and knock down that man that hangeth on my back.' So the boy did strike him one blow on the head which made him fall. . . . Then I looked about for a marlin spike or anything else to strike them withal. But seeing nothing, I said, 'Lord! what shall I do?' Then casting up my eye upon my left side, and seeing a marlin spike hanging, I jerked my right arm and took hold, and struck the point four times about a quarter of an inch deep into the skull of that man that had hold of my left arm. [One of the Frenchmen then hauled the marlin spike away from him.] But through God's wonderful providence! it either fell out of his hand, or else he threw it down, and at this time the Almighty God gave me strength enough to take one man in one hand, and throw at the other's head: and looking about again to see anything to strike them withal, but seeing nothing, I said, 'Lord! what shall I do now?' And then it pleased God to put me in mind of my knife in my pocket. And although two of the men had hold of my right arm, yet God Almighty strengthened me so that I put my right hand into my right pocket, drew out the knife and sheath, . . . put it between my legs and drew it out, and then cut the man's throat with it that had his back to my breast: and he immediately dropt down, and scarce ever stirred after."—I have slightly abridged Lyde's narrative.

Concerned about the centrality of feeling in religious experience, James's pragmatic philosophy is constantly in the background of his thinking. Pragmatic has been defined as: "The true is that which works well on the whole." What people's religion did to them was of the greatest importance to James. He was far more concerned with the outward manifestations of religious experience than with inner feelings. With scant regard for the origins of religion, he displayed great interest in the activity resulting from it. "Fruits, not roots" has been seen as a description of his basic concept. One of his most illuminating phrases was, "That is truth which works" (**105**, p. 48).

An illuminating evaluation of William James comes from the pen of one of his students, H. V. Kaltenborn, later to become the famous news commentator. Of him Kaltenborn (**105**, p. 47) says, "He was probably the most genuinely open-minded person I have ever met." Kaltenborn (**105**, p. 48) illustrates by recounting that when a famous spiritualist medium named Eusapia Palladino was in the public eye, James, anxious to investigate her theories of the spirit world, invited her to Cambridge. At a controlled seance the German psychologist, Hugo Münsterberg, who was teaching at Harvard at that time, caught her in the act of ringing a bell with her naked toes. As a result, a

jingle was heard around the campus of the famous university. It
went:

> Eenie, meenie, minie, moe,
> Catch Eusapia by the toe,
> If she hollers, that will show
> James's doctrines are not so.

Even the credulity displayed in the incident was apparently typical
of the open-mindedness of William James.

There have been many criticisms leveled at William James's famous
book, the main one being that it is founded on exceptions. Uren
(**179**, p. 72) says, /"One rises from the perusal of this fascinating
volume with the impression that none other than the extremely vicious
or the extremely neurotic can have a religious experience which is
worth notice."

In justification of William James, it may be said that he sees the
abnormal as the exaggeration of the normal and conceives the possibility of seeing mental mechanisms elaborated, for a closer examination than was possible in their normal state. It must be acknowledged
that William James sees little value in the intellectual aspects of religion. Nevertheless, he still remains a giant, and the words contained
in a letter of thanks written to Kaltenborn (**105**, p. 49) so many
years ago give a measure of James's true stature: "I have tried all
my life to be good, but have only succeeded in becoming great."

More Recent Developments

The development of the study of psychology of religion has been
very uneven. After James's great work, there came a spate of other
volumes, and then interest died away. Robert Thouless' *An Introduction to the Psychology of Religion* was published in 1923. The influence of Freud is obvious with one chapter on the "conscious" and
another on the "unconscious." MacDougall's instinct theory of motivation is seen in the chapters on instinct, sex instinct and religion,
and herd instinct and religion. The book has an attraction for the
scholar in these reflections of the psychological emphases of the day.
Over thirty years old, it has recently been reprinted in a soft cover,
and is still one of the best books on the subject.

In 1929, Elmer T. Clark reported his extensive research on conversion in the book, *The Psychology of Religious Awakening*. Clark

tried to compare the results of Starbuck's research in religious awakening with his own carried out in the twenties. Another significant volume is *The Psychology of Christian Personality* by Ernest M. Ligon. It is a study of the religious life taken from the Sermon on the Mount. Ernest Ligon has been in the forefront of research in religious experience, and is presently the leader of the "Character Research Project." The most recent development of his thought about research is found in his *Dimensions of Character*.

Anton T. Boisen broke a new and different pathway in psychology of religion and helped to develop a revolutionary concept in theological education. Boisen had studied at Union Theological Seminary, specializing in the field of psychology of religion. As the result of an emotional illness he spent some time as a patient in a mental hospital. Compelled to remain after his recovery, his careful observations led him to conclude that in many forms of mental illness there were religious rather than medical problems, and he determined to give his life to helping the mentally ill.

Five years later, after much study and many discouraging experiences, Boisen was appointed chaplain of the Worcester State Hospital in Massachusetts. He became the first minister ever to hold such a position. The unique feature of Boisen's work was in introducing theological students to the work of the mental hospital. The hospital director, Dr. William B. Bryan, was the decisive personality. When Boisen sought permission to introduce theological students to the work of the hospital, Bryan responded he would gladly open the hospital doors to a horse doctor if it would help his patients. At first they worked as attendants or aids, and in time the program developed into clinical pastoral education. Concerned about the patient's needs, Boisen also edited a hymnal he felt would be an adjunct to both worship and the recovery of the patient.

In the field of literature Boisen's best known work is *The Exploration of the Inner World*. It is a remarkable book in many ways. Boisen opens by frankly recounting his own emotional difficulties in hospitalization. He then tries to trace the development of others who have had a similar experience. With remarkable facility he discusses patients hospitalized at the same time as himself and draws into the discussion George Fox, John Bunyan, Swedenborg, Jesus, and Paul. For Boisen it is a simple matter to compare Albert W., whom he met in the hospital, with George Fox, the founder of the Quaker movement. Altogether it is a stimulating, thought-provoking, and significant writing.

Boisen has been called "the father of clinical pastoral education" which has now spread across the nation and represents an effort to unite the insights of both psychology and religion. Boisen (21, p. 250) describes the birth of the idea:

I had . . . watched with interest the medical internes who came to the hospital to work under guidance as part of their medical training. I had seen how real, how vital, such instruction became as they and their teachers dealt together with the actual raw material of life, and I had become convinced that the theological student might well spend less time with his books and more with the human documents found in a mental hospital. I had become convinced that clinical experience should be just as important to the man who is to be charged with the cure of souls as it is to the man who is to care for the bodies of men.

In clinical pastoral education the student learns to work with other professionals—doctors, nurses, dietitians, physiotherapists, and social workers, gaining insight into their work and coming to see himself as a member of the "healing team." Supervision is an essential feature of clinical pastoral education, with the trainee working under the supervision of a chaplain supervisor. Reports of his contacts are written up and discussed with the supervisor. There is a three-fold outcome as the trainee discovers himself, learns to work in an interdisciplinary relationship, and gains skills in helping others.

The fascinating story of the evolution of the whole pastoral care movement has been written by Charles Kemp in *Physicians of the Soul*. As an active teacher in the field, after years of practical church work, Kemp has emphasized the relationship of the guidance movement to the work of the pastor, as is shown in his book *The Pastor and Vocational Counseling*.

Much of the newer writing on psychology of religion has laid a stronger emphasis on the study of personality. Gordon W. Allport, well known for his outstanding writings on the subject of personality, contributed a definite work to the field in *The Individual and His Religion*. Paul E. Johnson has written *Personality and Religion* and *Psychology of Religion,* among other works. Wayne E. Oates has been responsible for a whole series of helpful books on the subject, including *Religious Factors in Mental Illness* and *Religious Dimensions of Personality*.

O. Hobart Mowrer, already accepted for his wide accomplishments in psychology, has caused a stir in the psychological world with his work *he Crisis in Psychiatry and Religion.* The book has come out st ̣gly in defense of the orthodox religious position with regard to ̣n. However, Mowrer claims, he has been left straddling the fence between the religious and psychological world because of his rather unorthodox views in other areas of religious conviction. Walter Houston Clark's *Psychology of Religion* is probably the definitive introductory work in the field.

The steady trickle of books seeking to relate psychology to religion, or vice versa, has grown to a flood. In 1961 the magazine, *Pastoral Psychology,* listed a bibliography for the year of some 236 books which were related in some way to psychology and religion. *Pastoral Psychology* itself, with its firmly established reputation and large circulation, stands as a monument to the ever-growing interest in the relationships of psychology and religion.

Summary

Although a thorough examination of the literature in the field has not been possible, an attempt has been made to look at some of the great writings, with particular emphasis upon those of the early days. The objective has been to try and isolate trends obvious with passing time.

Psychology of religion has been seen as a part of the development of the over-all field of psychology, which was influenced by the scientific spirit of the late nineteenth and early twentieth centuries. G. Stanley Hall comes in the van as with tireless energy he involved himself in so many pioneering enterprises, devised means of research, and focused attention on childhood adolescence. The first full-length book on psychology of religion came from Starbuck and gave attention to conversion, distinguishing between gradual and sudden experiences and establishing age averages which are still used today. A great leader in the field of religious education, George Albert Coe, made a striking advance in research technique by hypnotizing his subjects as a part of his investigation. The giant of them all, William James, whose name was already established as an authority in the fields of psychology and philosophy, by brilliance of mind and literary ability called attention to the field with his *Varieties of Religious Experience.*

In this all too brief sketch of the high lights of the history of the study of psychology of religion, it will be seen that the interest ebbs and flows and is in a constant state of flux and change. However, the research which is being carried on and the significant new books which are being published, plus the ever-growing interest in clinical pastoral education, all serve to indicate that at least one branch of psychology is returning to its historic role and is in search of a soul.

3

The Techniques Used in the Search

In two chapters of his book, *Introduction to Research,* Hillway draws an analogy between the work of the scholar and that of the detective. Hillway (**84,** p. 57) summarizes by saying:

The successful scholar must be just as painstaking in his investigations and just as precise in his methods as a detective engaged in the search for clues leading to the solution of a crime or a district attorney engaged in prosecuting a criminal in the courts. What the scholar seeks—as the detective or the attorney does—is evidence of every kind that can be shown logically to be linked in a cause-and-effect relationship with the problem or question under consideration.

Like the detective, the scholar often encounters problems in isolating causal relationships. Students of psychology of religion have found particular difficulty at this point. They have had to either borrow techniques from other disciplines or occasionally devise some special methods of their own in their search for the elusive soul.

As one of the youngest disciplines in the modern sense, psychology has struggled for the right to be called a science. It has accepted the aims of science, which Allport sees as: (1) understanding, (2) prediction, and (3) control. Application of these aims to the physical science is relatively easy, but it is more difficult in the behavioral sciences. An excellent example of applying the aims to a social science situation is seen in the work of Sheldon and Eleanor Glueck (**75**) on crime and delinquency. The Gluecks aimed first of all at understanding. They examined the cases of thousands of delinquents, seeking to discover the causes of their delinquency. They then moved to prediction and developed prediction tables, by which they could examine factors in a young person's life and determine with a high degree of accuracy whether or not he would become a criminal or a delinquent. The next move was control. The Gluecks maintained that if two of the five "highly decisive" factors in delinquency could be altered, the chances of delinquency could be reduced. Thus research, which might at first have seemed to be largely academic as it sought for understanding, had a final practical outcome in control.

Munn (**134**, p. 20) claims that the scientific status of psychology rests on its methods rather than its subject matter. Scientific method itself has grown through a process of trial and error over a long period of time, as investigators have sought ways to discern cause-effect relationships. The development has taken place mainly in the physical sciences. Thus, it is apparently far removed from either psychology or religion. But scientific principles have many applications, and though originally used in the physical sciences they can often be adapted and utilized by the behavioral scientist. Although scientific method may seem a dry and uninteresting subject, some of the experiences which have taken place in its formulation have been as full of drama and suspense as a mystery story.

Ignaz Philipp Semmelweis (1818-1865) lived in a day when surgeons wore bloodstained frock coats to the operating room and wiped their scalpels on their coat sleeves. Becoming concerned about the high mortality rate among women in childbirth, Semmelweis tried to discover the cause of "childbirth fever." Comparing two clinics in the same hospital he discovered a remarkable difference in the number of deaths. The first clinic had a mortality rate which was three or four times that of the second clinic. His biographer, Morton Thompson (**174**, p. 199), describes the investigator's search for a cause for the high mortality rate:

He worked harder. In the evenings he read whatever work on obstetrics he could find. He consulted the greatest authorities. He explored overcrowding as a possible cause. And found that the safe Second Clinic was more overcrowded than the deadly First. A week later he assembled all his research on the depression natural to unmarried mothers. The cause of greater mortality was not here. The same types of patients were in both the First and Second Clinics. There were as many unmarried mothers in one division as the other. He made a study of medical treatment. He found that it was the same in both clinics. The laundry was the same. The ventilation was the same. The same caterer supplied identical diets to both clinics. Patients rose after labor at the same interval in either clinic. The First Division continued to suffer three and four times as many deaths from childbirth fever as the Second.

After long consideration Semmelweis at last discovered a difference. The medical students attending women in the first clinic went straight from the dissecting room where they had been working over cadavers to examine women in the clinic. He concluded that infection was being carried on the students' hands and developed his now famous idea, that all must wash their hands and become aseptic before examining patients in the clinic. Finally, he was able to work in a hospital where all the physicians and nursing staff were scrupulously careful in their hygiene, thus virtually abolishing childbirth fever from the clinic.

Another example of experimental method was the work of Walter Reed, for whom the Army Hospital in Washington, D. C., was named. Speculation was rife about the transmission of yellow fever. Going to Cuba to investigate, Walter Reed met Carlos J. Finlay who had been trying for many years to convince people that yellow fever was spread by the female *Aëdes aegypti,* a mosquito living in and around human habitations. Finlay had experimented, studying the life cycle of the mosquito, and felt convinced it was the culprit.

To prove his theories Finlay conducted experiments on human beings, using homegrown mosquitoes that had bitten yellow fever victims, but for some reason only sixteen of those bitten contracted what Finlay thought was yellow fever. For nineteen years the whole scientific world had rejected his findings. Reed, although interested in the mosquito theory, could not accept the doctor's experiments as proof, since Finlay's volunteers all had opportunity to contract the disease from sources other than his experimental mosquitoes.

Reed had an ever-growing conviction that the mosquito was the cause, but the theory was very much criticized. According to Ralph Hill (**83**, p. 73), the *Washington Post,* November 2, 1900, said:

Of all the silly and nonsensical rigmarole about Yellow Fever that yet has found its way into print—and there has been enough of it to load a fleet—the silliest beyond compare is to be found in the mosquito hypothesis.

The doctor realized that to prove his point he would have to set up an experimental situation giving positive proof that the *Aëdes aegypti* was causing the trouble.

In the year 1900, three groups of volunteers were housed in separate quarters built by the army engineers. The Infected Clothing Building was some eighty yards away from the others, poorly ventilated but protected from mosquitoes. Into it were put articles used by yellow fever patients—sheets, blankets, clothing, eating and drinking utensils. Here the aim was to discover if a germ transmitted the disease. The Mosquito Building was screened but designed to allow the passage of fresh air. The volunteers were bitten by infected *Aëdes aegypti* mosquitoes.

A section of the second building housed the third group. Thoroughly screened, the inhabitants could not be bitten by mosquitoes or infected by germs from the clothing and, thus, constituted a control group.

In due course, the men in the Mosquito Building contracted the disease while the others remained in good health. It was concluded that the cause-effect relationship of the bite of the *Aëdes aegypti* and yellow fever had been shown.

Examining the two experiments, it will be seen that they were both designed to find the one cause-effect relationship, but their work was complicated by a multiplicity of possible causes. In experimental method the investigator tries to keep all factors constant except one.

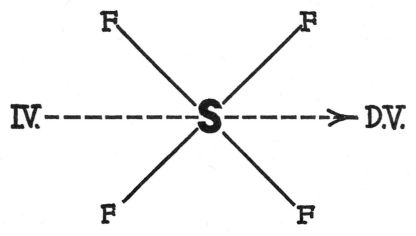

In the above diagram of experimental method, all the factors (F) are kept constant in the situation (S) except the independent variable (I.V.). Changes in the independent variable bring some predictable change in the dependent variable (D.V.). In Semmelweis' example the factors are the same in both cases, including overcrowding, the unmarried state, types of patients, food, laundry, and treatment. The independent variable was the coming into the clinic directly from the dissection of bodies to care for women in the first clinic. Semmelweis postulated germs were carried on unwashed hands. This became the independent variable which was changed, and the dependent variable was the reduction in the number of deaths.

An important consideration in isolating the causal factor is the control group. In Reed's experiment he had three groups: one with infected clothing, another with mosquitoes, and a control group. Allport insists upon the necessity of a control group, and it has a bearing on investigation in psychology of religion. Applying research methods to the behavioral sciences, Allport discusses the measurement of prejudice. Measurement of an attitude is even closer to the study of psychology of religion than the previous examples, and Allport's exposition of method is relevant. After discussing a program aimed at the reduction of prejudice, Allport (6, pp. 481-82) states the case:

The ideal essentials for evaluation research are three in number: (1) There must be first an identifiable program to be evaluated (a course of instruction, a law, a moving picture, a new type of contact between groups). This factor is called the *independent variable.* (2) There must be some measurable indices of change. Attitude scales might be administered before and after the experience, or interviews conducted, or indices of tension within the community computed (for example, the number of group conflicts reported to the police). Such yardsticks are known as the *dependent variable.* (3) Less vital, but still important, is the use of control groups. When the independent variable is applied we should like to prove that the measured change is unquestionably a result of this fact. We can do so best if we have a control group of people (matched for age, intelligence, status) who are not submitted to the impact of the independent variable. If they too (for some mysterious reason) show an equivalent amount of change, then we *cannot* conclude that it was our independent variable that was effective but rather that some other influence was reaching both groups.

Investigators do not always recognize the necessity of a control group, and it must be acknowledged that attempts to achieve such groups are not uniformly successful. For example, the things learned by an experimental study group may be passed on to those in the control group informally outside of school, thus rendering the control ineffective. However, no serious researcher would ignore their potential usefulness.

Allport (6, p. 482) finally sums up the desirable design for evaluation research as follows:

Group	Dependent Variable	Independent Variable	Dependent Variable
Experimental Group:	measure of prejudice	exposure to program	measure of prejudice
Control Group:	measure of prejudice	no exposure to program	measure of prejudice

Allport's emphasis on the necessity for a control group will be a factor for consideration in any research work.

Application of experimental principles to a religious situation is seen in an experiment reported by Parker and St. Johns (145) in *Prayer Can Change Your Life,* in which the writers tell of an experiment conducted at Redlands University in California. The forty-five volunteers in the experiment were divided into three equal groups of fifteen individuals. The groups were known as the psychotherapy group, the random prayers group, and the prayer therapy group.

The psychotherapy group undertook a course of psychotherapy consisting of weekly individual counseling sessions aimed at helping the members of the group handle their emotional difficulties. Religion was not discussed as the people selected for this category either expressed a definite preference for psychotherapy, or had been specifically recommended for this type of treatment by their physician.

The random prayers group consisted of individuals who were all practicing Christians. Each expressed confidence in prayer as a means of handling emotional and physical ills. Each felt that psychotherapy was unnecessary and that he already knew how to pray. The members of the group agreed to pray every night before retiring for the duration of the experiment which lasted for nine months of the college year. Their objective was to solve their problems with prayer, so no psychological help was offered nor technique of prayer suggested.

The third group was the *prayer therapy group* which met weekly for two-hour sessions. This group set about to incorporate psychological insight with improved prayer techniques.

The criteria used for evaluating the work was incorporated in five generally accepted psychological tests—the Rorschach, the Szondi, the Thematic Apperception Test, the Sentence Completion Test, and the Word Association Test. The tests were given privately, off campus, to each individual in the entire experiment, at the beginning and at the end of the project, by a skilled psychometrist who was in no way involved in the work of the experiment.

After the final test evaluations had been made, the following results were observed: Group one, the psychotherapy group, showed a 65 per cent improvement. Group two, the random prayers group, show no improvement. Group three, the prayer therapy group, showed a 72 per cent improvement. It was concluded that prayer therapy had been shown experimentally to be superior. Whether there was a statistical significance is open to question, but the experimental design is the important consideration.

While the student of psychology of religion may try to use scientific method, he has peculiar problems. The subject matter of the study constitutes a major difficulty. In psychology of religion the basic study is focused upon personality, or the "living human document," which does not lend itself to simple study. Even within the framework of psychology itself, students of personality have not always felt at home. Hall and Lindzey (**79**, p. 2) show that the personality theorists have a long tradition of clinical observation as the favored method of study. Impressed by the unity of behavior they have been unwilling to study segmented aspects of personality, preferring to examine the whole of life. The experimental psychologists, on the other hand, are concerned about the findings of the laboratory. Their inspiration has come from the natural sciences and experimental methods. Thus, smaller segments of behavior, or reaction, have been their major concern.

Fromm claims psychology as a whole lost its sense of direction by trying to stay close to scientific methods. Fromm (**71**, p. 6) says: "It was more often concerned with insignificant problems which fitted an alleged scientific method than with devising new methods to study the significant problems of man."

All this complicates the study of psychology of religion, already the "shotgun wedding" of two fundamentally different disciplines. It has had to adapt generally used techniques, occasionally devising new methods for its purposes. Following the processes of the evolution of these methods brings insight into the complexity of the quest for the soul.

The Personal Documents

Allport (10, p. xii) maintains that an adequate study of the religious life is only really possible by using "personal documents." "Personal documents" have been defined as "any self-revealing record that intentionally or unintentionally yields information regarding the structure, dynamics, and functioning of the author's mental life." These include autobiographies, diaries, letters, and verbatum recordings. Rather unfortunately, a variety of motives function in these productions, including special pleading, exhibitionism, literary appeal, catharsis, monetary gain, and the desire for immortality. The bewildering array of motivations complicates the work of the researcher.

Autobiographies are valuable as they frequently contain confessions of inner experiences, thus revealing the motives in the writers' lives. One of the best-known autobiographies in Christian literature is that of Augustine. Hunt (90, p. 117) says that Augustine's *Confessions* is the first autobiography in Western literature. It was in the year 388, when he was thirty-two years of age, that Augustine reached a critical point in his religious experience. After living for years with concubines, while visiting his friend Alypius and sitting in the garden, he was overcome with a fit of weeping and rushed to the end of the enclosure. He relates how he heard the voice of a child saying, "Take up and read." He seized a copy of Paul's writings and opening them his eyes fell on the passage, "Not in rioting and drunkenness, not in chambering and wantonness, not in strife and envying, but put ye on the Lord Jesus Christ, and make not provision for the flesh" (Rom. 13:13-14). In his own words he tells of his reaction.

No further would I read; nor needed I: for instantly at the end of this sentence, by a light as it were of serenity infused into my heart, all the darkness of doubt vanished away . . . for Thou convertedst me unto Thyself, so that I sought neither wife, nor any hope in this world (176, pp. 199-200).

Writings of this type have been a fruitful source of study for investigators of psychology of religion.

Boisen utilized personal documents in *The Exploration of the Inner World*. He refers very frequently to George Fox's *Journal* and makes an exhaustive study of Fox's religious experience from the entries in the *Journal*. Similarly, he takes the case of Emmanuel Swedenborg, an outstanding Swedish scholar of the early eighteenth century. Swedenborg wrote a *Spiritual Diary* in which he recorded his dreams during a period of conflict. Consulting the diary and his other writings, Boisen reconstructs Swedenborg's religious experience.

Personal diaries are the most intimate of all documents and generally less restrained than other sources of information. It sometimes seems as if we are looking over the writer's shoulder as he pours out his heart. Allport (**7**, p. 405) shows that diaries escape the fallacy of attributing to earlier years the thoughts, feelings, and interpretations of life seen from the perspective of later days. Several investigators have noted that adolescents have a tendency to keep diaries, with girls more likely to do so than boys. A study of diaries has shown that religion is often the topic of concern, thus spelling opportunity for the investigator of psychology of religion.

There are some disadvantages in using personal documents. Some of these were stated by Felix Frankfurter when he pointed out that writers all fall prey to "the fallibility of the human memory, the infirmities of the human mind, the weakness of the human understanding and recollection" (**146**, p. 50). Even people who have been referred to by a great church as saints have had a tendency toward exaggeration, and often mixed fact with fiction in their letters and memoirs. Passing time often causes the writer to forget details, and he is unaware of the unconscious determinants which overshadow any recording experience.

Re-creative Methods

Stolz (**170**, p. 139) used the term, "re-creative," and stated very simply that it represents an effort to reconstruct primitive man's experiences of religion with the aid of anthropology, social psychology, and genetic psychology. A study is made of the origin and significance of religious ceremonies, rites, creeds, cults, and it is used along with other available material to reconstruct the past.

Writers belonging to the Marxist school have been particularly adept at this kind of work as they have reconstructed history and the part religion has played in its development. Rather unfortunately, they have shown that they not only intend to change history in the future but have the ability to change its past course. The facts of the past are manipulated with amazing facility to fit the philosophical and economic concepts of dialectical materialism. The historical writings of Marxism stand as a warning of the possible perversions of the re-creative method.

However, with a fair and unbiased attitude toward early history and primitive peoples, it is possible to learn much about both personality and religion. In *Totem and Taboo,* Freud displays a remarkable familiarity with writings on anthropology. Freud (**69**, p. 3) claims that in a sense primitive man is still our contemporary.

We can thus judge the so-called savage and semi-savage races; their psychic life assumes a peculiar interest for us, for we can recognize in their psychic life, a well preserved, early stage of our own development.

Primitive forms of religion are forever with us, and a knowledge of the early development of religion helps us in the evaluative process.

The method has been used by some outstanding students in the field of psychology of religion. Such men as Ames, Stratton, and Leuba used the technique, but it has serious limitations. The amount of material available is often far too meager, and the historical imagination easily takes off at a tangent. Also complex inferences are often drawn from rudimentary materials.

Literature

Though not obvious as a resource, literature has offered a fruitful field for psychological investigation. At least one psychologist feels that writers of literature can show the way to psychologists in investigating personality. Allport (**8**, p. 13) indicates three superiorities of authors over psychologists: (1) Writers of literature very frequently identify and define ·traits manifested in their subjects in their reactions to life. (2) Authors generally portray their characters as being self-consistent and displaying an underlying unity despite obvious contradictions in their adjustments to life's experiences. (3) Writers generally follow one life experience over a long period of time. Allport concludes that the study of literature by psychologists will lead to an improvement in psychological investigations.

The writer does more than record facts. His literary efforts often constitute an act of self-revelation. The Thematic Apperception Test consists of a series of pictures about which the testee is invited to compose stories. In the process, more is revealed about the person taking the test than the picture which he interprets. Henry A. Murray (**79**, p. 199), the author of the T.A.T., has shown his liking for the documentary method in a brilliant interpretation of *Moby Dick*, which apparently has a strange attraction for psychologists. Jung (**103**, p. 154) considered it the greatest novel ever written in America. Murray sees Captain Ahab, named for the infamous King Ahab of the Old Testament, as representing Satan or the forces of evil. In psychological language Ahab represents the primitive and largely evil forces of the id. Moby Dick, the great white whale, portrays the moral forces and religious conventions of Melville's day and thus is the personification of the superego.

Jung (**103**, p. 154) insists that the literary quality has little to do with the value of a writing for psychological research. It may be of very poor literary value but of the greatest interest to the psychologist. Similarly, the so-called "psychological novel" may not offer much help. The psychologist is more concerned with the free-flowing story which unwittingly reveals underlying psychological factors.

Freud (**68**, p. 68) made use of literature, and Shakespeare attracted him. "Theme of the Three Caskets" is the title of an essay discussing the scene in the *Merchant of Venice* where there is a contest for the hand of Portia. She is to marry the man who chooses the casket containing her portrait. After two suitors have chosen unsuccessfully, Bassanio decides on the one made of lead and so wins the bride. Developing his essay, Freud finds many parallels of the scene in literature and gives a psychoanalytic interpretation of the theme. *Macbeth* and *King Richard III* were veritable mines of illustrations of psychoanalytic principles for Freud.

Ibsen's plays and Goethe's writings presented similar opportunities to him. One whole paper by Freud (**68**, p. 111) is given to the discussion of an incident taken from Goethe's autobiography. As a boy Goethe had thrown the family china out the window. Encouraged by three men who lived across the street, the young boy had hurled the crockery out piece by piece, and rejoiced to see it smashing on the paving stones. Freud noticed a resemblance to a case he had treated, where a man in childhood days had acted in a similar way. He concludes that in both Goethe's and his patient's case throwing crockery was a symbolic action of trying to be rid of brothers and sisters who were seen as intruders.

More specifically, religious literature presents possibilities for study. *Journey into Self* by M. Esther Harding (**80**) is a psychological interpretation of *Pilgrim's Progress*. The author seeks to show that Bunyan's immortal allegory is not so much a story of mankind's spiritual pilgrimage as it is a revelation of Bunyan's psychological development.

Some investigators take tne sacred literature of a group of people and subject it to an intense study in an effort to find psychological aspects of religious experience. Gerber (**73**) has made a study of the psychological aspects of the book of Job in his work, *The Psychology of the Suffering Mind*. Examining the experiences of Job in the light of psychological theory, Gerber tries to diagnose Job's difficulties and discusses the techniques of Job's friends as they tried to counsel with him. Leslie D. Weatherhead in *Psychology, Religion, and Healing* made a study of the healing miracles of Jesus and formulated the psychological principles indicated. Another recent book, *Counseling for Church Leaders* (**49**), has a chapter on "Counseling in the Bible" and makes a brief examination of counseling techniques utilized in both the Old and New Testaments.

The study of literature opens possibilities for the investigator of psychology of religion. Biblical literature is a particularly promising field which might be explored by an enthusiastic student.

Observation

Possibly the simplest and the oldest way of investigating psychology of religion is for the student to observe religious people and their activities, and then write up his impressions. It has been refined to the point where the observer sometimes lives with a group, making tape recordings, taking careful notes of their activities, having interviews with the participants. Finally, the observer gives a detailed account of the whole experience, making evaluations and reaching conclusions.

In the small booklet, *The Modern Tongues and Healing Movement*, Carroll Stegall, Jr., tells of his experience with Holiness groups and tries to evaluate the practices of faith healing. He attended the meetings, observed what was taking place, and then wrote up his detailed conclusions. His book is somewhat critical of the movement, but he claims that at the beginning of his investigations he was open-minded and sympathetic. There is a freshness about his writing, and the reader feels that he has been brought face to face with the total situation in which these particular groups function.

There are dangers in the approach. It is hard to remain objective and impartial. An observer with a group of people is liable to feel either sympathetic or antagonistic toward them, thus letting his observations and interpretations be colored by his personal bias. Wolfe (**151**, p. xxxii) shows how even an eyewitness account can be made to tell a story. John Reed, who wrote *Ten Days that Shook the World,* described the events of the Bolshevik revolution. His friend, the artist Boardman Robinson, reproached him, saying, "It didn't happen that way." Reed replied that Robinson had missed the point, seized hold of one of his sketches and, pointing to the figure, said, "She didn't have as big a bundle as that." Robinson replied that he was not aiming at photographic accuracy but an over-all impression. Reed answered that that was what he was trying to do.

Because religion is such an overpowering force in personality, it can easily cause the interviewer to report only the results of interviews which fit in with his preconceived ideas. In the latter half of the fifteenth century two Dominican priests, Jacob Sprenger and Henry Kramer, who were professors of Sacred Theology at the University of Cologne, were named by Pope Sixtus to investigate witchcraft. The result of their investigations was the monumental *Malleus Maleficarum* which could be translated *The Witches' Hammer* or "a hammer with which to strike witches." Hunt (**90**, p. 195), describes its contents:

From actual testimony of witnesses and confessed witches, Sprenger and Kramer had learned that, by means of their incantations and brews, evil-doing women could summon plagues of locusts to destroy a harvest or bring a hailstorm to ruin it, make men impotent or women frigid, induce abortions or dry up a mother's milk. They could see at a distance, fly at night, and leave a duplicate body behind to fool people; sometimes they could turn themselves into cats or other creatures; some of them turned men into animals and kept them at hard labor; and some kidnapped children, and roasted and ate them.

The answer to the criticism of these findings was that the investigators had actual testimony; yet it was just as wrong as ever it could be.

One writer points out another danger of which we might not be aware. He tells of attending a meeting of a "shakers group." It seems that these people shook vigorously when emotionally aroused. The writer, who had always thought of himself as an unbiased observer, found that after meeting with them on several occasions he began to shake himself. He thus felt that the time had come to put an end to his investigations of this particular group. He could no longer be objective in his observations.

There is a wide scope for the use of the observational method. If the approach were planned, with recording and interviewing procedures carefully worked out, much valuable information could be gained.

Case Studies

The case study is a technique which is both old and new. Hippocrates the Great, known as "The Father of Medicine," was the master of the case history method. Burton and Harris (**28**, p. 10) claim that no physician has ever surpassed him in its use. From this early start it has been the medical man's preferred way of accumulating medical knowledge.

Hall and Lindzey (**79**, p. 2) show that personality theorists owe much to the medical profession, and the early giants in the field like Freud, Jung, and McDougal were medical men as well as psychologists. While psychology as a whole has been lukewarm toward the case study method, personality theorists have seen its value, and the medical training of the early theorists may have played a part in this appreciation.

Fromm tells of Freud's realization that his work was taking him further from orthodox medicine and compelling him to study the soul of man. Using the case study method in a new way, Freud fostered and developed a whole new technique of investigating personality. Fromm (**71**, p. 7) states:

Freud's method of psychoanalysis made possible the most minute and intimate study of the soul. The "laboratory" of the analyst has no gadgets. He cannot weigh or count his findings, but he gains insight through dreams, fantasies, and associations, into the hidden desires and anxieties of his patients. In his "laboratory" relying only on observation, reason, and his own experience as a human being, he discovers that mental sickness cannot be understood apart from moral problems.

The term "case study" is often loosely used, and its most in-

clusive nature compounds the difficulty of the definition. English and
English (57, p. 75) describe the case study:

> A collection of all available evidence—social, psychological, physiologi-
> cal, biographical, environmental, vocational—that promises to help ex-
> plain a single individual or a single social unit such as a family. It is
> especially used in psychopathology, guidance, and social work. Since
> it emphasizes the single case or instance, it differs in aim from an experi-
> ment and from statistical studies. But the case study often incorporates
> data from experiments or tests, and a series of case studies may be sub-
> jected to statistical study and generalization.

Although some of the disciplines have devised set forms for case
studies, it is a highly individual technique, with the form of the case
study varying according to the individual involved. Allport (9,
pp. 391-94) says that the only inviolable rule is "fidelity to life,"
but most case studies fall into three sections: (1) a discussion of the
individual in his present status, (2) an account of past influences and
successive stages of development, and (3) an anticipation of future
trends.

New ground was broken in the case study method with the appearance of *Counseling and Psychotherapy* by Carl Rogers. The last
section of the book contains "The Case of Herbert Bryan," a complete, phonographically recorded counseling experience. It is claimed
to be the first verbatum presentation of a case from the beginning
to the end. A further refinement of the case study method is the use
of "verbatum reports" in clinical pastoral education. The trainee
chaplain writes up the experience of his encounter with a patient, as
far as possible recording "verbatum" the total exchange. Later, the
whole process if reviewed with his supervisor.

The value of the case study, as seen by Allport (9, p. 398) for the
study of personality, also applies to the study of psychology of
religion. First, it provides a framework within which many considerations of an individual's life can be arranged and systematized. Second,
the attention of the whole process is focused upon one individual.
Criticism has often been leveled at psychology because of its failure
at this point. Third, because of the perspective of the whole of life,
single acts and individual instances are seen as in integrated part of
the whole.

Writers on the subject of psychology of religion have turned increasingly to case study materials. A comparison of the original and revised editions of Johnson's *Psychology of Religion* shows this trend. In the revised edition, the chapter on conversion has been expanded with a fifteen-page case study of the conversion experience of Toyohiko Kagawa. A similar emphasis is found in many of the more recent writings on psychology of religion.

As with other methods there are limitations to the case study technique. With many subjective factors involved, the personality of the investigator is very influential. Strang (**172**, p. 468) claims that personal maturity is vital. If the investigator is not fairly well adjusted, he will have a tendency to interpret the case in terms of his own personality problem. Personal bias is also a hindrance, and the writer is always tempted to utilize the writing of a case as a means of getting across his own personal ideas.

Perhaps the best summary of the assets and liabilities of the case study can be found in the words of Allport (**9**, p. 390):

This method is . . . the most comprehensive of all, and lies closest to the initial starting point of common sense. It provides a framework within which the psychologist can place all his observations gathered by other methods; it is his final affirmation of the individuality and uniqueness of every personality. It is a completely synthetic method, the only one that is spacious enough to embrace all assembled facts. Unskillfully used, it becomes a meaningless chronology, or a confusion of fact and fiction, of guess-work and misinterpretation. Properly used it is the most revealing method of all.

The Questionnaire

Hillway (**84**, p. 175) classifies the questionnaire under the general heading of surveys and includes both questionnaire and individual interviews. He says that the first major survey in history was when Augustus, the emperor of Rome, issued his decree requiring every person in the empire to report on a given day to the city or village of his birth and there enrol upon the tax lists. When we remember that this was the occasion of the birth of Jesus Christ, it is easy to conjure up images of the association of the survey and religious experience.

The questionnaire is probably the oldest formal method of investigation employed in the study of psychology of religion. Much of the literature on the subject would not be in existence today if it had not been for the use of the questionnaire as a technique of research.

The questionnaire consists of a series of questions to be answered by the respondent. Questionnaires are of two kinds: (1) open-ended, and (2) close-ended. In the first type, questions are asked in such a way as to enable the person answering to state the facts in his own words. An example of this type of questionnaire is seen below. This is a section of the instrument that was used by Elmer T. Clark (**32**, p. 25) in gathering the basic information used in his book, *Psychology of Religious Awakening*.

III. Conversion

15. Have you ever undergone the experience commonly called conversion? (If not, see question 22.) _____

16. When? _____ 17. Where? _____

18. Describe the circumstances and your feelings leading up to the experience.

_____

_____

_____

19. Describe the experience itself and your feelings during and immediately following it. _____

_____

_____

_____

20. What were the immediate aftereffects of the experience? _____

_____

21. Are you conscious of any influence of the experience remaining in your life today? _____ What? _____

_____

_____

The close-ended questionnaire, on the otherhand, suggests possible answers for each question, and the respondent replies by circling, checking, or underlining the answer with which he agrees. This may be a yes or a no; it may be true or false. In some instances, there may be a third category such as uncertain, undecided, or just a plain question mark. Below is a section of a questionnaire of this type:

Experiences Immediately Before Your Religious Awakening

Check column 1 if this was a very important factor.
Check column 2 if this was a moderately important factor.
Check column 3 if this was of no   importance.

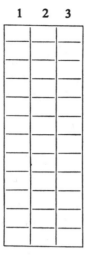

(53) A sense of sin
(54) A feeling of estrangement from God
(55) A feeling of incompleteness
(56) A desire to live a better life
(57) A depressed feeling
(58) A feeling of resentment
(59) An anxious feeling
(60) A feeling of conflict
(61) Weeping
(62) A desire to pray
(63) Loss of sleep
(64) Loss of appetite

A refinement in the process of giving answers to statements on a questionnaire is found in *rating scales,* by which degrees of intensity of feeling can be checked.

Ernest M. Ligon (**118**, p. 335) warns us about the care necessary in preparing a questionnaire when he says, "A questionnaire is one of the most difficult of all instruments to construct." After deciding upon the subject, a decision has to be made as to how much information is required, and none should be sought which is available from other sources. The number of questions asked will vary with the information sought, but it should be kept as brief as possible. The respondent must develop confidence, so certain information should be given, including:

1. A descriptive general title of the study.

2. A brief description of the purpose of the study. State that the questionnaire is being sent to a select group of authoritative people and that the study is to make a definite contribution.

3. The name of the sponsoring institution or agency.

4. The name and address of the person to whom the completed questionnaire is to be returned.

5. Definitions of difficult terms.

6. Clear instructions as to how the questions are to be answered.

The wording of the questionnaire needs particular attention; the following suggestions may help:

1. It should ask for simple, objective, concrete information.

2. It should ask for a minimum amount of writing. This also helps in the tabulation of results.

3. Each question should be complete in itself. It should not depend for its meaning on some preceding question.

4. The statement of the question should not suggest the desirable answer.

5. The wording of every item ought to be understandable and familiar in order to insure the respondent's comprehension of what is being asked.

6. The items should be arranged in a neat and logical order. Items at the beginning should be simple and encourage the respondent to continue answering.

To determine the suitability of the questions, the whole questionnaire should be pretested. A preliminary draft may be made, and the following criteria of evaluation used:

1. Are all questions on the subject?

2. Do all of the questions pull or have extractive power?

3. Do all response choices show a reasonable range of variation?

4. Is the general tone of the questionnaire friendly and courteous?

5. Are directions clear and complete, important terms defined? Does each question deal with a single idea? Are all questions worded as simply as possible? Are questions presented in a good psychological order?

Following evaluation the questionnaire can be given to a small group for their reaction and criticism. When the content is satisfactory, the questionnaire should be neatly set out on good paper in order to have an attractive physical appearance.

There are a number of difficulties involved in using the questionnaire in research. There is always the problem of introspection, as people find it difficult to take a look within and accurately report what they see. Lapses of memory, unconscious exaggeration, or suppression further complicate the use of the questionnaire.

Even if the questionnaire is well designed and constructed and submitted to people who are capable of making objective evaluations, the difficulty of sampling remains. It is impossible to submit the questionnaire to the total population, so a sampling process is followed. A small number of people or a "sample" is chosen. Theoretically, the selection is made so that every individual in the group being studied has an equal chance of being chosen in the sample. The names of all the people may be put in a hat and a number of them drawn out, or the list of names of members of the group may be taken and every tenth (or some other number) selected. In the census taken in the United States in 1960, census takers sought detailed information at every fourth house, utilizing a sampling technique. In technical language, a "random sample" was used.

A further refinement of this process is the use of "stratification." People for the sample are chosen so that they will be representative of the total population. The investigator might make sure that his sample comes from different age levels, educational standards, vocational callings, or geographical locations. Then, within these groups, a random sampling would be taken which would be called a "stratified random sample." In any case, sampling is one important aspect of any research project.

Despite the many criticisms leveled at the questionnaire, it is one of the best techniques available for simple research, but the investigator must work carefully to eliminate possible errors. It still remains true that the questionnaire has been more frequently used than any other technique of research in the study of psychology of religion.

The Challenge of Research

There are many areas of research altogether untouched in this chapter. Despite the shortcomings, it may serve to stir an interest in research. Too many leaders in religious work have been "playing the game by ear." On the other hand, many are covering the same ground, not realizing that others have passed the same way and that their experience can give us a jumping-off point for our work.

In a changing society we need to know the "why" of our work so that the Christian enterprise can move forward more expeditiously. Research can furnish some of the clues we need and give us instruments for measuring the effectiveness of our work.

Ernest Ligon, leader of the Character Research Project, has used the term "co-scientist" to describe people at work within a church situation who are interested in research. Ligon (118, p. 1) states the challenge:

Research is neither impersonal nor dull. It has all the personal interest of a political campaign, all the thrills of a championship football game, and can be engaged in at some level by everyone from Junior High to an Einstein.

Some reader may catch a vision of the possibilities and embark on a career of research. If so, tomorrow's church work may be more effective because someone has become familiar with the techniques used in the search for a soul.

PART TWO

The Search for a Soul in Personality Development

The first section of the book was devoted to the examination of the history of the techniques used in the search for a soul in psychology of religion. Attention now turns to the heart of the matter—personality development.

Literature on personality is profuse; there are almost as many theories as there are writers. To choose the most important and helpful concepts from among these is not easy, but this has been attempted in the chapters of Part Two.

After an inquiry is made into the basic concepts of personality and religion, a definition of each field is stated and expounded. Six basic personality concepts are chosen and set out as postulates containing the kernel of the discussion which follows in the successive chapters.

The third determinant is discussed in chapter 5, which takes note of the emphasis on heredity and environment that frequently makes man a pawn of these impersonal forces. Attention is focused on the third determinant—the self. Economic determinism is challenged, and consideration is given to the Weber thesis and to the more recent developments and formulations of the idea.

Unconscious factors in personality are evaluated in chapter 6. Evidences for the concept and the nature of the unconscious are considered in a discussion leading to an evaluation of religious aspects of the unconscious.

Chapter 7 takes up the discussion of love. The close association of love, sex, and religion, the necessary differentiation of levels of love, and the consideration of love objects are an integral part of the chapter.

Maturity, the much used but frequently misunderstood word, is the central concept of chapter 8. Although physical growth is virtually automatic, emotional and religious development is far otherwise. An examination of the characteristics of a maturing person closes out the chapter.

The conflict between psychiatry and religion has ebbed and flowed, and it is frequently charged that religion is an escape mechanism and accordingly not conducive to healthy personality development. An evaluation of the situation is attempted, with a final formulation of religious factors ministering to mental health.

Chapter 9 goes to the heart of the matter and deals with the "self" or ego. Systems of personality and their relationship to biblical concepts, the conflict within personality, and the development of a value system are all necessary ingredients in the discussion.

4

Basic Concepts of Personality and Religion

Although sputniks and satellites whirling in space cause us to talk about the present space age, the tendency of man to turn his eyes to the sky and speculate concerning the happenings in outer space is not really new. For centuries people have been concerned about the surrounding universe and have endeavored to find an explanation for the happenings among the heavenly bodies.

Living his lonely life on the mud flats of Mesopotamia, primitive man noted that life was in some way ruled by the heavenly bodies. The moon coming over the horizon sent him to bed, and with the rising of the sun he left his place of rest to go to his work. The fertility of the soil was, in a large measure, dependent on the sun shining from the heavens. The destructive storms and inundations also came from the skies. Consequently, heavenly bodies loomed large in early man's thinking.

One effort to discover the relationship of stars and men was the formulations of astrology. The heavens were separated into twelve divisions or "boxes." One of these was said to be "in the ascendency" at a person's birth, and this sign guided his destinies. Despite the explosion of the basic presuppositions of astrology by modern astronomers, many people still feel their lives are governed by the stars. They may need to be reminded of Cassius' famous words from Shakespeare's *Julius Caesar,* "The fault, dear Brutus, is not in our stars, but in ourselves."

The really amazing thing is that while man has been so interested in the mechanics of the universe, he has shown little concern about the workings of his own personality. Preoccupied with searching the skies, only in comparatively recent times has man turned to look within himself. Oddly enough, some of the interest in the workings of personality came through celestial observation. In the nineteenth century, astronomers created a widespread interest by their accidental discovery of individual differences in reaction time. While making records of the transit of stars, it was noted that there were variations in the speed with which observers pressed a key to indicate the transit. A study of reaction times followed in an effort to better understand the "personal equation." In a sense man discovered that he had to learn something about the workings of his own personality if he were to make adequate observation of the firmament above. Thus, in the more scientific investigations of personality, man began to look *within* his own self because he found difficulty in looking *out* at the stars.

The Nature of Personality

When at last man took a look within he experienced difficulty in describing what he saw. American investigators favored the use of the word "personality," although different terms have been used in other parts of the world. In its development the meaning of the word "personality" has had a number of changes. Personality comes from the Latin *persona,* a word which is derived from the verb form, *personare,* meaning "to sound through." Historically, the word had two meanings. It meant either the mask or the person who played a part in the Greek drama. The Grecian theater had no girls on the stage, and men played all the parts. They dressed to call attention to the characters they played. High heels made them look taller; padded shoulders caused them to appear more impressive. On their faces they wore masks. The masks, carefully fashioned, indicated the character of the person portrayed.

The idea of masks came to be closely associated with the concept of personality. Some scholars think the word had particular reference to the crude type of megaphone in the mask. As the theater of that ancient day had no amplification, the mouth of the mask was shaped to help throw the actor's voice to the audience in the amphitheater. It is easy to see how the word came to mean "sound through."

Allport (**7**, pp. 22-25) discusses the classes into which personality definitions can be divided and labels the categories *external effect, internal structure,* and *positivist.* As positivist definitions are presently beyond our consideration, the first two will serve as the basis for a discussion of the salient concepts of personality.

External effect.—This class of definition emphasizes what Hall and

Lindzey (**79**, p. 7) call "social skills or adroitness." An individual's personality is evaluated in terms of his effectiveness in calling forth positive reactions from others. As a natural consequence, a person who does not develop his social skills is sometimes said to have a "personality problem." The concept has value. Paul E. Johnson (**99**, p. 25) calls it "the interpersonal axiom," with the emphasis that the individual moves into the broadening fields of interpersonal relationships to discover himself and his possibilities in his reactions to others.

However, the mask idea has frequently been taken too literally in personality, with the predominant emphasis laid on "stimulus value." Someone with a gushing manner, a back-slapping technique, or a mouth full of syrupy compliments is thus said to have a "good personality." Allport (**7**, p. 23) shows that advertisers have capitalized upon the idea. The freely propagated ways to develop personality range all the way from the charm school through the public speaking course to certain clothes or cosmetics, all alleged to develop the "personality." Commenting on this Allport (**7**, p. 23) laments that in the latter instances "personality is not even skin deep." Helen Joseph (**102**) has expressed a legitimate misgiving about people whose personalities are masks and no more.

> Always a mask
> Held in the slim hand, whitely,
> Always she had a mask before her face—
> Smiling and sprightly,
> The mask.
>
> For years and years and years I wondered
> But dared not ask.
>
> And then—
> I blundered,
> I looked behind,
> Behind the Mask,
> To find
> Nothing—
> She had no face.
>
> She had become
> Merely a hand
> Holding a mask
> With grace.

Taken to its logical consequences, it may mean that an individual has no personality apart from that provided by the response of others. The person living a solitary life like a hermit poses a problem. Allport (7, p. 24) asks about Robinson Crusoe. Did he not have a personality before the arrival of his man Friday? All sorts of fascinating possibilities present themselves. Crusoe, mixing and mingling with and relating himself to others before his shipwreck, had personality. After the shipwreck and living in isolation, he was without personality. Friday's advent on the island meant the restoration of some personality, and a return to civilization with the renewed multiplicity of relationships with people of higher cultural standards meant the possibility of Crusoe's fully blossoming personality once more. Theories of personality based just on external effect will always be inadequate.

Internal structure.—While many American personality theorists have favored personality as a descriptive term, European psychologists have shown a preference for "character." There is an essential difference. For while *persona* means "mask," character comes from the Greek word *charaktēr,* meaning "an engraving" and suggesting a deep and fixed basic structure. Allport (7, p. 31) maintains that the American usage stresses environmentalism while the European term indicates the deeply etched nature of man.

Personality is more than a reaction to others. It has an inner reality as dynamic forces effect an individual's decisions. Each person has his own life history and existence apart from other people's estimates. Value in personality is implied. Each peculiar individual exists in his own right and may not be exploited by others. Religious concepts may enter. Allport (7, p. 26) credits the Judeo-Christian ethic with the initiation of this concept. A recent writer shows that the study of personality has a unique place in the field of psychology.

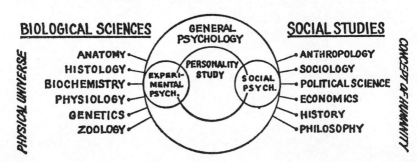

As seen in the above drawing of the central role of personality study in the social and biological sciences, Baughman and Welsh (16, p. 16) have noted that the study of personality bridges the gap between two basic branches of psychology: (1) experimental, which tends toward the biological sciences, and (2) social, which is closely related to the social sciences. The implication is that both the internal nature of the organism and the social setting are involved in any concept of personality.

It becomes obvious that defining personality is a complex assignment. Allport undertook the task and summarized some fifty definitions in his own book, *Personality: A Psychological Interpretation.* Allport (9, p. 48) finally came up with his own definition of personality: "the dynamic organization within the individual of those psychophysical systems that determine his unique adjustments to his environment." Interestingly, Allport has slightly changed this definition in his latest book, *Pattern and Growth in Personality.* The alteration is a commentary on the flexibility of personality theory and the futility of dogmatism. As the change has been small, and the older definition is used frequently by personality theorists, it will be retained for this present discussion. Five emphases—dynamic organization, psychophysical systems, determining, uniqueness, and adjustment—will be considered to show some essential elements in a concept of personality.

Dynamic organization.—The old practice of dividing personality into discreet elements came from the natural sciences and the laboratory where it has done a yeoman's service. The Negro scientist, George Washington Carver, used to tell of analyzing the peanut and then putting the constituent elements together in a new way to make his discoveries of the multitudinous uses of the nut. But personality is more than a peanut, and people cannot be taken to pieces and reassembled. Consequently, reductionism has done little to help the final understanding of the personality. Students in the Gestalt tradition have led us to a healthy emphasis on the unity of behavior and have shown the futility of studying its segmented aspects. The classical formulation is that the whole is *more* than the sum of its parts. Rogers makes a like emphasis when he says, "The organism is at all times a totally organized system in which alterations of any part may produce changes in any other part" (155a, p. 478). A similar organizational pattern is seen in Freud's relationship of the id, the ego, and the superego. Yet the organization is itself constantly changing.

Also inferred in Allport's definition is the possibility of disorganization. Abnormal psychology sees the maladjusted individual as having a disorganized inner life.

Psychophysical systems.—Some not so well informed enthusiasts for psychology have an unfortunate tendency to separate "mind" and "body" as if they were two separate entities. All evidence indicates far otherwise, with the mental aspects affecting the physical and vice versa. Some of the older ideas about behavior have been related to the physical make-up of man. The Greeks were concerned about the four "humors"—blood, black bile, yellow bile, and phlegm. If any of these humors predominated, the individual was a particular type of temperament as seen in the chart below on the relationship of humor and temperament. (7, p. 37)

Humor	Temperament
Blood	Sanguine
Black bile	Melancholic
Yellow bile	Choleric
Phlegm	Phlegmatic

Although modern science has rejected these categories, it is nevertheless recognized that body chemistry plays a large part in determining temperament.

Of more recent days, Sheldon (161) has developed a system of classifying three major body builds: (1) the *endomorphic*, a round-

SHELDON'S CONSTITUTIONAL TYPES

 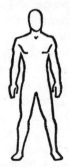 

ENDOMORPHIC   MESOMORPHIC   ECTOMORPHIC

ish build but relatively weak in bony and muscular structure; (2) the *mesomorphic,* having large bones and muscles with a squarish build; and (3) the *ectomorphic,* with long slender extremities and lacking in muscular development. Refining the major divisions with other factors, Sheldon held that it was possible to distinguish some seventy types of constitutional build and postulated a correspondence of temperament to body type.

The generally accepted concept of body-mind relationship is subsumed under the term "psychosomatic," a word referring to the close and intricate relationship of body and mind. Psychosomatic illnesses are sometimes called "organ language," indicating that the mind says something through the body. Difficulties like peptic ulcers, migraine headaches, bronchial asthma, skin disorders, and obesity often have their origin in psychological difficulty. In all formulations about personality the body-mind relationship must be seen as an inextricable unity.

Determining.—Within personality there are factors which constantly push the individual, and the student of personality always faces the problem of motivation. Development of the instinct theory with its formulations, varying all the way from the simple threefold division of self, sex, and social to long lists of drives and motives with associated emotions, is evidence of the reality of the forces. Freud's demanding, pleasure-seeking "id" and his concept of instincts represent his effort to account for motivating forces. Maslow (**126**) sees man as a "perpetually wanting animal," with a series of needs: physiological needs, safety, love, esteem, and self-actualization. These needs are in a hierarchy and are never satisfied. As soon as physiological needs are satisfied, the individual becomes aware of his safety needs, and so on right through the scale of love and esteem to the urge for self-actualization. Constant pressure from within is a characteristic of human personality.

Uniqueness.—Hall and Lindzey (**79**, p. 262), in their comparison and contrast of the various personality theories, emphasize Allport's reference to the word "unique." Allport (**4**, p. 23) makes a plea for personality theorists to pay more attention to the feature of personality which is most outstanding—the uniqueness of organization. He notes that science speaks about differences; for example, how that every stone in the field is different from all other stones. But stones are purely reactive and do not change unless they are manipulated, whereas man has all the potentialities of becoming. After considering the animal forms of life, Allport maintains that they are psychologically less distinct from one another than one man is from other men.

The factor of uniqueness can be overplayed, for no man is unique in every aspect of life. Kluckhohn and Murray (**110**, p. 53) say: "Every man is in certain respects (a) like all other men, (b) like some other men, (c) like no other man." An individual is *like all other men* to the extent that he shares a common heritage, with a physical make-up which is akin to all other members of the human family. He is *like some other men* in the respect that he lives within a certain cultural group, feels the pressures of that society upon him, and conforms to a large extent to what is expected from him by the group. However, in all of this he is *unique,* because no other person has undergone exactly the same experience as he. His heredity is unique, and the responses he makes to his environment are peculiarly his. The emphasis upon individual uniqueness must overshadow theorizing about personality.

Adjustment.—Man is constantly adjusting to his environment. Sometimes he masters it, and sometimes he is mastered by it. Allport (**7**, p. 153) says adjustment should not be thought of in mere reactive terms, as it has the possibility of being a creative activity by which the individual aims at mastering his environment. A valid distinction in adjustment, made by Allport, is that adjustment may be thought of in two ways: *confrontation* or *escape.* The wholesome aspects of adjustment are to be seen in *confrontation.* The individual faces the reality of the situation and makes an appropriate adjustment. The following drawing shows Shaffer's (**160**, p. 9) schematic presentation of adjustment.

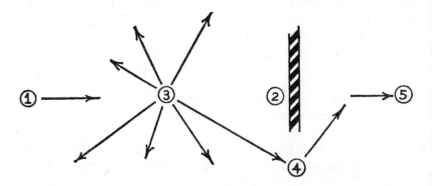

Shaffer expounds his concept:

You are proceeding in some course of motivated behavior (1) when your activity is thwarted or blocked (2). You make various exploratory trials (3) until one of them (4) overcomes the obstacle and you proceed as before (5). The principal steps of normal adjustment process are therefore the existence of a *motive,* the operation of some *thwarting* that prevents its immediate satisfaction, giving rise to *varied responses,* and leading eventually to a solution.

This process of adjustment involves mastery rather than just mere passive adaptation.

The other method of adjustment is by *escape.* Whereas the method of confrontation is mainly a conscious process, escape is largely an unconscious process. In the early days of motoring, the driver was proud of being able to shift gears without clashing. His skill at knowing when and how to shift was an important factor in rating his driving ability. The modern automobile, with its automatic transmission, has removed this consideration in driving skill. Like the automatic transmission which, in consideration of the power of the engine, the grade of the hill, and the pressure on the accelerator, engages the appropriate gear without the driver's help, so there are self-corrective devices within the personality. The "automatic transmission" of personality is the mental mechanisms, dynamisms, or adaptive mechanisms.

There are numerous classifications and different definitions of these defense mechanisms, but they all serve to help the ego cope with the reality of the situation. Thorpe (**175**, pp. 130-142) classifies escape mechanisms in categories of forgetting reality, distorting reality, atoning for reality, retreating from reality, and attacking reality. The following list sets out some of the more frequently used ego defense mechanisms.

Fantasy:	The process of gratifying frustrated desires by imaginary achievements.
Compensation:	A mechanism used to make amends or atone for some weakness or loss in personal characteristics or status.
Identification:	The gaining of increased feelings of worth by identifying self with a person or institution of illustrious standing.

Projection: The placing of blame for difficulties upon others or attributing one's own unethical desires to others.

Rationalization: The process of concocting plausible reasons to account for one's practices or beliefs when they are challenged by oneself or others.

Repression: The mental activity by which painful or dangerous thoughts or ideas are unwittingly relegated to the unconscious.

Reaction formation: The establishment of a trait or regular pattern of behavior that is directly opposed to a strong, unconscious trend.

Displacement: A mechanism by which strong emotions are shifted from one area to another where they can be better tolerated. This is sometimes called the "kick the cat" mechanism.

Regression: Retreating to earlier developmental level involving less mature responsibility and usually a lower level of aspiration.

Sublimation: The referment or redirection of the energy belonging to a primitive tendency into a new, noninherent and generally higher channel.

Everybody uses escape mechanisms to some degree. Sometimes there is a fine line of difference between normal and abnormal use. Murphy (**136**, p. 154) uses a simple illustration:

If one pushes a chair backwards a few inches, pivoting it upon the rear legs, he can remove his hand and the chair will fall forward to resume the old equilibrium. But let him pass by a hair's breadth beyond a given point, and the old equilibrium cannot be regained. The chair falls backward to the floor, to come to rest in a completely new position with no tendency to return to the old.

It is the same with personality. Most people escape the grim realities of existence at some time or other and later return to the normal confrontation of life. But if escape becomes the characteristic mode of reaction, lasting difficulty may result. Some psychotherapists see the aim of psychotherapy as being to enable the individual to develop the capacity to confront and adjust to his society.

Turning from the stars to look within himself, man has made some strange discoveries. The mere reactions of the individual which were the starting point of the investigation soon led to the complexities involved in Allport's definition. Our examination of the aspects of this definition has given us a starting point for our further investigations.

The Nature of Religion

Defining and categorizing religious experience is even more difficult than dealing with personality. According to Miller (**129**, p. 134), in Jonathan Edwards' day people were put into three categories of religious experience. The small inner circle consisted of those who could give testimony to their experience of conversion, and they were known as the "church." A second circle was made up of children of church members who had been baptized and had come into the church under the "Half-Way Covenant" but were denied church membership, the title of saint, and the Lord's Supper. It was hoped that the members of this group would one day have a conversion experience and come into full church membership. The third circle were the people of the town who had the privilege of attending church and paying for its support but little else. If supporting a church or attending it constituted "being religious," then all qualified. But if religious experience was the criteria, only the professing church members could be said to be religious.

However, even among the church members there are shades of belief. Clark (**34**, pp. 23-25) suggests that religious behavior can be divided into three categories: (1) *primary religious behavior,* which is an authentic inner experience leading the believer to activity aimed at harmonizing his life with and pleasing his deity; (2) *secondary religious behavior,* that which may have been primary and vital but has cooled off and become dull, routine, and habitual; and (3) *tertiary religious behavior,* which is the mere acceptance of religious routines from someone else. In this book it is assumed that we are talking about the primary type of religious behavior.

As formidable as the task of defining personality was, that of defining religion is more difficult. In one early book the author gathered over one hundred diverse definitions. Clark (**34**, pp. 18-20) suggests that the definitions can be subsumed under three headings: (1) Those which refuse to mark off religion from any other aspects of the psychic life. These will be of little help to us. (2) Statements emphasizing the social aspects of religion. Once again, this type of definition will be of more value to the sociologist than to the psychologist. (3) The definitions that stress the individual and his experiences. The third category will be the focus of our attention in our search for a soul.

Perhaps the best known of the latter type is William James's (**97** p. 31) definition, in which he describes religion as "the feelings, acts, and experiences of individual men in their solitude, so far as they apprehend themselves to stand in relation to whatever they may consider the divine." The psychoanalyst, Fromm (**71**, p. 21), gives his definition as "any system of thought and action shared by a group which gives the individual a frame of orientation and an object of devotion." With an emphasis more akin to that of James, Clark (**34**, p. 22) states his definition:

Religion can be most characteristically described as the inner experience of the individual when he senses a Beyond, especially as evidenced by the effects of this experience on his behavior when he actively attempts to harmonize his life with the Beyond.

There is in Clark's definition a threefold emphasis on inwardness, mysticism, and effect that offers a convenient starting point for the discussion of the nature of religion.

Inwardness.—Religion in an individual can be the result of a response to many factors. It could be a reaction to the group or an effort by the individual to gain status, by aligning himself with a certain church in much the same way as he would join the country club or a similar organization. However, if there is no inner response, it will probably have little or no effect upon his personality. In many ways this is the crux of the problem of the much vaunted objectivity of the investigators, who have had no such inner experiences themselves and find it impossible to comprehend the inward religious experience of others.

Mysticism.—Clark does not name the deity but simply uses the term "beyond." Neither does James nor Fromm. Religious people become concerned at this point, as there is a conviction at the heart of every devout believer that his deity and his alone is the one true and only God. But men worship all types of gods, some of which will be encountered in later chapters. It will be seen that people not only have gods of wood and stone but also abstract virtues, such as reason, as objects of worship. Even more remarkable, the denial of all religion —atheism—can itself become a religion.

Results.—Clark's definition agrees with James's emphasis on the

pragmatic aspect of religion. James was concerned with what religion did to people, and it has been said that the phrase "Fruits not roots," expresses James's attitude. Jung (**104**, p. 4) made a similar emphasis:
Read.

Religion, as the Latin word denotes is . . . a dynamic existence or effect, not caused by an arbitrary act of will. On the contrary, it seizes and controls the human subject, which is always rather its victim than its creator.

Similarly, Fromm (**71**, p. 26) feels that psychology is tempted to spend too much time looking for the psychological roots of religion rather than being concerned about its value for the individual.

The emphasis on results serves to highlight the difference between faith and belief. Clark (**34**, pp. 224-25) shows that belief is a static term which does not have the emotional connotations of faith. Faith is a more dynamic word. A person may believe that Pluto is a planet, and it has little effect on his behavior. Whereas, faith in God has implications of loyalty and obligation. Fosdick (**64**, p. 542) says of Martin Luther's faith, that for him, "Faith means not so much 'a believing about God' as 'a lively, reckless confidence in the grace of God.' " Erasmus, on the other hand, was a great intellectual contemporary, but his belief did little to upset life's easy pathway. Speaking of the great Reformation movement, when men were committing themselves to one side or the other, he defined his own position by saying, "The wise navigator will steer between Scylla and Charybdis. I have sought to be a spectator of this tragedy" (**13**, p. 198). With academic detachment he could stand off and survey the scene. But faith involves commitment and sometimes at a great risk. Without final certainty, the man of faith takes the risk in an effort to please the deity that he worships.

A discussion of the nature of religion raises almost as many questions as it answers and leaves a vague apprehension as to whether a clear and satisfying formulation will ever be made. Nevertheless, we all have the feeling that we know what religion *is* even though we may not be able to define it. Inwardness, mysticism, and activity are always an integral part of the experience.

Postulates of Religious Factors in Personality

One of the most helpful concepts in educational theory is Robert J. Havighurst's "developmental tasks." Havighurst (**81**, p. 2) shows

that in the developing personality there are certain tasks to be ac-
complished. He defines developmental tasks:

A developmental task is a task which arises at or about a certain period
in the life of the individual, successful achievement of which leads to his
happiness and to success with later tasks, while failure leads to unhappiness in the individual, disapproval by the society, and difficulty with later
tasks.

Developmental tasks involve three factors: (1) Physical maturation.
At a certain stage in his growth and development the individual is
"ready" to learn a particular physical or social skill. (2) Cultural pressures which demand that the person develop abilities and skills to fit
into his society. (3) The personal values and aspirations of the
individual.

The mentioning of personal values and aspirations opens the way
for a discussion of religion and personality development. Each of the
factors inherent in a "developmental task" is also a factor in religious
experience.

Physical maturation.—This is involved in the differing types of
religious experience through which the individual passes at various
stages of his physical development. The relationship between puberty
and conversion is the most obvious of the formulations involving
physical maturation.

Cultural pressures.—Havighurst's second factor has its counterpart in the "religious culture" of the individuals' lives. Although
colored by surrounding society, the religious community has its own
particular set of expectations for both children and adults, and these
expectations will influence the individual.

The individual's personal values and aspirations.—These represent
the area of personality where religion plays its most telling role. What
is accepted as a value, the conflict between desire and conceived
duty, and the vital life decisions are all tied up with religious convictions.

It might be said that there are "religious developmental tasks"
which concern the religious educator. At what age can we expect a
child to have a significant religious experience? When should an individual be baptized, confirmed, or received into the religious community? How should the picture of God be presented to the child?
What image is to be projected at what particular stage of growth?

Are these skills in religious living to be learned at appropriate stages of development? The concept of the *teachable moment,* so important in secular education, will be equally important in religious education.

For convenience, the thought in the following chapters on personality and religion will be gathered around postulates. According to Allport (**9,** p. 6) the founder of experimental psychology, Wilhelm Wundt, stated that "there is no psychological law to which the exceptions are not more numerous than the agreements."

If this were true of the laws set out by Wundt after such careful laboratory consideration, it will naturally follow that our basic postulates will be far from final, and open to challenge and question. However, they will serve as starting points for our thinking. The basic postulates for consideration are:

1. Man's genetic endowment and his physical and sociocultural environment are an important but not determinative factor in the development of personality.

2. The recognition of unconscious elements is vital in considering religious factors in personality.

3. The focusing of one's love on the right object at the appropriate time is of moment in studying religious factors in personality.

4. Religion is an important ingredient in the maturing of personality.

5. The development of mental health is facilitated rather than inhibited by a mature religious faith.

6. The development of ego-strength in personality is assisted by religious motivations.

These postulates will form the basis for the discussion in chapters 5 through 11.

Points of Agreement

Religion and personality must have a close relationship, as a man simply uses the capacities of his organism in his religious experiences. With characteristic perception William James (**97,** pp. 27-28) noted years ago:

There is religious fear, religious love, religious awe, religious joy, and so forth. But religious love is only man's natural emotion of love directed to a religious object; religious fear is only the ordinary fear of commerce, so to speak, the common quaking of the human breast, in so far as the notion of divine retribution may arouse it; religious awe is the same organic thrill which we feel in a forest at twilight, or in a mountain gorge; only this time it comes over us at the thought of our supernatural relations; and similarly of all the various sentiments which may be called into play in the lives of religious persons.

The old idea of a religious instinct or sentiment which was an extra to the religious individual's personality has been dropped by modern investigators. Religious experiences come through the same avenue that all other experiences come to the human being.

From the examination of both the concepts of personality and religion some common grounds become discernible, and eight similarities emerge.

1. Both religion and personality are intangibles. Efforts to define both of them have met with little success, and any formulation is open to question.

2. Personality and religion are highly subjective areas of life, and it is not easy to devise objective means of evaluation. The report of the individual will always constitute a significant part in the evaluation of both religion and personality.

3. Personality and psychology of religion have each experienced difficulty in finding their place in the field of academic psychology. The antipathy of psychology to religion has already been encountered, and Hall and Lindzey (79, p. 4) note that personality theory has never been deeply embedded in the main stream of academic psychology.

4. The functional orientation is characteristic of the two. Personality theorists are concerned about how an individual reacts and adjusts to life. Religion, although often charged to the contrary, points to changed behavior and attitudes as the evidences of its veracity.

5. The whole person is the focus for personality theory, and more and more there is a rejection of a segmented idea of personality. Religion, too, is emphasizing an influence which covers the whole of life.

6. Wayne E. Oates (141, p. 47) notes that religion and personality can both be defined in terms of man's uniqueness which separates him from other species, and the individual from other members of his race.

7. Personality theorists have been concerned about motivation, and the "why" of behavior has a strange attraction for Hall and Lindzey

(79, p. 5). Religion, too, has been vitally interested in life's motivations.

8. Religion and personality affect each other. An individual's personality affects his cognizance of his religious experience, and his religious experience changes aspects of his personality.

With so much common ground there is possibility for a creative relationship between personality and religion. But it may be just love at first sight or an infatuation. Can these two be really united? Can they bear to be close to each other? Will the match bring forth a new and vigorous feeling? The following chapters may serve to show whether it was a short-lived marriage, or whether they settled in the first stage of "living happily ever after."

5

The Third Determinant

Wordsworth in his *Intimations of Immortality*, conjectured about the newborn babe and what it brought into the world and concluded:

> Not in entire forgetfulness,
> And not in utter nakedness,
> But trailing clouds of glory do we come.

While the nature of Wordsworth's "clouds of glory" may be uncertain, we do know that each individual enters the world with inherited biological equipment. At the time of fertilization, the ovum has about forty-six chromosomes, half of which come from the mother and half from the father. The chromosomes, in turn, contain the genes, the real carriers of heredity. The processes by which the respective legacies of both parents are passed on are complex, but factors such as bodily structure, latent skills, and intelligence comprise a goodly part of the individual's inherited assets.

To the genetic endowment must be added the influences of environment. In the appropriate environment inherited factors find the conditions for optimum development. Environment may be divided and classified as *physical*, referring to the natural world surrounding the individual, and *sociocultural*, including the world of people, customs, and values.

Some of the hottest controversies of the past have raged about the roles of heredity and environment in the developmental process. Resolution has sometimes come by viewing the two factors as inextricably intertwined, it being virtually impossible to tell where one ends and the other begins. We will use the word "environment" in its broadest sense to describe an individual's total life situation.

An easy oversimplification of life is contained in the statement, "A man is just a product of his heredity and environment." The determinism implied in the statement is often thoughtlessly propagated. Determinism has been defined by Horace and Ava C. English (57, p. 147) as

the doctrine that an event is completely explicable in terms of its antecedents. Applied to human actions it holds that, given complete knowledge of conditions, one would have complete knowledge of precisely how a person will—indeed *must*—act.

Determinism has psychological, sociological, religious, and even political implications. Psychology of religion must concern itself with determinism, for both psychology and religion have felt its impact. We will commence by considering the almost monotonous regularity with which the emphasis has been made in psychology, sociology, and religion.

Psychology

The overtones of determinism are noticeable in the theorizings and formulations of a great number of the schools of psychological thought. Although psychological theories show wide variance in their speculations about the factors affecting individual growth and development, it is probably inherent in the nature of psychological theory that causality should be an overshadowing factor, with the individual viewed as the product of life's multiple forces.

Genetic determinism is the expression often used to describe Sheldon's theory of personality. Each person's bodily shape and structure is of a certain type, and this body type has been shown statistically to correspond with a type of reaction to life. Behavior and body type are thus closely related to each other. Even in the matter of rewards and punishments, the body type of the individual determines the manner in which the subject responds. These relationships are so close that, not only does a difference appear between the physiological characteristics of delinquents and normals, but there are distinctive differences between the various subvarieties of delinquents. The individual's body structure determines in a large measure the sort of person he is going to be.

Freud's scientific background and training paved the way for his deterministic emphasis. Jones (101, I, 366) says Freud would certainly have agreed with the statement of his teacher, Neynert, when he said, "Even the freedom we feel within ourselves is only apparent." The individual is unconscious of the background factors operative in his decision making, but his choice has been determined by a whole series of causal events. The events of early life lay down the patterns for later adjustment. The experiences of breast feeding, toilet training, child-parent relationships, and infantile desires all pave the way for later adjustment to life. It has been commented that for Freud the drama of life was but a repetition of the plot of infancy. Freud (**69**, p. xvi) himself declares: "Thus the civilized adult is the result of his childhood or the sum total of his early impressions; psychoanalysis thus confirms the old saying: The child is father to the man." It is generally agreed that Freud sees the foundations of character as being established by the time the child is three years old. Freud's painstaking work on the unconscious and his belief in the regular chain of mental events made him the pre-eminent example of *psychic determinism.*

Alfred Adler, a disciple of Freud, left the Freudian fold and replaced the Freudian emphasis on sex with one on the social aspects of life. A primary social grouping is the family, and the position in the family becomes a crucial factor in the development of the child's "style of life," which may become a lasting influence by the age of four or five. The oldest child tends to be conservative and, having the total love of the family for so long, wants to maintain his original status unchallenged. The second child is constantly trying to catch up with the pacesetter before him. His twofold temptations are (1) that he will develop an exaggerated ambition and (2) that he may tend to be a revolutionary endeavoring to upset the status quo.

A particularly difficult situation is that of the youngest child. He has all the love of the family lavished upon him and, consequently, grows up expecting to be loved by everybody. Adler's formulations came from his clinical experience, and not all investigators agree with him. Nevertheless, the conclusions reached in this area of his theory showed the heavy social emphasis on the deterministic influence of the family environment.

The behaviorist psychologists made an entirely different emphasis from the constitutional, Freudian, or allied schools. Seeing man as a stimulus-response mechanism, making him akin to a machine, they reject concepts such as the conscious, and have developed a heavy environmental emphasis. The environment of infancy and childhood helps the conditioning processes, which in turn build in habit patterns functioning in later reactions to life. Watson's (**182**, pp. 104, 94) most dogmatic statement was:

Give me a dozen healthy infants, well-formed, and my own specified world to bring them up in and I'll guarantee to take any one at random and train him to become any type of specialist I might select—doctor, lawyer, artist, merchant—chief, and, yes, even beggar-man and thief, regardless of his talents, penchants, tendencies, abilities, vocations, and race of his ancestors. . . . There is no such thing as an inheritance of capacity, talent, temperament, mental constitution and characteristics.

Here environmental influences reach their zenith in Watson's emphasis on the all-powerful molder of the character of man.

The positivistic ideas of personality are also attacked by Allport because of the emphasis on environment. Positivists see man as primarily a reactive being. Busy studying white rats in laboratories, the reaction inference is easily drawn. The psychologist's vocabulary is studded with terms like reflex, reaction, response, and retention, which are a hundred times more frequently used than terms with the *pro* prefixes—programing, propriate, proceeding, promise. The inference is that man just reacts to his environment rather than acting upon it.

Religion

Turning from psychology, we are not altogether prepared for the strong religious emphasis on environmental factors in personality, but it is there for all who have eyes to see. In Old Testament times the atmosphere of the home was to influence the children to grow and to take on their parents' religious convictions.

The classical passage in the book of Deuteronomy is:

Thou shalt love the Lord thy God with all thine heart, and with all thy soul, and with all thy might. And these words, which I command thee this day, shall be in thine heart: And thou shalt teach them diligently unto thy children, and shalt talk of them when thou sittest in thine house, and when thou walkest by the way, and when thou liest down, and when thou risest up. And thou shalt bind them for a sign upon thine hand, and they shall be as frontlets between thine eyes. And thou shalt write them upon the posts of thy house, and on thy gates (Deut. 6:5-9).

Much of the symbolism of the Old Testament was geared to impress-

ing the developing child mind. The Feast of the Passover concluded with the child asking, "What mean ye by this service?" and the father would accept the responsibility of explaining the rite to him.

In modern times both Roman Catholics and Protestants have stressed environment. The Roman Catholic Church, with its insistence upon parochial schools, has been credited with claiming that given the child for the first seven years of its life, he would remain a Roman Catholic for the rest of his days. Similarly, the emphasis upon programs of religious education within Protestant churches is an acknowledgment of the importance of the early environment. An investigation carried out at Southwestern Baptist Theological Seminary with leaders in the field of religious education revealed that most of the superior leaders came from devout religious homes, while many of those not successful came from homes with little Christian influence. The modern institutional emphasis in church life is a continued recognition of the belief in environmental influences.

Forces opposed to religion pay their tribute to the environmental influences. In Communist Russia children may not be taught religion, and no one is permitted to join a church until he is eighteen years of age.

Some commentators have seen deterministic influences in some of the churches' theological formulations. Calvinism has been viewed as a determinism concept, in which the individual is predestined to follow a certain pathway in life, and nothing that he ever does will change his ultimate destiny. Seldom overt, the deterministic emphasis constantly lurks in the background of religious concepts.

Sociology

Lenski (116, p. 3) shows that there were two influences in the development of sociology. A child of the French Englightenment, from its beginning sociology was committed to the positivist idea that religion in men is a survival of the past which is doomed, and will ultimately disappear. A second influence came in sociology's formative years, when the theory of economic determinism brought its emphasis on the economic institutions of society which determine all social change.

Because of the very nature of their work, sociologists give a good deal of thought to environmental influences. One example of a sociological investigation indicates this emphasis. In *Predicting De-*

linquency and Crime, Sheldon and Eleanor Glueck have developed a system of predicting criminal behavior. After many years of careful investigation, this husband and wife team has come up with the startling premise that criminal behavior can be forecast almost as accurately as an insurance company figures the odds on accidents and deaths.

By studying elaborate statistics on thousands of criminals, the Gluecks isolated key factors to be used in predicting delinquency. They have pinpointed the "five highly decisive factors" in family life: father's discipline, mother's supervision, father's affection toward his son, mother's affection, and cohesiveness of the family. It is claimed that these environmental factors are so important that, using them as a basis, predictions were made and compared with case histories of two thousand delinquents in New York. The predictions were found to be 90 per cent accurate. It was also discovered that the tables were just as useful when used as a basis for prediction in Japan and France.

The Gluecks indicate that it may be possible to head off delinquency by changing the environment. If even two of the "five highly decisive factors" are altered, the prospects of delinquency may be reduced from nine chances out of ten to six chances out of ten. The manipulation of environment is obviously a vital factor in the Gluecks' predictions about delinquency.

Economic Determinism

We have already noted Lenski's statement that economic determinism has influenced sociology. But it affects not only sociology. The concept, like a furtive thief operating under the cover of darkness, has crept into many areas of thought. Stated very simply, economic determinism means that the institutions of society are determined by the prevailing mode of economic production. It is a Marxian idea. Engels, writing in the preface of the *Communist Manifesto,* states the basic proposition which underlies the whole writing:

That in every historical epoch, the prevailing mode of economic production and exchange, and the social organization necessarily following from it, form the basis upon which is built up, and from which alone can be explained, the political and intellectual history of that epoch (**125,** p. 7).

He then claims that this proposition of Karl Marx was destined to be as important for history as Darwin's theory was for biology.

Schwartzchild (**159**, p. 121) says that economic determinism rises in a three-story structure. The ground floor is the productive forces—the tools, machines, and technical processes which man has at his disposal. From the productive forces comes the second floor, which is the economic and social system. The third story of the structure is made up of the laws, ideas, and morals of a given society, which develop out of the previous two. It might further be added that the whole structure has an atheistic foundation, for it is materialistic through and through. It is built upon the basic premise that there is no God and that men and women are merely animals.

The concept has even been given biological significance. Commenting on the work of the great biologist, Michurin, his biographer, Bakharev (**14**, p. 77), says:

Michurin's general biological theory is based on dialectical materialism, the world outlook of the Marxist-Leninist Party. Materialist dialectics teaches that views and beliefs, and the whole outlook of man are determined by the conditions of material life of society.
"The order of ideas . . . depends on the order of things."

These formulations went so far as to effect the official views on heredity for many years. Mendelian ideas in genetics were rejected, and Lysenko's concept that acquired characteristics could be inherited was officially adopted. Environment was seen to be so powerful that it was felt that the official doctrine should allow the benefits of one generation to be passed on to the next, and the theory was accepted despite the opposition of reputable scientific evidence.

In its extension of the doctrine of economic determinism, Marxism has postulated that the ideas of man come from his economic environment. "Your very ideas are but the outgrowth of the conditions of your bourgeois production and bourgeois property" (**125**, p. 47). The *Manifesto* declared that the institution of the family is a product of economic environment. "On what foundation is the present family, the bourgeois family, based? On capital, on private gain" (**125**, p. 48). But it comes even closer to home for us when it goes on to postulate that religion is the product of the economic environment of the individual. Even the cherished value of religious liberty is accounted for by Marx when he says, "The idea of religious liberty and freedom of conscience, merely gave expression to the sway of free competition within the domain of knowledge" (**125**, p. 52).

There are important implications here for personality theory. Marxism presupposes that under the rule known as "the dictatorship of the proletariat," a man may be placed in the "correct" environment. Here human nature can be miraculously transformed, and the processes of perfection take place until he becomes a fit member of the idealistic state of communism. So heavy has been the environmental emphasis, without any respect for the distinctives of the individual, that it has called forth the derisive remark of Max Eastman:

In building a model hen-house a Marxian would have the good sense to consider the instinctive nature of the hens, but in building an ideal social structure for mankind, he is prevented by his religion from even asking a question about the natural tendencies of this animal (**63**, p. 194).

Significantly, the day the Communists have looked for to usher in "the withering away of the state," and bring a paradise on earth, has continually receded into the distance. The constant purges, the continually consolidating class system, and the overshadowing, all-powerful dictatorial state have shown that this materialistic concept is inadequate to bring about a change in personality. Even in Communist countries, economic determinism has been weighed in the balance and found wanting.

Rather than being an example of the validity of economic determinism, religion is, as Lenski points out, an illustration of its lack of validity. The argument is that ideas are only a reflection of the prevailing method of economic production. But when we examine the characteristics of the major religions of the world, we are impressed with their continuity rather than their flexibility. Creeds formulated fifteen hundred years ago are accepted by major groups this very day. Scriptures that are two or three thousand years old continue to be the guides for faith and practice. Ideas about the nature of God, formulated over three thousand years ago and believed by primitive people living in distant societies, are accepted and believed by people in urban industrial societies of today. There have been some changes in religion. But the same form of production is associated with different types of religion, and the same type of religion with different forms of production. Continuity rather than change is the predominant characteristic of religion.

Many thoughtful people are questioning the over-simplification involved in deterministic views of personality. Sometimes the whole argument runs in circles, as is shown in the interchange between Archbishop Temple and a questioner.

A reckless young student, who had a smattering of psychology, once attacked Archbishop Temple with the accusation, "You only believe what you believe because of your early upbringing." The Archbishop promptly dispatched him with the reply, "You only believe that I believe what I believe because of my early upbringing, because of *your* early upbringing." Thus the boomerang returns (5, p. 109).

An article in a national magazine called, "The Cop with the Criminal Brother," told the story of two boys from the same family. There were five in the family, and the eldest boy became a lieutenant in the police department of a big American city, while the other developed into a much-wanted criminal in the same city. There was obviously more than either straight heredity or environment at work in the situation. The individual has a perspective and part to play in life, which cannot be discarded for mere deterministic considerations.

The Third Determinant

Coleman (**38**, p. 61) discusses the determinants of personality and, after referring to man's genetic endowment and his physical and sociocultural environment, calls attention to " 'self' as the third determinant." Far too long, the major consideration has been given to the factors of heredity and environment. Allport (**4**, p. 83) maintains that it is possible to look through hundreds of American books on psychology and find absolutely no mention of the words "will" or "freedom." Now comes the overdue recognition by some that an individual, becoming conscious of his own separate identity, interprets life's experiences from his own peculiar perspective.

The attack on determinism has come from different fronts. Some of the leading personality theorists have declared themselves. Hall and Lindzey (**79**, p. 543) state the situation:

In contrast, Allport, Lewin, and to some extent Rogers, explicitly stress the lack of continuity in development and the relative independence of the functioning adult from the events of childhood or infancy. . . . All of these theorists suggest that somewhat different principles may be needed to account for what takes place at different stages of development.

Allport's (**9**, p. 200) concept of "functional autonomy" buttresses the attack, as he insists adult motivations are not just a continuation of those in infancy. The neurosis is one of Allport's most convincing pieces of evidence. Certain acquired modes of behavior, such as tics, stammering, sexual perversions, and anxieties, are stubborn and difficult to rectify. Frequently spoken of as "symptoms," the inference is that discovery of the original cause will lead to their disappearance. But the finding of the cause often makes no difference, and the neurotic reactions carry on in their own right. Therapy just based on the discovery of the cause is not necessarily effective. The individual has to learn new ways of reaction, learn how to handle his symptom, and gain insight into what it is doing for him at this present moment, apart altogether from the original cause.

The burgeoning counseling services of our day, with types of counseling assistance of which our grandparents never dreamed, have been seen as a symptom of this "age of anxiety." But they represent more than that. A counselor is motivated by a faith in the relative independence of the individual, his capacity to change and realize his potential. Rogers (156, p. 30) sees the counseling relationship, not just as setting the stage for new activity, but as a growth experience in which the individual develops and gains momentum in handling life at this moment, apart from past experiences or present circumstances.

Marriage counseling represents an effort towards adjustment. Two relatively normal individuals may have an unsatisfactory marriage because they cannot adjust to each other. If human nature is seen as rigid and unchangeable, assistance will be futile. Mudd (133, p. 35) expresses the alternative view:

If, however, the counselor views personality as an unfolding, evolving, ever-growing, and developing expression of almost limitless potentialities and inner strengths which only need assistance to achieve fruition, he himself, as well as his client, will envision broad goals and will marshal the inner resources of the client toward their realization.

This view of personality is, by and large, familiar to counselors and more particularly marriage counselors.

The amount of success coming from their efforts has justified the confidence of marriage counselors.

Education has been greatly influenced by the stimulus-response concept. However, Ernest Ligon (118, p. xi), one of the outstanding research workers in the field of religious education, lays down as one of his basic concepts, "that the individual influences his environment far more than his environment influences him." Later, Ligon (**118**, p. 78) considers stimulus-response concepts and says:

Traditionally we have thought of the S [stimulus] as something to which the individual must adjust. He is almost a pawn in it. Now, we suddenly discover that in a far more real sense the individual decides what S [stimulus] he will face.

Coming as Ligon's statement does from a lifetime of research in education, he shows his faith in the changeability of human nature and the motivation back of his emphasis on character education.

The horrendous catastrophe of World War II came from Hitler's concept of a master race which could be made to order. Frankl (**65**, p. xxi) writes: "The gas chambers of Auschwitz were the ultimate consequence of the theory that man is nothing but the product of heredity and environment—or, as the Nazis liked to say, of 'blood and soil.'" Frankl, a Viennese psychiatrist, went through the horror of a concentration camp. From the awful experience of watching the behavior of both guards and victims, he lifts his voice in a plea for the consideration of factors other than heredity and environment in determining personality patterns.

A devastating attack on Freud's determinism comes from a former follower. Making a survey of the distinctive contributions of the depth psychologists, Ira Progoff discusses the "big four": Freud, Adler, Jung, and Rank. Each of the latter three was originally a follower of Freud but later developed a distinctive system. These had some elements in common with Freud but also strong disagreements, which alienated each man from his former teacher. A series of names developed. Freud's theory was called *psychoanalysis;* Adler's, *individual* psychology; Jung's, *analytic* psychology; and Rank's, *will* psychology. Progoff claims that the basic attack on Freud was against his determinism and materialistic interpretation of personality. Otto Rank particularly took issue over the place, nature, and influence of the will. He even went so far as to say that the realm of willing was the actual ground of psychology.

For Rank, the conflicts of life serve to develop the will, which reveals itself as the heart of individuality. He claimed that any avoidance of a formulation of an idea of a will may represent an attempt by mankind to evade the responsibilities of life. According to Progoff

(**149**, p. 199), he spoke enthusiastically about "a constructive will psychology, in the center of which we again place the ego, with its old rights and newly won prerogatives." Progoff feels that the peculiar insights of Rank into the nature of the will are the key to the understanding of all his work, both therapeutic and theoretical.

An analogy may help. The first launching of a man into orbital flight around the earth by the United States of America represented a triumph of scientific technology. Automation had been highly developed, and the astronaut seemed to be just "going along for the ride." However, once in flight there was a slight malfunction, and the astronaut, instead of spending his time making observations, took control of his spaceship. Man's biological inheritance may be likened to the spaceship, and the programed flight with its automatic controls may be seen as being similar to the pattern of life determined by factors of environment. But man can take control if he will. After the first space flight, Colonel Glenn said, "Now we can get rid of some of that automatic equipment and let man take over" (**166**, p. 11). Glenn's advice might well be given to personality theorists. It is time for a recognition of the will and the actively functioning ego.

Alfred Adler developed the widely popularized term "inferiority complex" and showed that feelings of inferiority were often the very stimulus leading to change. A popular writer expounded Adler's idea and titled his writing, "The Importance of Feeling Inferior." The very feeling of inferiority was a motivating force. Adler was concerned with the mental mechanism of *compensation*. He referred to "the human being's power to turn a minus into a plus." The classical illustration used is Demosthenes, the Greek who stammered and stuttered. Becoming conscious of his disadvantage, he went to the edge of the seashore where he put a pebble in his mouth and cried out against the voice of the waves. Ultimately, he became the greatest orator of antiquity. A set of circumstances which dramatized his disadvantage motivated him to do something about changing his life situation.

The will used to be the center of controversy in theology, as writers like Jonathan Edwards struggled with the problem of man's will. In those days the concern was whether or not man could exercise his will against God. The question has now turned in a strange new direction, and the concern in theology and psychology of religion is whether a man can exercise his will against his environment. The mounting evidence shows that he can.

The possibility of changing the environment is developed in Max Weber's essay, *The Protestant Ethic and the Spirit of Capitalism,* in which he seeks to show that without the Protestant ethic Western capitalism may not have developed. According to Weber, capitalism developed not so much through the spirit of greed which has always characterized mankind but through the spirit of dedication and commitment to work. For him the spirit of Protestantism was distinguished by two main characteristics: (1) a conviction that work was a worthwhile activity in its own right, and not merely a means to material comfort or wealth; and (2) a distaste for personal indulgence. An almost inevitable accumulation of wealth followed.

Weber found the genesis of the spirit of capitalism in Protestantism in general, and more specifically in Calvinism and Puritanism. It was an unintended by-product of these religious movements. The followers of Luther and Calvin saw work, not as a penalty for sin, but as a means of glorifying God. Self-indulgence was a deadly sin for a Calvinist or a Puritan. The Methodists shared the same idea, and John Wesley in one of his sermons stated the situation:

Wherever riches have increased the essence of religion has decreased in the same proportion. Therefore I do not see how it is possible in the nature of things for any revival of religion to continue long. For religion must necessarily produce both industry and frugality, and these cannot but produce riches. But as riches increase, so will pride, anger, and love of the world in all its branches. How then is it possible that Methodism, that is a religion of the heart, though it flourishes now as the green bay tree, should continue in this state? For Methodists in every place grow diligent and frugal; consequently they increased in goods. Hence, they proportionately increase in pride, in anger, in the desire of the flesh, the desire of the eyes, and the pride of life. So, although the form of religion remains, the spirit is swiftly vanishing away. Is there no way to prevent this—this continual decay of pure religion? (**165**, pp. 305-6).

Wesley's answer to the problem he posed was, "Gain all you can, save all you can, give all you can," with the idea that the Methodists once again enter the cycle of starting to earn again.

For us the significant factor is that man's religious motivation caused him to alter his environment rather than conform to it. In his studies in Detroit, Lenski (**116**, p. 322) found substantial confirmation for the Weber thesis that religious motivations were more important than environment. Within given social situations motivations were found to be different, and even the type of religion effected the intensity of the drive of an individual.

The spell of psychological determinism is being broken. Human nature is not just like concrete, made with a predetermined mixture, poured into the mold of environment, set into rigidity, and henceforth unchangeable. The ego or decision-making self will always have a potential role in personality's development. The individual's ideas and concepts are more than a mere reflection of his environment, and they have a tremendous inherent power to bring about a change in one's situation. As Weber and, more recently, Lenski have shown, a religious motivation brings a new power, enabling the individual to turn from his environmental prison, tear it down, and reconstruct it into anything from a cottage to a mansion.

The Self as Theme

Like a musical composition which has a theme or a motif, this book, by its very nature and purpose, has a constantly recurring concept of the soul or self. Periodically it will appear, and reappear, as part of the quest of psychology in search of a soul.

In this chapter the first muted tone of the theme is heard in the protest against the determinism so freely taught, and unthinkingly accepted. It has been said there is nothing so practical as good theory, and the practical outcome of a deterministic theory is a lack of respect for the rights, privileges, and responsibilities of the individual. Democracy has had a long and often troubled development, but it is based on the premise that an ordinary man has the ability to make the decisions necessary for the well-being of the state. A theory of personality which fits the facts of experience must recognize the peculiar abilities of the decision-making self. Heredity and environment are both important, but man is never their helpless pawn. The ego or self is revealed in its executive functionings.

The unconscious is considered in chapter 6, which deals with the concealed aspects of psychic life. Seen along with the cosmological and biological insults, the psychological blow to man's self-love can be considered as devastating. However crippling the first comprehension of the pushing, purposive, and primitive forces of the unconscious may seem to be on the ego or self, it still retains its importance. The ego must ultimately make the unconscious its servant rather than submit to it as a master.

The developing love life discussed in chapter 7 again focuses on the ego. All that is known of love begins with the dawning of self-consciousness, as the individual becomes aware of himself and then a series of love objects. In the strange and often bewildering vicissitudes of the developing love life, ego involvement and ego protection are in a constant interplay in the necessary adjustments of the individual.

Growth is a key concept. Ego growth and development are the result of many factors as the individual becomes aware of his body, develops his communication skills, reckons with reality, and learns to tolerate delay. Failure to grow represents the most fruitful source of maladjustment and ego weakness. Maturity is the center of discussion in chapter 8.

Mental health is essentially ego strength. The ego either manages the situation or is overwhelmed by it. Chapter 9 makes an effort to set the self in its psychological and religious setting as it seeks for optimum mental health.

A discussion of the systems of personality in chapter 10 brings us to the heart of the whole matter. In any discussion of this type the ego will of necessity come to the front. The complex interrelationships of impulses, ego, and value system focus on the essential role of the ego in the functioning of personality.

6

The Psychological Insult

In his book, *A General Introduction to Psychoanalysis,*
Freud (**67**, p. 289) claimed that science had dealt a number of blows
that hurt man's pride. Karl Stern elaborates the three insults to man's
self-love: (1) The cosmic insult. The discoveries of Copernicus
showed that, contrary to man's fondly held view, the earth was not
the center of the universe but only a speck in a tremendous celestial
system. (2) The biological insult. For Freud, the formulation of
Charles Darwin's theory of organic evolution, claiming man was not
different from the animals, was an insult to his self-love. (3) The
psychological insult. In Freud's view this was the bitterest blow of all.
It came from his own psychological research, which he claimed
showed that man is not master of his own house, as he so fondly
imagines, but in a large measure is motivated by unconscious forces
of his personality.

Unconscious behavior is that about which the individual is unaware
of the motives or reasons. Consequently, the investigation of its acti-
vating forces presents a formidable task. Despite this, however, in our
search for a soul we must take cognizance of unconscious factors as
they affect both personality and religion.

The Topography of Mental Processes

Dynamic psychology sees the mind as functioning at three levels:
(1) the conscious, (2) the preconscious, and (3) the unconscious.
Not to be thought of as watertight compartments, nor unmovable divisions, one shades off into another. It is difficult to be dogmatic about
the specific details of any of the levels.

The *conscious* is that part of the mental processes which is concerned with immediate awareness. You know who you are and what
you are doing. At this moment you are conscious that you are

reading, and your attention may be turned to any number of objects of which you are immediately aware.

The *preconscious* is that area which has material in it that is recallable by focusing attention upon it. The name of a friend, the address of a house in which you live, the mental image of someone you know, what you had for breakfast this morning. Each is now conscious. A moment ago it was preconscious but available for recall.

The *unconscious* contains material not recallable at will. It may be likened to the basement of a home, having space for both the accumulation of articles in storage and also the heating system. It is a vast storehouse of material, once conscious but now relegated to the unconscious. Within it, too, like the furnace and the boiler, are the primitive strivings and emotionalized but forgotten experiences of earlier days. Carrington (**29**, p. 22) gives a summary of the unconscious concept:

The whole pattern of the Freudian concept is built on the existence and power of this deep unconscious part of the mind, without which the field of consciousness would be so cluttered up with useless material that the ego could not function properly. But however necessary the unconscious part of the mind may be for normal psychic function, it may provide some complex problems when psychic function is disturbed.

Several analogies have been used to depict the unconscious. One is the iceberg, six-sevenths submerged and one-seventh above the water. The one-seventh above the water and in full view represents the conscious, available for examination. The larger six-sevenths, hidden from view below the water, illustrates the powerful unconscious, proportionately greater than the conscious area.

Freud used the illustration of two adjoining rooms. He saw the conscious as an observer in the smaller room. The room itself is the preconscious, and the larger, curtained off, adjoining room is the unconscious. This larger room is full of mental excitations, crowding upon each other like anxious shoppers trying to get into the clearance sale. At the curtain leading into the smaller preconscious area stands a doorkeeper, called by Freud "the censor." Some of the excitations manage to enter the preconscious room, but others are turned back. Even if the excitations gain admission to the preconscious, it is still necessary for the observer to focus attention on them before they become conscious.

Jung adds another depth to the unconscious. A strange phenomenon may be seen in the Arbuckle Mountains in Oklahoma. Probably due to some catastrophic upheaval of a bygone day, a great section of earth has been torn up and laid flat, so that it is possible to walk along the surface of the mountain and see the various strata of the depths of the earth. It could be said that Jung's formulations are similar to the work of nature in the Arbuckle Mountains. He has gone beyond Freud in the development of the unconscious concept, and divides the totality of the unconscious into the "personal unconscious" and the "collective unconscious."

Once again, not to be thought of as hard and fast divisions, Progoff (149, p. 146) likens the layers of consciousness to a geological formation. The thin layer on the surface is the conscious. Thicker than the first but relatively thin, the next layer is the personal unconscious. Below these two is a deep formation of rock extending to the Plutonic core of the earth itself which is called the collective unconscious. The collective unconscious contains archetypes, which are psychic patterns present in all mankind as a species. These psychic patterns manifest themselves in the symbolism of myths which represent the transmission of unconsciously held beliefs in national cultures.

Jung produced evidence to substantiate his postulation of the collective unconscious. From a study of the mythology of primitive races, he was impressed by the similarity of their myths and tales, even though the people concerned lived in widely separated parts of the earth. Moreover, in his observations in his psychiatric practice, he found that clients utilized the same symbols as he had found in the ancient myths and tales. He also discovered that schizophrenic patients produced archaic and primitive images in their delusions and hallucinations. From these and other sources Jung was led to conclude that people everywhere had the same set of inherited potential ideas, and these constituted the collective unconscious.

Evidences of the Unconscious

It is not easy to prove the existence of the unconscious. Most of the conclusions have been arrived at from clinical experience. Although many of these would be difficult to demonstrate in a laboratory, a number of evidences have been produced to strengthen the concept of the unconscious.

Hypnosis is a fruitful source. A subject who has been hypnotized can often recall events of childhood of which he previously had no conscious knowledge. Age regression is a technique of hypnotherapy, in which the subject is put into hypnotic trance and it is suggested that he is living at an earlier age level. In the trance he may recount incidents which occurred at that earlier age, even though he had no conscious memory of the experiences previously. It is inferred that knowledge of the early part of life was stored somewhere, the hypothesis being that it was in the unconscious.

The phenomenon of posthypnotic suggestion offers helpful leads. The individual, having been put into a hypnotic trance, is given a suggestion of something he will do thirty minutes later. Coming out of the trance, exactly thirty minutes from the time when he was told, the subject performs the act, even though unaware of the reason. The explanation offered is that his unconscious was at work, even to the detail of measuring off thirty minutes of time.

It has long been noted that many people evidently have a built-in timing device, enabling them to wake from sleep at any time previously decided upon. The device is by no means infallible. One experimenter put it, "Sure I can wake up at 5:30 A.M. if I tell myself to do so before going to sleep. The only difficulty is that I also awaken at 1:30 A.M., 2:30 A.M., 3:30 A.M., and 4:30 A.M. just to check up on myself." Even though a student suggested that this capacity demonstrated "the power of mind over mattress," for inquirers, another particle of proof is added to the idea of the unconscious.

Slips of the tongue, which can be so humorous or so embarrassing, may demonstrate the work of the unconscious. The hostess, worn from all her tensions, says goodnight to her guests with the words, "I am so sorry you came." Although embarrassed, she has nevertheless unconsciously said what she really felt after her entertaining ordeal. A man who would rather have played tennis was cajoled into attending a prayer meeting. Called upon to pray, he said several times, "Lord we play—uh—uh—pray," thus revealing his really preferred way of spending the hour.

One of the early printings of the King James Version of the Bible is called the "Wicked Bible," because the "not" was left out of the Seventh Commandment, causing it to read, "Thou shalt commit adultery." Investigation into the embarrassed printer's personal life might have been very revealing. Interestingly, it was Jesus who said, "But I say unto you, That every idle word that men shall speak, they shall give account thereof in the day of judgment" (Matt. 12:36). Apparently, for Jesus, the unpremeditated word was the one which showed the true intent of the heart.

Another evidence of the unconscious is the mental process of incubation in which an idea develops with the lapse of time. After sleeping on a problem, the answer may become obvious. Amy Lowell tells of her procedure:

What I had really done was to drop the matter into the subconscious, much as one drops a letter into a mailbox. Six months later, the words of the poem began to come into my head, the poem—to use my private vocabulary—was "there" (12, p. 58).

John Dewey warned about the futility of keeping on past a certain limit, and he wrote about the necessity of putting the problem to one side:

Then after the mind has ceased to be intent on the problem, and consciousness has relaxed its strain, a period of incubation sets in. Material rearranges itself; facts and principles fall into place; what was confused becomes bright and clear; the mixed up becomes orderly, often to such an extent that the problem is essentially solved (12, p. 63).

Albert Einstein said that the implications of his theory of relativity came to him while he was strolling through the woods in Germany. The process of incubation was obviously important in each of these examples. Whether the individual is awake or asleep, it seems that his unconscious processes continue.

The phenomenon of dreaming may also be seen as an activity of the unconscious. In Freud's illustration of the conscious, preconscious, and unconscious, he showed that the mental excitations were crowded in the unconscious and were trying to push their way past the curtain into the preconscious section where the observer, representing consciousness, could focus attention upon them. In the dreaming process, Freud saw the censor at the curtain as temporarily off guard. The excitations in the unconscious, like people going to a Halloween party, changed their appearance and entered consciousness.

A dream has two aspects. The *manifest* content is the form of the image, while the *latent* content represents the dream's real meaning. A man dreamed that he was constantly chased by a small, curly-haired dog which continually snapped at his heels. Recounting the dream to his wife, she asked him to describe the dog, whereupon she said, "Do you mean it has curly hair like mother's?" The dreamer replied, "Er . . . er . . . yes." Unconscious resentment normally kept under control had manifested itself in the dream. Freud claimed that the dream was the fulfilment of a wish; the wish often buried deeply in the unconscious expressed itself in the form of the dream.

Dreaming is further complicated by the mechanisms used in transforming the unconscious wish into the manifest content. *Condensation* is the process by which the manifest content is more abbreviated than the latent idea. Some elements are omitted, and others are combined in the actual dream. A second mechanism is *displacement,* in which elements of the dream may be replaced by something more remote and less dangerous. *Symbolism* is the third and possibly most interesting aspect of dream work. Symbols are divided into two classes: (1) universal and (2) individual. Freud claimed that certain symbols are common to all, and these mainly have a sexual connotation. Individual symbols are distinctive to each person and must be interpreted in consideration of the dreamer's experience, conflicts, and relationships. Dreaming is so significant for some investigators that it has been called the royal road to the unconscious.

Forgetting may be an activity stemming from the unconscious. Intense preoccupations can cause forgetfulness, but forgetting may also be a purposeful activity, providing an avenue of escape. Counselors find that counselees facing difficult problems easily forget their appointment. In many instances people forget quite sincerely as their unconscious helps them out of difficult situations.

It is sometimes claimed that Freud discovered the unconscious, but this is obviously not so. There were many other thinkers who had postulated a similar phenomenon. Nevertheless, he did popularize the idea, although it was not as significant for him in his later thinking as in his earlier work. Altogether, the evidence from hypnosis, slips of the tongue, forgetting, problem solving, and dreaming builds a fairly solid case for the hypothetical unconscious.

The Nature of the Unconscious

The nature of the unconscious may be conveniently summed up in three words: (1) primitive, (2) purposive, and (3) pushing. The words illustrate the dynamic aspects of the unconscious.

The unconscious is *primitive*. Contained within it are forces that were necessary in the infancy of civilization, but which have troublesome possibilities for a twentieth-century culture. Walter Murdock illustrates with his essay, "Beasts in the Basement," in which he tells of inheriting a house from an eccentric aunt. At the reading of the will he discovered, to his dismay, that he was obliged under its terms to keep alive the strange collection of animals gathered by his aunt and housed in the cellar. A tiger had been brought from India by his grandfather; a parrot was given by his Great-aunt Celina; a donkey had been donated by Uncle Henry; and sundry other animals in the motley assortment had been donated by deceased relatives.

Compelled under the terms of the legacy to keep the menagerie alive, Murdock tried to conceal their existence, but he had some difficult moments. While entertaining friends, a lion would roar, a parrot screech, or a donkey bray. As they did, Murdock would shuffle his feet, clear his throat, turn up the radio, or in some way try to distract his guests' attention. Murdock (**135**, p. 184) interprets his parable:

> Now the figure of the private menagerie, to represent the subterranean workings of our minds, is so obvious that I expect it has been scandalously overworked. Caged within us, and kept in normal circumstances invisible to others and even to ourselves, are numerous wild primitive urges, tendencies, instincts, call them what you will, which we have inherited from savage forebearers. Civilized society implies their repression, but they are there all the time, alive and active. In certain circumstances, an old ancestral tiger of aggressiveness will wake in me and roar; try to make me do something distasteful to me, and an ancient mule will plant his hoofs firmly on the ground and refuse to budge; touch my vanity, and an atavistic porcupine will raise all his bristles; tickle one of my appetites, and you will hear the grunting of an immemorial pig; try to argue me out of an unreasonable prejudice, and a patriarchal donkey will lift his head to heaven and bray. . . . It is the survival, in civilized times, of impulses which were useful and indeed indispensable to savage man, but which are not compatible with civilization, that causes the trouble in the world today.

The New Testament has references to this part of personality. In the Pauline writings there are three references to "the old man," as when Paul says, "That ye put off concerning the former conversation the old man, which is corrupt according to the deceitful lusts" (Eph. 4:22). Similarly, Paul uses the word "flesh," with overtones of the primitive forces of man.

Another characteristic of the unconscious is its *purposiveness*. This primitive element of personality seeking self-preservation is fundamentally self-centered, striving to get the best deal for the individual even though he is unaware of the reality of the situation. A man asked by his wife to mow the lawn works at it for ten minutes, then staggers in to announce he is exhausted and stretches out on the couch to recuperate. A few minutes later a friend calls and invites him to play golf. His strength is miraculously restored, and he sallies forth to play a strenuous eighteen holes. The student, bored with his subject, feels too tired to study but after retiring cannot sleep for hours. The sleeplessness gives mute evidence of the purposive activity of the unconscious.

Illnesses known as functional have no physical basis but beautifully illustrate the purposiveness of the unconscious. The soldier in a difficult spot develops a paralysis of the leg necessitating his evacuation, the housewife tired of the never-ending routine gets a sick headache, and the preacher in a difficult church situation loses his voice. None of these things is done consciously. Each brings suffering, but it nevertheless offers the way of escape and is a manifestation of the purposive workings of the unconscious.

The unconscious is also *pushing*. In the spring of 1513 the Spaniard, Ponce de Leon, set sail westward from Puerto Rico seeking "The Fountain of Youth." Three small ships constituted the expedition which sighted land at a spot to be known in another age as Cape Kennedy. Turning south it seemed to them as if they were in the middle of a mighty river pushing against their small craft. In the words of the historian, Clarke (**35**, p. 80) says:

Although they had a great wind, they could not proceed forward, but backward, and it seemed that they were proceeding well, but in the end it was known that it was . . . the current that was more powerful than the wind.

The last two of the ships managed to anchor, but the third in deeper water was swiftly borne away northward. Little attention was paid to Ponce de Leon's experience. There was more interest in the mythical Fountain of Youth than in the amazing natural phenomenon which changes life in great areas of the world's surface.

Two and a half centuries later this was recognized as the Gulf Stream.

Ponce de Leon's ships, with sails bellowed out by the powerful northerly wind while traveling northward at a rapid rate, illustrate the power of the unconscious. The unrecognized forces of the unconscious, like the powerful moving Gulf Stream, are a constant, impelling force difficult to comprehend and harder still to manage. Like Ponce de Leon questing for the Fountain of Youth, it is easy to be preoccupied with unreal and superficial aims, overlooking the submerged and pushing forces of the unconscious.

Insights into unconscious motivations have even permeated advertising techniques. Rapidly developing M. R. (motivational research) finds that people prefer artificial flowers, renamed permanent flowers, because the wilting of natural flowers reminds them of death. Merchandisers are thus aiming to satisfy the hidden needs. Packard (**144**, p. 8) says, "The cosmetic manufacturers are not selling lanolin, they are selling hope. . . . we no longer buy oranges, we buy vitality. We do not buy just an auto, we buy prestige." The motivating power of the unconscious has had a belated recognition.

Repression and the Unconscious

Repression is the term used by dynamic psychologists to describe the mechanism which probably gives most trouble in the unconscious. *Repression* should not be confused with *suppression,* a word used to describe the voluntary process whereby material is recognized as unacceptable and excluded from the conscious. Repression represents the manner by which the mind unwittingly relegates painful memories and conflict to the unconscious. The process or mechanism of repression is depicted in the diagram below.

Repressed ideas are continually striving toward consciousness. Driven upward to consciousness by the unregulated urges, they are kept under control by the combined action of the ego, or self, and the value system. However, repression is never complete. It is as if a group of ruffians keep entering the house. The husband does not mind particularly, as he might have enjoyed their company under different circumstances, but his wife objects and insists that they be thrown out. The ruffians represent the repressed material striving for expression; the insistent wife depicts the individual's value system; the reluctant husband symbolizes the self, or ego.

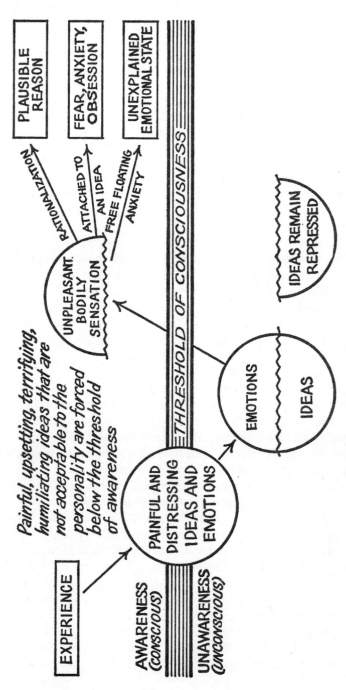

THE MECHANISM OF REPRESSION (ADAPTED)

Weatherhead (**184**, p. 252) suggests another analogy to illustrate difficulties coming from the highly emotional experiences in early life which have been repressed into the unconscious.

These forgotten, and psychologically traumatic incidents, charged with repressed emotion, are not allowed into consciousness because they are obnoxious to the patient's peace of mind, to his self-respect, to his ideal of himself, and so forth. But they do not lie dormant in the unconscious mind as mud lies at the bottom of a pond. Although withheld from consciousness, they revenge themselves, as it were, by expressing their energies in terms of mental symptoms of anxiety, or fear, or physical symptoms. . . .
To keep the analogy of the pond, we may imagine that the mud at the bottom contains fermenting material which sends up bubbles to the surface. So, on the surface of the mind, symptoms like the emotion of fear or the pain of asthma may be experienced, as different from their origin as bubbles are different from mud, but also as consequent.

Repressed ideas may continue to color life's experiences. A soldier in the army had difficulty in adjusting because of his submissive spirit. A psychiatric investigation revealed a deep-seated antagonism to his father. While undergoing narcotherapy, an altogether forgotten incident was revealed. In boyhood days his father had attacked him in the woodshed and beaten him into unconsciousness. Though forgotten, the emotion of the incident remained, and extensive therapy was needed before an adequate adjustment could be made.

With a characteristically thought-provoking approach, Jung (**103**, p. 31) says that psychoanalysis is a development of the basic ideas underlying the confessional. There is no causal relationship, and both go in different directions. But they may have the same psychic root. When man first became conscious of his shortcomings he tried to cover up. Jung calls the process "psychic concealment." Everything concealed is a secret, and the maintenance of a secret acts as a psychic poison which alienates the individual from others.

Secrets are essential for individuality and help to differentiate the individual from the community. Primitive man often found it necessary to invent secrets so that he would not have to dissolve into the mere unconsciousness of community life and so suffer a fatal psychic injury. Many of the ancient mystery cults with their secret rituals served this necessity for differentiation. Jung claims that the sacraments were looked upon as mysteries in the early church, and initiation gave a sense of belonging to the Christian community and sharing its secrets.

A secret shared with several persons may have values, but a private secret can be dangerous. If we are conscious of what we conceal, the harm done is less than if we do not know what we are repressing, or do not know that we have repressed at all. In the latter case we not only keep the matter consciously private, but we conceal it even from ourselves. It then splits off from consciousness as an independent entity to lead a separate existence in the unconscious where it can neither be corrected nor interfered with by the conscious mind. Jung sees repression in this autonomous role, developing a peculiar and destructive fantasy life of its own.

Religious Aspects of the Unconscious

The relationship of religion to the unconscious is an unexplored area. What has been done is peripheral and incidental. It may be that the crass materialism of Freud, the popularizer of the unconscious concept, has frightened off students of religion. The time is far overdue for a more systematic and comprehensive examination of the religious aspects of the unconscious. Tillich (85, p. 14) claims that the ideas of the unconscious have created a whole new climate for theological disciplines. Consequently, religious formulations concerning the unconscious are vitally important.

Creativity and religion have traditionally been associated, and the place of the unconscious in creativity demands attention. In the introduction of a recently published volume of Freud's (68, p. x) essays on cultural subjects, *Creativity and the Unconscious,* the editor says, "Freud discovered the way to the heights (of creativity) was by way of the depths" of the unconscious. But not all writers are agreed that Freud had a creative view of the unconscious. Allport (7, pp. 148-149) has said that in his work of exploring the unconscious, "Freud goes down deeper, stays down longer, and comes up dirtier than any other psychologist." Chaplin claims that psychoanalysis has brought about a deterioration in the quality of art. Recalling Aristotle's emphasis on unity, structure, and form in art, Chaplin (31, p. 179) pessimistically surveys the present scene.

With the coming of the age of analysis and the spread of psychoanalytic doctrines among the avant-gardé of literary and artistic circles, a profound change occurred in the structure and function of art. In literature, classicism gave way to naturalism. Naturalism, in turn, was displaced by realism which then evolved into the novel of the stream of consciousness. Painting, too, lost its formal structure and sought to mirror the unconscious. Drama gave up classical forms and turned from traditional themes to the exploitation of pathological problems. Generally speaking, human nature, as portrayed in the arts, has fallen from the zenith of heroic classicism to the nadir of contemporary beatnikism. Nature, once glorified in art, is now mocked by the dribble-and-drool school. Man, who appeared with the face of a thousand heroes in the literature of the past, is portrayed as a shadowy, irrational object of pity, crushed by his environment and inner conflicts. All gods have failed; we are ruled by the murky depths of the unconscious.

Freud's pessimistic, deterministic view of man's irrational, animalistic side has dominated twentieth-century aesthetics.

Turning from this somewhat depressing scene, Chaplin looks to Jung's idea of the creative unconscious. For Jung, the creative forces of art and religion lie buried beneath the more superficial layers of the unconscious. Jung's *collective unconscious* is a creative concept. It is defined by Clark (**33**, p. 9): "The collective unconscious is an inheritance of the possibility of ideas." Raised in the tradition of German and French psychiatry, Jung accepted this stress on heredity factors in mental development.

Orthodox psychoanalysts, on the other hand, revolted against the idea. A. A. Brill claimed that the mind was a clean slate at birth. Jung tried to wed the idea of inheritance to that of the personal unconscious. He contended that the structure of the brain was inherited in much the same manner as the structure of the body, and the brains of all human beings have a resemblance to each other.

An unusual facet of Jung's concept of the unconscious is his emphasis on its feminine aspects. According to Jung (**103**, p. 170), the creative work of the poet grows from him as a child from its mother: "The creative process has feminine quality, and the creative work arises from unconscious depths—we might say, from the realm of the mothers." Jung rejects the concept of the unconscious as a mere receptacle for material discarded from the conscious. It does contain this material, but it also carries on its own creative activity.

The *dynamic* aspects of the unconscious were considered as a part of the evidence for its existence earlier in the chapter and are relevant to any discussion of creativity. Testimony has accumulated to show that put into operation the dynamic unconscious continues its work. John Dewey expressed it:

Many persons having a complicated practical question to decide find it advisable to sleep on the matter. Often they awake in the morning to find that, while they were sleeping, things have wonderfully straightened themselves out. A subtle process of incubation has resulted in hatching a decision and a plan.

But this bringing forth of inventions, solutions, and discoveries rarely occurs except to a mind that has previously steeped itself consciously in material relating to its question, has turned matters over and over, weighed pros and cons.

Incubation, in short, is one phase of a rhythmic process (12, p. 58).

The incubation process reveals the unconscious as essentially creative, albeit quite *amoral*. A Hitler can conceive the idea of a master race, and his unconscious works on the plan as he produces schemes of world conquest and the destruction and elimination of races of people.

Creativity is not just a simple entity but a complex activity resulting from the interaction of many forces. A happy compromise

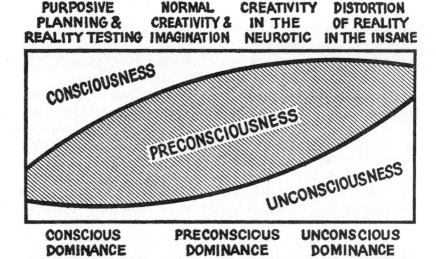

THE ROLE OF THE PRECONSCIOUS IN CREATIVE ACTIVITY (7, p. 153)

has been formulated by Kubie who sees a balance between the conscious, the preconscious, and the unconscious elements in the various types of creativity.

A truly neurotic person is largely dominated by the unconscious, while the person with ego strength lives more within the bounds of the conscious. The preconscious, representing the area of material available for recall, plays a pivotal part in the process. Creativity in the normal person is more the co-operation of the conscious and preconscious, while in the neurotic the unconscious is more compulsively in control. However, the ego may be active, even in the shady borderland of the preconscious, and participate in the creative process.

A strange aspect of creativity in the unconscious is shown by Jones (**101,** pp. 304-5) in his biography of Freud, where he indicates the connection between a period of Freud's creativity and his neurotic reactions:

However unpalatable the idea may be to hero-worshipers, the truth has to be stated that Freud did not always possess the serenity and inner sureness so characteristic of him in the years when he was well known. The point has to be put more forcibly. There is ample evidence that for ten years or so—roughly comprising the nineties—he suffered from a very considerable psychoneurosis. An admirer might be tempted to paint this in the darkest colors so as to emphasize by way of relief Freud's achievement of self-mastery by the help of the unique instrument he himself forged. But there is no need to exaggerate; the greatness of the achievement stands by itself. After all, in the worst times Freud never ceased to function. He continued with his daily work and with his scientific investigations, his care and love for his wife and children remained unimpaired, and in all probability he gave little sign of neurotic manifestations to his surroundings (with the sole exception of Fliess). Nevertheless, his sufferings were at times very intense, and for those ten years there could have been only occasional intervals when life seemed much worth living. He paid very heavily for the gifts he bestowed on the world, and the world was not very generous in its rewards.

Yet it was just in the years when the neurosis was at its height, 1897-1900, that Freud did his most original work. There is an *unmistakable connection between these two facts. The neurotic symptoms must have been one of the ways in which the unconscious material was indirectly trying to emerge, and without this pressure it is doubtful if Freud would have made the progress he did. It is a costly way of reaching that hidden realm, but it is still the only way.*

That Freud dimly perceived this connection even at the time is shown by several allusions to his mode of working. He did not work well when he felt fit and happy, nor when he was too depressed and inhibited; he needed something in between. He expressed this neatly in a letter of April 16, 1896: "I have come back with a lordly feeling of independence and feel too well; since returning I have been very lazy, because the *moderate misery necessary for intensive work* refuses to appear" (italics supplied).

Jones's frank acknowledgment of the situation opens the door for further investigation into the relationship of the unconscious and creativity.

The power of the unconscious may complicate the methodology of psychology of religion. Previous discussion has shown that personal documents, biographies, diaries, and letters, along with literature and the questionnaire, provide a large proportion of materials used in the study of psychology of religion. All these methods lean heavily on introspection. Dynamic psychology indicates that answers given and responses made are notoriously unreliable, and they may not provide an adequate basis for accurate generalizations. To obtain more valid material, it may be necessary to utilize more controlled situations and employ observational techniques, along with some form of standardized testing.

Possibly the most potent way to influence the unconscious is by suggestion. The matter is discussed at length in chapter 11, but here we might note that suggestion plays a large part in religion. Autosuggestion is operative in prayer. Group worship experiences raise the suggestibility of the participants. Faith healing has strong overtones of both autosuggestion and heterosuggestion. Conversion involves incubation in the unconscious, and the subject's suggestibility often determines the type of experience. In all religious activities suggestion, and its influence on the unconscious, remains a continuing factor.

Estabrooks likens the unconscious to a steam boiler, with an ever-expanding pressure build-up which seeks release. The unconscious may express itself in a variety of what Estabrooks calls "automatic activities," in which the subject is in a type of hypnotic state. If a shell is placed to the ear a roaring noise is heard and interpreted as the roaring of the sea. Voices are sometimes heard in "shell hearing" as the unconscious gains expression. In crystal gazing a suitable subject can look into a crystal or a glass of water and see material from the unconscious. Automatic writing is a process in which the subject releases all conscious control of the pencil in his hand. A good subject expresses himself through his writing, all the while unaware of what he is doing, even to the extent of reading a book while writing. The finished writing is sometimes in a strange hand, with unusual words and forms manifesting the activity of the unconscious.

Estabrooks sees the phenomenon of "speaking in tongues" as "automatic speech." Technically known as "glossolalia," speaking in tongues is found among Pentecostal groups. It is seen as an indication of the baptism of the Holy Spirit, or an act of worship. A common misapprehension is that the tongue spoken is in some recognizable language and to be used in the propagation of the gospel. This is generally not so. Speaking in tongues is more frequently seen as a "sign" and need not be in any particular language. Estabrooks (**59**, p. 104) remarks on the experience:

What happens in automatic speech is the same sort of thing we have already seen in automatic writing. It is a case of dissociation, only here it is the muscles of the throat which are no longer under control of the normal waking personality. The individual starts talking just as the automatic writer writes, the throat muscles appearing to run themselves without any conscious control from the person in question. The words the subject utters may be utterly unintelligible, a language of his own, a "divine language" as it is sometimes called, or he may speak his own native tongue, expressing what is in the unconscious mind.

From this perspective glossolalia is an activity in which control is relinquished and the unconscious expressed. The meetings where glossolalia is generally seen and heard are highly emotional, with suggestion freely used and a strong emphasis on passivity and releasing all control. However, much glossolalia is probably just imitated behavior, and many of the manifestations have a remarkable similarity.

A somewhat related matter is the type of preaching heard in many churches. Niebuhr (**137**, p. 141) shows that the religion of the frontier gave rise to a certain type of preaching. The formal logical discourse was looked upon with suspicion, and the "language of excitement" was the utterance which brought forth the best response. Much of this legacy is carried over into American religion today, and in many churches the "language of excitement" is frequently heard.

Among some preachers there is almost a fetish on "preaching without notes," and a leading Episcopalian personality recently declared that his sermons were delivered in this way. The unconscious thus enters in. An extract from Jones's (101, I, 341) biography of Freud shows the way in which the great psychologist viewed his own personal utterances.

He never used any notes, and seldom made much preparation for a lecture; it was mostly left to the inspiration of the moment. I remember once while accompanying him to a lecture asking him what the subject was going to be that evening and his answer was, "If I only knew! I must leave it to my unconscious."

For Freud, the dynamic unconscious was ready to facilitate his expression. In the religious setting the quality of the unprepared utterance is said to be the result of the work of the Holy Spirit. This relationship of the Holy Spirit and the unconscious opens an avenue for further discussion later.

Thouless (176, p. 114) has emphasized *symbolism* in the unconscious. Of more recent days, Paul Tillich (177, p. 4) claims that one of the greatest impacts the unconscious has made upon our theological climate has been a new appreciation of the symbol.

The decisive factor was the breakdown of the belief in the power of reasoning to determine the direction of the will. Intellectual and moral preaching fail to reach those levels of the personal life which can, however, be opened by authentic symbols—symbols which themselves have roots in the unconscious depths of individuals and groups. The impact of symbols on the totality of the personal life gives them revealing as well as healing power.

Jung claims that the symbols most frequently used by man are projections of the collective unconscious. He calls these symbols archetypes, or primordial images which have religious connotations. In his *Psychology and Religion* he tells of studying the religious implications of the symbol for some fourteen years before publicly alluding to them. He expresses the fear there will be a reluctance to accept the idea. However, he maintains that he and his colleagues have so frequently observed people developing the same kind of symbolism that he can no longer doubt it. He feels that the symbol of quarternity is a direct representation of God and elaborates on the frequency with which symbols center around four or the multiples of four. Many references are given, such as the old idea that God created four elements, four rivers in Paradise, four winds, and the symbolism used for the Four Gospels of the eagle, lion, man, and ox.

For Jung (104, p. 72) the quarternity means "the God within." He comments on the psychological importance of this:

> It would be a regrettable mistake if anybody should understand my observations to be a kind of proof of the existence of God. They prove only the existence of an archetypal image of the Deity, which to my mind is the most we can assert psychologically about God. But as it is a very important and influential archetype its relatively frequent occurrence seems to be a noteworthy fact for any theologia naturalis (104, p. 73).

Jung discusses the fact that the central Christian symbolism is a trinity, while the formula of the unconscious mind is a quarternity. It is easily accounted for in his theory, because the Christian formula is incomplete, having failed to mention the evil principle and the fourth aspect of deity, the devil.

A discussion of symbolism raises the matter of the relationship of the Holy Spirit to the unconscious. Mowrer (132, pp. 125-29) likens the unconscious to the Holy Spirit and partially advances the idea that the Holy Spirit resides within the unconscious. The idea of God entering through the unconscious is not new. William James advanced a similar idea. The following figure shows Uren's (179, p. 71) diagramatic presentation of James's theory of the entrance of the transcendental. James felt that the subconscious (unconscious) was the fountainhead that fed all our religious experiences. He maintained that there was some power beyond the unconscious but impinging on it. The inner circle was the region of the conscious experience adjacent to the area of the subconscious (unconscious), where there were various psychic elements having the potentialities of the snake or the seraph. The next area was the region of the transcendental, from which religious experience came. Religious experience was the result of the transcendental element flooding into the subconscious (unconscious), and finally into the conscious.

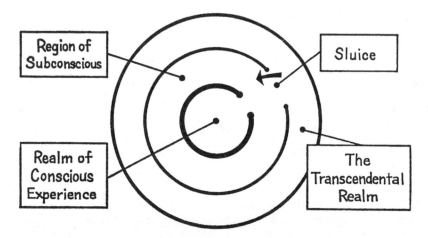

One of the most intensive treatments of the relationship of the Holy Spirit and the unconscious is contained in Dewar's (47) book, *The Holy Spirit and Modern Thought.* Seeing no possibility in Freud's idea of the unconscious, Dewar notes Jung's dynamic concept. Jung claims that even when psychotherapy comes to a conclusion, the therapeutic process often continues with the unconscious apparently carrying on. For Dewar, the goal-seeking activity of the unconscious can easily represent the working of the Holy Spirit on a natural level within the individual. He notes the analogy between psychotherapy and the work of the Holy Spirit, referred to in the Bible as the Paraclete, "one called alongside to help." Thus, he sees the work of the psychotherapist and the work of the Holy Spirit as being similar.

Another point of interest for Dewar is the place of dreaming in biblical revelation. One example is the incident of Peter at Joppa. Peter, hungry and anticipating his midday meal, fell asleep to dream of a sheet let down from heaven containing all kinds of animals and insects. A voice told him to rise, kill, and eat. When Peter refused, the heavenly voice said, "What God hath cleansed, that call not thou common" (Acts 10:15). The word translated "sheet" means "mainsail," so it can be supposed that the sight of sailing boats in the harbor had supplied the imagery and stimulation.

Awakening from the dream, the Holy Spirit tells Peter that three men are seeking him, and the incident is followed by the descent of the Holy Spirit upon the Gentiles. Recounting the incident to the church at Jerusalem later, Peter said, "Then remembered I the word of the Lord, how that he said, John indeed baptized with water; but ye shall be baptized with the Holy Ghost" (Acts 11:16). Dewar sees this as the fulfilment of the Johannine account of the work of the Holy Spirit, which was to recall the teachings of our Lord to the disciple's mind. According to Dewar's interpretation, the Holy Spirit is working on the unconscious and using the symbolism contained therein.

Another interpretation of the religious significance of the unconscious is found in the writings of Alexander Maclaren, known as the "prince of expositors." Maclaren made no claim to being a psychologist, but in one of his sermons entitled, "Memory in Another World," he shows psychological insight. His text is the words, "Abraham said, Son, remember" (Luke 16:25), spoken to the rich man in hell. Maclaren in his *Expositions of Holy Scripture* develops the widely accepted idea of the unconscious as the storehouse of life's experiences, every man having within him a sort of recording angel. Incidents altogether forgotten can be recalled with great vividness, and in the recall the events of the whole life can flash before the screen of the mind in a moment. Maclaren claims that memory in a lost world may be eternal punishment and quotes Milton, "Which way I fly is hell—myself am hell." The unconscious with its stored memories, material available at a moment, and the remorse associated with the experience of recall represent for Maclaren the possibility of what Christian theology calls "lost."

In the well-developed personality the unconscious must be the servant rather than the master of the ego. Mastery is achieved in a large measure by the use of the mechanism of sublimation, defined by English and English (57, p. 533) as "refinement or redirection of the energy belonging to a primitive tendency into a new non-inherited channel." The primitive pushing and purposive forces of the unconscious must be redirected, if we are to live meaningful and purposive lives in our day and age. A community settled on the side of a mountain, where prolonged rains sent a destructive stream of water tearing away the foundations of the homes and buildings. Efforts to dam the torrent were unsuccessful until someone conceived the idea of rechanneling the water, sending it down over the other side of the mountain where it ran to the farm lands. There it was used to irrigate the crops and make the earth fruitful. Referring specifically to the sex drive, Thouless (**176**, p. 124) says:

> His sex-instinct may lead him to marry a wife, and devote the rest of his life to the maintenance and protection of her and her offspring. In this case, he is forming on his sex-instinct a habit which is its biological intention. But it may also drive him (particularly if his first or repeated attempts to form a habit of the above kind are frustrated) to write poetry, to shut himself up away from the world, to devote himself to scientific research, to paint pictures, or to engage in a variety of other activities which are as remote as can well be imagined from the kinds of habit which other animals found on the same instinct. In this case, we may say that he is redirecting the energy of this instinct to other (perhaps we may think to higher) ends. It is now usual, when the end is recognized to be of value, to call this process *sublimation*.

Freud was critical of all forms of religion. Yet, there were sometimes moments when he saw it in a different light. Writing to Pfister after the publication of his book, Freud discussed ideals and ethics and with an almost wistful note said, "From a therapeutic point of view I can only envy you the possibility of sublimation that religion affords" (**101**, II, 199). Religious motivations are vital for sublimation. Psychology can teach us sublimation, but it takes religion to put meaning into it. Years ago I conducted church services among the natives on the island of New Guinea and was amazed to hear some of the strange tunes the people had to their hymns. Further inquiries revealed that they had originally been war chants, but missionaries had given the new converted natives the Christian message of peace for all men, and they sang it to the tune of the primitive war chant. Similarly, the mechanism of sublimation will function best within people who have new lives, new objectives, and new motivations that come through faith in Jesus Christ.

Summary

Trying to explore and map out the areas of conscious, preconcious, and unconscious processes is at the same time rewarding and frustrating: rewarding, because it promises a rationale for behavior hitherto inexplicable; frustrating, because all the formulations have a certain atmosphere of speculation and haziness about the details. Although at first blush it might seem that the primitive, pushing, and purposive unconscious would undercut religion, a closer examination shows that the concept may have some significant implications for the student of religion. Aspects of repression are religiously involved; creativity has religious associations; religious phenomena such as glossolalia and the "language of excitement" have obvious close relationships with the unconscious. The place of the symbol, the possibility of a clearer understanding of the Holy Spirit's functioning, the peculiar place of religious motivations in sublimation, and the warning of the complications in the methodology of psychology of religion brought about by unconscious factors—all of these things point up the necessity of a harder look at religion and the unconscious.

7

The Developing Love Life

Love and religion have had a close association. Some critics of religion claim it is nothing more than a misinterpretation of the sex drive, but that conclusion has all the earmarks of gross oversimplification. Nevertheless, it must be acknowledged that there is a close relationship between the two ideas.

The Bible opens with a discussion of man-woman relationships; the standards of sex conduct come from religious sources; the concept of the marriage bond and its degree of permanence has religious roots; the obligations of parents to children and vice versa are frequently within the context of religious ideals.

In the Old Testament, the prophet Hosea saw his domestic relationships with his wife, Gomer, as a symbol of the relationship between God and Israel. In the New Testament, Paul, sometimes referred to as a crusty old bachelor, sees the marriage bond as showing the relationship between Christ and his church.

Thouless maintains that there are four lines of evidence for the close association of sex and religion.

1. In the development of the sex instinct there are periods of growth and decay. These periods show at least some parallels with the peak periods of religious experience, such as the number of conversions taking place in the adolescent period of life. But there is often religious experience in childhood, before adolescence. Also, there is little evidence to show that in old age the diminishing of the sex drive causes the disappearance of religious fervor.

2. Religious emotion often expresses itself in the language of human love. Many of the mystics have been particularly adept at using human love metaphors to express their spiritual aspirations. However, there are also other types of symbols and metaphors used in describing the experience.

3. In some religious groupings a high value is placed upon chastity. The implication is that the suppression of the sex drive opens the way for it to be channeled into religious expression. But again, there are other drives which are denied to religious living. Aggression is put aside in favor of meekness; physical appetites are rejected for fasting; the company of others is given up for the solitude of life in monastic seclusion.

4. In some forms of religion there is a tendency for sexual license to develop. Despite the beginning with demands of sex suppression, some of the highly emotionalized forms of religion are characterized by uninhibited sexuality. The very contrast with the accepted standards of Christianity highlights this type of behavior as exceptional and apart from the normal expectations from a professed religious person. There is no clear-cut evidence that religion is just a manifestation of the sexual drive, but there are obvious associations.

Sigmund Freud probably wrote, or caused to be written, more on the subject of love than any other mortal. Yet, even though he bared his soul on so many other matters, he told very little about his own love life. His biographer, Ernest Jones (101, I, 98), says, however, that Freud's love life must be probed because

No man's inner life, the core of his personality, can be comprehended without some knowledge of his attitude towards the basic emotion of love. Nothing reveals the essence of his personality so piercingly and completely as the gross, and subtle, variations of the emotional responses in this sphere, since few situations in life test so severely his mental harmony.

Another parallel point of interest between psychology and religion manifests itself. Obviously the psychotherapist sees love as intimately related to his discipline, and no serious student of religion can afford to ignore the central place of love in his field of interest.

Any discussion of love faces difficulties of definition. The problems of semantics have never loomed larger. People speak of loving such dissimilar objects as God, pecan pies, cats, old shoes, money, and mother. The difficulty is that one English word must cover so many different ideas. Hunt (90, p. 15), who claims the Greeks had a word for everything, also states that they invented love. It thus follows that the names which they gave to the various aspects of love are probably the most accurate we possess. Three Greek words trans-

lated love—*eros, philia,* and *agape*—can serve as a basis for definition, although even in the Greek the meanings are not always as
precise as may be indicated.

Eros is *selfish* love. It is the physical attraction between the sexes,
and the individual involved has the expectation of gaining some personal experience, release, or expression. In the writings of the Greeks,
eros was the "love of desire" or acquisitive love. It wants something.
Consequently, for Plato, love was a middle state between having and
not having. It follows then that when the object of desire has been
possessed, *eros* love dies away. The word *eros* is nowhere used in
the New Testament.

The act of sexual experience is frequently spoken of as "making
love." While it is true in the *eros* sense, there is a question as to
whether the word "love" is not wrongly used in this connection.
Writers as far removed from each other as Reik (**152**) and Duvall
(**54**) have shown that love and sex are not only not the same but
often quite different from each other.

1. Sex is basically physical and, as in masturbation, there can be
a solitary physical sexual response. Love, on the other hand, is psychi-
cal and involves the response of personality to personality. It is possible to love without physical contact.

2. Sex may involve only a fragment of the personality, but love
at its best is the response of two personalities.

3. Sex is mainly concerned with satisfying its own desires, seeking
physical satisfaction and release, without regard to the welfare of
others. Love at its best is unselfish, and if love conflicts with sex, the
lover may forego sexual experiences altogether. Duvall concludes that
love and sex are not only not identical but can be exactly opposite
to each other. However, combined, like steel and concrete, they build
the solid structure of interpersonal relationships.

Philia may be thought of as the *mental* level of love. It represents
the attraction of similar intellectual and cultural interests. *Philia* is
used in the New Testament. The Phillips' translation indicates the
difference between *philia* and *agape* in the incident of Jesus and Peter:

When they had finished breakfast Jesus said to Simon Peter, "Simon,
son of John, do you love me more than these others?"
"Yes, Lord," he replied. "You know that I am your friend" (John 21:
15).

The use by Jesus of *agape* and Peter of *philia* is shown in the respective translations of love and friend.

Some of the most unusual love affairs of history had very little of the *eros* element about them. The affair of Robert Browning keeping up his correspondence with Elizabeth Barrett, a spinster in her late thirties, living as an invalid and postponing the day of meeting, had very little *eros*. Similarly, Walpole, the English parliamentarian, a bachelor of about forty-eight years of age, spending so much of his time with a blind seventy-year-old French woman showed a *philia* love. Marriage counselors often inquire of husbands and wives in difficulty as to what mutual friends they have, and what they do together. The similarities of mental affinity play a large part in enriching the physical *eros* urge.

Agape is the *altruistic* level of love. It is the great rich word of the New Testament predominantly used to describe the love of God towards men and that which Christians are to have for each other. The altruistic or unselfish note is the characteristic of *agape*. Paul sets it out in all its glory in 1 Corinthians 13, where there is the constant refrain of the altruistic attitude of love:

> This love of which I speak is slow to lose patience—it looks for a way of being constructive. It is not possessive: it is neither anxious to impress nor does it cherish inflated ideas of its own importance.
> Love has good manners and does not pursue selfish advantage. It is not touchy. It does not compile statistics of evil or gloat over the wickedness of other people (vv. 4-5, Phillips).

Paul's exposition is like a towering mountain in a desert wasteland when compared with the literature of antiquity on the subject of love. The main differentiating point is the essential unselfishness of love in Paul's portrayal.

With the exception of *eros,* the levels of love are not necessarily exclusive of each other, and there is an interplay of the three elements in most expressions of love. The biblical book called The Song of Solomon is a good example. The book is a love song. Aglen, in the conservative Ellicott *Commentary* (**56**, IV, 385), says of it:

> The subject of the book is the sentiment of love. The language is like that of all love poetry, passionate, sensuous, voluptuous, and in some cases with oriental license passing the bounds of the Western standards

of sobriety and propriety. . . . From beginning to end there is not a single word in it which suggests any connection with religion.

In the opinion of Aglen, as of others, the writer of The Song of Solomon deals primarily with the *eros* level of love. It may go to the *philia*. However, through the years great saints of the Christian faith have found in this book an expression of Christ's love for his church and the relationship of the people of God to him. Thus, the three concepts intermingle and intertwine.

The complexity of the concept makes consideration of other aspects necessary. Four features of love, not always obvious, are: (1) it is mobile, (2) object seeking, (3) uniting, and (4) reciprocal.

Love is mobile.—In the parlance of romantic love, "falling in love" implies a condition into which an individual enters and remains henceforth. It is a static situation. Menninger (**128**, p. 261) tries to correct the misconception when he says, "One does not 'fall' in love: one *grows* into love and love grows in him; and this starts not in adolescence nor in maturity, but in infancy." Love is a living, vital part of personality, and like everything else that lives, it can be nourished or neglected. It can be flexible and variable. Developmental factors in personality are no more significant in any other area of life than in our thought about love.

Love's relationship to objects.—Blanton (**19**, p. 108) reminds us, "Love, in its widest meaning, is simply *an intense, positive interest in an object.*" The singer can enthusiastically announce, "I'm in love, I'm in love, I'm in love," but in love with whom? The growing and developing individual finds his mobile love life focusing on different objects. Development of personality depends in a large measure on the individual focusing his love on the appropriate object at the right time. In the long haul from infancy to maturity, inappropriate objects will always be available, and failure to discern the correct object at any given stage is a constant hazard for the growing individual.

Love is union.—Man without love lives in isolation. An experience of love breaks down this isolation, allowing him to feel at one with another. Fromm (**70**, p. 8) claims that in the story of Adam and Eve the sense of shame which came upon them was from their sense of separation. He says, "The awareness of human separation without reunion by love—is the source of shame. It is at the same time a source of guilt and anxiety." In his dilemma of separateness, primitive man lived close to nature and the earth. He tried to identify with animals by wearing animal masks and worshiping totem and animal gods. With increasing sophistication these were gradually dropped, and modern man frequently seeks to escape isolation by conformity to the group.

Fromm claims that the desire for reunion and interpersonal fusion is the most powerful single striving within man. He prefers the term "symbiotic," used in biology to describe a relationship between two species, neither of which can survive without the others. In the *psychic,* symbolic union the bodies are separate, but there is a psychological attachment. Moreover, each of the persons involved must maintain his individuality. There are times when he can be a part of another, and there are times when he can stand alone entirely. Nevertheless, love provides for the individual what Allport (**4,** p. 32) calls his "affiliative needs."

Reciprocal aspects of love.—This must be stressed if one of the worst aspects of romantic love is to be countered. Too many girls feel that they must wait for the knight in shining armor who will come riding along on his white horse, see some unusual feature about this attractive creature, fall in love with her, and carry her off to his castle. The stress is on "being loved" rather than "loving." Too many people feel that "to love" is simple, but "to be loved" is difficult. Criticising the attitude, Fromm (**71,** p. 66) says that it comes in part from our "marketing orientation." In much the same manner as goods are packaged, dress, make-up, hairdos, and all the rest are techniques to make us more "marketable," so that someone will fall "in love" with us. We must learn to love before we can ever really be loved. Both aspects are important. It is essential to both love and be loved, and our relationship is at its best when the two elements are present.

In the later days of his life, Robert Louis Stevenson, the famous author, went to Samoa in pursuit of good health. There he built a house on an elevated spot overlooking the sea. He endeared himself to the natives by his acts of kindness and interest in their affairs. When he was restricted in his movements by sickness, the natives showed their gratitude by building a road from his house to the sea. It was called "The Road of the Loving Heart." There is a sense in which every individual must climb the road of the loving heart, and the features of mobility, object seeking, union, and reciprocity are all involved in the climb.

To climb the road is normal. Multitudes have managed very successfully by just "doing what comes naturally." However, the complexities of the emotions associated with love makes it tragically easy for the individual to stumble, try to climb too quickly, or slip back down. As Blanton (**19**, p. 167) states it:

Our mistakes are not due simply to love or hate in themselves. We commit errors because, under the urgent pressure of these accumulated emotional forces, *we are driven to love or hate the wrong people, at the wrong time, for the wrong reasons.*

An understanding of the appropriate love objects may serve to save one from this pitfall.

Self-Love Comes First

The infant loves himself. A newborn babe has much in common with other forms of animal life, and his main drive is physiological. He must ingest food to grow. A fond mother feels that it is a manifestation of love when the baby snuggles into her breast, but it is truer to the facts to say that he generally follows this line of activity in the hope of getting food. The pleasure in the infant's life comes first of all through his mouth, and "oral activity" is as necessary for the infant psychologically as it is physiologically.

Making seven statements of the needs of the infant, Menninger (**128**, p. 39) puts first: "He should have the opportunity for frequent sucking periods not limited in time, not artificially interrupted, and preferably at the mother's breast." Oral activity and its pleasures, encountered so early in life, will remain to both enrich and bedevil the infant throughout his developing life.

The infant is the complete egotist. All of life exists to minister to him. The attitude is natural and essential in a small child, but it becomes inappropriate in the full-grown adult. An individual may become fixated or regress to this earlier stage of development. Thumb sucking is one of the earliest forms of regression. Later it can be overeating, smoking, or some other form of oral activity. Many people who are overweight obviously eat for pleasure and psychological reassurance rather than for nourishment. The current fad of liquid diets and their remarkable successes may indicate that the milky fluid being ingested provides some infantile satisfaction for the frustrated "fatty."

Turning back to the story of the young Greek, Narcissus, we are told that looking into the pool he saw a reflection of himself and fell in love with his own image. Thus, some psychologists have used the term "narcissism" to describe the preoccupation of an individual with himself. It can take many forms. Jealousy, which at first sight seems to be an overevaluation of a love object, can in reality be a narcissistic estimate of the individual's own self and a fear that he will not get enough attention from his love object. Masturbation may be ·a turning in of one's love life upon himself. The self-centered woman, displaying her scantily clad body, spending all of her money on clothes, and dissolving into tears to get her own way, may be regressing to this earlier stage of the development of the love life. For many of these people a pacifier might have been the appropriate solution to their problems.

A certain amount of self-love is absolutely essential for the adequate development of the ego. But this evaluation of one's self must be made in the context of reference to other people. Jesus said, "Thou shalt love thy neighbour as thyself" (Matt. 19:19). In his criteria of mature religion, Clark (34, p. 256) states it clearly: "Is it socially effective? Does the individual's religion strengthen his sense of community with others in such a way as to be ultimately creative of a more wholesome society?" Cain, with his question, "Am I my brother's keeper?" becomes the representative of an infantile self-centeredness which is the antithesis of the Christian religion.

Mother-Child Relationships Develop

Discussing some of the difficulties encountered by women, Menninger (128, p. 41) emphasizes their place in society and says:

To place the major responsibility for the formation of the child's personality upon the mother is to put woman in the center of the universe, psychologically. This is not in contradiction to biological concepts; in many of the lower forms of life, there are no males but only females.

For the infant, his mother is the center of the world *physically*. She takes care of him, gives him food, and is with him most of his waking hours. The relationship with his mother is also the first *social* relationship the child ever has. She is also the center of his world *psychologically*. Freudians see the male child as having an Oedipus complex, falling in love with his mother and seeing his father as a

rival. However, most impartial observers see the little girl's relationship with her mother as being equally important.

Mother love, with its accompanying physical and psychological
contact, fosters an adequate personality development. In one of the
best-known studies, Rena Spitz tells of two groups of babies in institutions. The institutions were evenly matched in all ways, except
one kept the babies with their mothers while the other cared for them
without the help of the mothers. In a two-year period it was shown
that the children whose mothers participated developed in every way
at a much more rapid rate than the others.

Thorpe (175, p. 338) quotes a similar study:

After making extensive studies of infants, Margaret Ribble came to the
conclusion that, even after birth, mother and infant are psychologically
still a unit and that a close physical relationship is as essential for mental
and emotional development as was the fetal connection for physiological
development.

In the work of the Gluecks, investigating the causes of crime and
delinquency, two of the "highly decisive factors" were "mother's supervision" and "mother's affection." More recently, a prominent psychologist has concluded that the rhythmic heartbeat of the mother
is beneficial for the child and may even serve as the basis for the
child's later appreciation of music. Studying groups of babies in hospitals, an experimenter found that when the rhythmic sound of a
normal heart beat was amplified into the hospital nursery, the babies
were more relaxed and gained more weight than those in a normal
nursery setting.

As necessary as a mother figure might be, the pitfalls of fixation
and regression remain. An over-protective mother dominating a child
becomes a hazard and a hindrance to personality growth. From his
work with the G.I.s during World War II, Strecker (173, p. 30)
popularized the idea of "mom," and says:

What constitutes a mom? . . . Mom is a maternal parent who fails to
prepare her offspring emotionally for living a productive adult life on an
adult social plane. A mom does not untie the emotional apron string—
the Silver Cord—which binds her children to her.

To cut the emotional umbilical cord is difficult, but it must be done.
One leading sociologist found that if a marriage broke up within the

first twelve months, it was probably because of in-law interference. It was the boy's mother who generally caused the trouble. The mother whose love was so necessary for the child's early development is now a hindrance to the proper growth of his love life. Similarly, the girl who decides to "go home to mother" as soon as difficulties arise in the marriage is just as surely regressing to an earlier love object. The situation is illustrated in the well-known story of the young husband who said, "You don't make biscuits the way Mother used to." His bright young wife replied, "And you don't bring home the sort of dough that Daddy did."

Father Comes into Sight

Like a man standing on the seashore watching a ship appearing on the horizon as a tiny speck and seeing it gradually grow into a distinguishable outline, the infant becomes increasingly aware of the shadowy figure of father, until he is delineated as a companion to the all-powerful mother figure. Some psychologists have seen the girl as becoming attached to the father in a relationship that is more significant than that of the father and son. In reality, however, it would be difficult to conclude that sex was a significant factor in determining the relative importance of a father in the realization of personality's potential.

How does a boy learn to be a man? By identifying with some masculine figure. The most obvious pattern is the father figure readily available in the framework of the home. For the son, the father represents masculinity, the outside world, the symbol of authority, the father-parent he will one day be, and the lover-husband he can become as he develops into the sexual male.

A vast body of evidence has been amassed to highlight the father figure. During the Korean conflict Americans were shocked when for the first time in United States history twenty-one Americans elected to remain in enemy hands rather than return home. Investigating the background of the twenty-one men, Virginia Pasley in her book, *21 Stayed,* showed that nineteen out of the twenty-one felt unloved or unwanted by their fathers or stepfathers.

An examination of the lives of the leaders of the world communism movement shows that Friedrich Engels constantly quarreled with his father, Stalin had an alcoholic father, and Trotsky was constantly at odds with his father. It might well be that much of the hostility engendered in a bad father-son relationship gave impetus to association with the outlawed revolutionary movement.

Similarly, the Gluecks included in the "five highly decisive factors" paving the way for delinquency two having to do with the father-child relationship—"father's discipline" and "father's relationship with his son."

Girls need an adequate father figure in their lives. In an article, "The Search for a Phantom Father," a writer discussed office romances in which a girl became involved with a man, not only much older than herself, but also obviously unavailable for marriage. The writer claims that in many instances the girls involved in the clandestine romances have had poor father figures in their family circle. Discussing the high incidence of abortion and some reasons for it, a writer noted that nearly all the aborted women whom he interviewed felt unwanted by their fathers. A promiscuous girl having psychotherapy finally reached a point where she confessed that her main interest in sexual relationships was that in the experience she had the feeling she could remember of being in her father's arms as a small child.

A newspaper report, concerning a shocking incident in which four boys and a girl assaulted a forty-five-year-old man in an apartment, told of the girl taking a pair of scissors and carving her initials in eight inch letters on the man's back. Apprehended, the girl was asked why she had attacked the man, and her reply was, "Because he looks like my father, and I hate my father." Elements of hostility in the father-child relationship obviously manifested themselves in the incident.

There are religious implications. Freud claimed that the child was searching for a "father figure" and in his search was ultimately led to the religious idea of God as a Heavenly Father. Undoubtedly, Freud tended to oversimplify religious experience, but it is nevertheless true that many people make God in their father's image. In the course of a counseling relationship a young man told of being constantly beset with doubts and uncertainties. As therapy progressed it was revealed that he was the son of a prominent clergyman who was exacting, demanding, and inconsistent in his relationship with his son. One day in a moment of insight, he spontaneously said, "I think of God in exactly the same way as I think of my father."

What does this mean for the church? The Old Testament portrays the father as an essential figure in the teaching of religion. Today we are faced with what one writer calls "the effeminization of American society" as women become increasingly important. Moreover, with more marriages breaking up than ever before and the custody of the children being given to their mothers, greater numbers of children will be without father figures in their lives.

Fortunately, the work of some investigators with surrogate parents has shown that emotional rather than biological bonds build the relationship. Substitute parents sometimes do a better job than the natural parents. A great responsibility is placed upon the church and its ministry, and it will have to provide at least some type of surrogate parent through its organizational life. Some Sunday school classes are divided by sex with men teaching the boys, and at younger age levels churches are increasingly putting men to work in close contact with the children. It is not an unusual sight to see a very masculine individual sitting with a group of tiny children. As churches enlist men and involve them in their organizational life, it may be that they will strengthen personality development and add significance to the child's concepts of God as he learns the Model Prayer, "Our Father which art in heaven."

Playmates Become Important

The growing child becomes aware of children his own age who are now the objects of his attention, and he enters into what is generally known as the "gang stage" of development.

Some psychologists use the term "homosexual," implying the satisfaction coming to children from associating with their own sex. A boy rebuked for not playing with his cousin was asked the reason and gave the simple explanation, "She's a girl." It is the age when boys prefer to be with boys and girls with girls. The boys prefer to play at masculine games, and the girls find their amusement in imitating the feminine roles of life. Organizations for boys and girls flourish, and the members frequently get crushes on their leaders. Group solidarity is characteristic.

Once again the activity is appropriate for the stage of development. Fixation may lead to the tragic dilemma of homosexuality. Men who neglect their families to spend all of their times with "the boys," or women who become so involved in their club that they do not fulfil their duties to their families, may be examples of regression to this level of the development of the love life.

The Opposite Sex Takes on New Significance

Adolescence comes with explosive force, and love objects change from homosexual to heterosexual as the latent sex drive becomes overt. Half child and half adult, the adolescent is like a beginning water skier, struggling desperately to get up and skim along the surface of the water but frequently slipping over, falling, and feeling hopelessly bogged down with the futility of the effort.

The metaphor of "falling" is particularly appropriate, and possibly the most dangerous fall of all in adolescence is "falling in love." Some authorities consider the unreal elements of romantic love to be the modern counterparts of the medieval concept of courtly love which Hunt (90, p. 151) traces back to the court of William X, the Duke of Aquitaine, born in 1071. Although the essence of masculinity, William had a romantic strain. An ancient historian described him:

The Count of Poitou was one of the most courteous men in the world, and a great deceiver of ladies; and he was a brave knight and had much to do with love affairs; and he knew well how to sing and make verses.

William's flattering ways with ladies began a fashion, and knights sang to their lady loves while troubadours made tours of the countryside, pouring out their songs of the agony and ecstasy of love. The names of some 460 troubadours have been preserved along with twenty-five hundred of their songs. One remarkable song went:

> Thus, lady, I commend to thee
> My fate and life, thy faithful squire;
> I'd rather die in misery
> Than have thee stoop to my desire.

The sentiments expressed were typical of the depiction of womanhood, with the female figure the unobtainable love object to be admired from afar.

Eleanor of Aquitaine, William's granddaughter, popularized the romanticism of her father and the wandering troubadours. An amazing woman, she became Queen of France and induced her husband Louis to embark on the Second Crusade, accompanying him and leaving behind strange stories of her amorous adventures. Divorced by Louis, she married Henry Plantagenet, Duke of Normandy, who by an unusual set of circumstances became Henry II of England, thus making Eleanor a queen for the second time in her life.

Eleanor had many elements of romance about her. The wife of two kings, she was mother of two more in the persons of her sons, Richard, the Lionhearted, and Prince John. Hers was a restless and rugged life. When her son, Richard, the Lionhearted, was captured in Austria, she undertook the journey across the continent to negotiate his ransom. But she is remembered mainly because of her gentleness, compassion, and courtesy. Living in the castle at Poitiers, Eleanor gathered a court thronged with poets, philosophers, clerics, and knights. With her daughter, Marie, the Countess of Champagne, she developed a Court of Love, where the relationships of men and women were discussed, personified, and magnified.

In the manner of the Middle Ages, religion played a part, and a cleric named André, Marie's chaplain, wrote a manual called *Treatise on Love and Its Remedy,* in which the devious practices of lovemaking were set out, including:

The unswerving loyalty of a lover to his beloved; the emphasis on pleasing habits, courteous conduct, and personal attractiveness; the subservience, in the courtship stages, of the man to the woman; the gentleness and considerateness required in actual love-making; the spiritual benefits of being in love (**90**, p. 157).

Kelly (**106**, p. 206) says André's literary effort is based on Ovid's Latin treatises on *The Art of Loving* and the *Remedy of Love,* with an essential difference. In Ovid's writings man is the master, employing his arts to seduce the woman for his pleasure, while in André's writing the woman is the mistress with the man her pupil.

Medieval man was confronted with an overwhelming ambivalence concerning woman. She was the daughter of Eve, the temptress of man. A celibate clergy, sexually frustrated, poured out denunciations of pleasurable sex, sex being for the propagation of children and that purpose alone. Pleasure obtained from sex was sinful. But a woman stood at the heart of Roman Christianity. The Virgin Mary had been exalted to the position of "Mother of God." She was the personification of purity and saintly virtue. People of Mary's sex both attracted and repelled, and courtly love gave medieval man a way out of his dilemma.

As ridiculous as much of the discussion of courtly love sounds to modern ears, it played a large part in the transition from feudalism to a new age, with at least three features prominent. (1) Courtly love brought a new status for women. Before its advent, man had a God-like dominion over his wife, but the new emphasis demanded that women be wooed, won, and pleased. (2) Sexual expression was refined by courtly love and linked with devotion, deep feeling, and gentleness. (3) Courtly love laid down character improvement and ethical value as a condition of loving. It has been said that in their formulations the women of Eleanor's court were rationalizing a scheme of conduct which had broken out of the strait jacket of feudalism, and was in Hunt's (**90**, p. 161) words, "The manifesto of an emotional revolution."

It is a long step from the eleventh century to our present day, but many of the foibles of courtly love live on in modern romantic love. Hunt says that the American credo of romanticism involves a series of fallacious "articles of faith."

The one person theory.—Somewhere in the big, wide world there is one perfectly matched person who is the "right one." The quest is to search until "Mr. Right" is discovered. However, research has shown that in all probability the "only one in the world" lives, not in Calcutta, Canberra, or Casablanca, but probably within twenty city blocks of the individual's residence. Rather than the son of a maharaja or a shah, he will probably come from the same economic level, social class, or religious background as the questing lover. Moreover, there are a number of people with whom a very successful marriage could be made.

Falling in love.—The strange experience overtakes it's victim with an alarming suddenness. In some respects, like an attack of fever with its associated delirium, the results are longer lasting, for the victims fall in love, get married, and live happily ever after. Impartial observers doubt if there is such an experience. Menninger says that people don't "fall in love" but rather grow in love, and love grows in them. As for living happily ever after from this one experience, investigators claim that most normal people have about six or seven love affairs before finally taking the marital plunge.

Love conquers all.—Love is the mighty force, overcoming every obstacle. Parents, friends, and advisers can point to the inappropriateness of the proposed love object, but it makes no difference, for love will find a way. Hunt says that the creed is in reverse, and it might be closer to correct to say "all conquers love." Obviously unsuitable partners are often taken as a gesture of defiance. Some psychoanalysts consider "being in love" as an obsessional state in which old forgotten angers, sadistic and masochistic tendencies, sibling rivalries and the like, all make the fond fool suppose himself in love, when he is merely in the grip of his unconscious motives.

The turmoil of adolescence is closely associated to sexual maturation. Biologically, the adolescent is prepared for his sexual functions, but society demands that he spend increasingly longer periods in the educational processes before becoming economically capable of supporting a wife. Consequently, sexual conflicts are the order of the day. Masturbation may give release but brings its increment of guilt.

Petting offers an opportunity to satisfy, in part, both the demands of the unregulated urges and the value system. The practice is not new. "Bundling" was carried on in Colonial times, and forms of masculine-feminine stimulation short of sexual relations have followed ever since. The automobile has brought complications, for it is not only a status symbol and a weapon of destruction for adolescents but provides a mobile ready-made situation for varying degrees of intimacy in petting.

With new attitudes toward sex, young people are questioning the values so tenaciously held by their parents. They are asking if they should not free themselves from the old-fashioned inhibitions and enjoy their sexual capacities. But sex is more than a biological process. It involves emotional ties and evaluations of a partner's worth. Popenoe (**148**, pp. 1-3) suggests criteria for evaluating petting experiences:

(1) Does it mean the same to both of you, or is one callously exploiting the other to get a feeling of power or a cheap thrill? (2) Is it primarily physical, or does it involve the total personality? (3) Is it unaesthetic, deceitful, furtive, shamefaced, or is it open, sincere, honest, and wholehearted? (4) Does it interfere with other more important activities? (5) Is it like a habit forming drug of which larger and larger amounts are required to produce the same effect? (6) Is it a satisfying fulfillment of life at its best, or does it leave one feeling wrought up, dissatisfied, frustrated? (7) Is it preparation for future married life?

The obvious answer to many of these questions is an indication of the turmoil, conflict, and confusions associated with petting.

Love play is a preliminary to sexual relationships, but preliminaries continually carried on without consummation bring strains. It is like the young man who just climbs into the cockpit of the airplane to play at operating the controls. One day he starts the motor and while "revving it up" the plane suddenly starts down the field. Any marriage counselor can tell of the oft repeated stories of "take offs" which complicated lives and brought tragedy. A realistic attitude towards petting will be an essential in the developing, adolescent love life.

Early adolescence is "polygamous" in character. Boy-girl relationships are short-lived, and changes of partners are frequent, a consideration which immediately raises the problem of "going steady." This craze has spread through high school, junior high, and even elementary schools. It bristles with problems. Social experiences are limited just at the time when a variety is called for. An uneven commitment may result, with the girl deadly in earnest and the boy taking the relationship casually, or vice versa. With two adolescents constantly thrown together and bored with the process, an emotional involvement easily ensues.

Adults must accept a share of the blame. Some parents will not let their children be children but insist on their becoming little men and women. These parents thus wittingly or unwittingly foster the "going steady" craze. High school marriages dramatize the dilemma. One mother plaintively put it when she said, "Before they were married we couldn't keep them apart; now they are married we cannot keep them together." Going steady flies in the face of the polygamous nature of the early adolescent love life.

Contact with reality is a widely used criterion for the evaluation of emotional health. Coleman (**38**, p. 81) describes the desirable pathway of human development as being "from pleasure to reality." If these presumptions be true, many aspects of romantic love are not only indications of emotional maladjustment but also have overtones of some type of insanity, for in its worst forms romantic love is pre-eminently unrealistic. The lover frequently builds such an idealized picture of his beloved that the expectations could never be fulfilled by a normal human. Marriage and sex are so envisaged that they cannot possibly be attained. The emotional elements of life are exaggerated, until the rational aspects are almost entirely excluded. Love becomes for many a *delicious insanity* and, like many other psychotic conditions, the road back to normality may be rough and rugged.

There are tough and difficult sections on the "road of the loving heart," and adolescence probably represents the toughest pull of all. Not only is it difficult to negotiate, but the roadblock of fixation and regression never loomed larger. The philanderer who drifts from one partner to another is still in the polygamous stage, while the individual forever looking for a "good time" may be fixated or regressed to the adolescent stage. Every group has its "eternal adolescent" who cannot be his age. Not unnaturally, too, many young people who skipped the polygamous period by going steady too young, or marrying at an early age, often feel that they were robbed of something in life. Dissatisfied married women will frequently lament that they never had a chance to be a girl and feel that they have been married all their lives. The developmental processes of life exact their toll when they are ignored or bypassed.

For Better or For Worse

The crisis moment comes in the growing love life when one person of the opposite sex is selected as a love object and a marriage relationship is established. Religion enters to play its part and hallow the relationship. The Roman Catholic Church sees marriage as a sacrament, and the involvement of the religious community is indicated by some of the European churches which insist on reading the banns for three Sundays prior to the wedding.

Moreover, Christianity brought a new concept of commitment and permanence to marriage. The old Roman idea had been divorce by consent, but the Christian marriage vow says, "For better, for worse, for richer, for poorer, in sickness and in health, till death us do part." Even in its more liberal attitudes toward divorce, the church has agreed with reluctance and seen it as a surgical procedure, cutting apart a single organism which should really be in one flesh.

So comes the monogamous stage of love, and it is amazing to see how casually people enter into a lifetime commitment. Other cultures see the dangers. In the East weddings are often arranged by the parents, and, as strange as it may seem, many of these marriages turn out remarkably well. However, in the West, with the emphasis upon the equality of the sexes, the freedom of individuals to make their own choices, and the anticipations of fulfilment, marriage becomes a somewhat hazardous procedure.

Emotionality is a roadblock. With the high premium placed on emotional response, the necessary rational processes that should be utilized in selecting a partner are bypassed. A comparison between love and infatuation shows some of the essential qualities of love that may easily be overlooked in this period. The following is a list of the differences between love and infatuation as revealed in representative research studies (**53**, pp. 40-41).

Love	Infatuation
1. Tends to occur first in late teens and in the twenties	1. Tends to be more frequent among young adolescents and children under teen age
2. Attachment simultaneously to two or more tends not to be frequent	2. Simultaneous attachments to two or more tends to be frequent
3. Most cases last over a long period of time	3. Tends to last but a short time (only a few weeks in most cases)
4. More slowly develops after a love affair has ended	4. More quickly reoccurs soon after a given involvement has ended
5. Often used to refer to present affair	5. Is often the term applied to past attachments
6. Object of affection is more likely a suitable person	6. Tends to focus more frequently on unsuitable person
7. Parents tend to approve	7. Parents more often disapprove
8. Broadly involves entire personality	8. Narrowly focused on a few traits, mostly physical thrill
9. Brings new energy and ambition, and more interest in life	9. Less frequently accompanied by ambition and wide interests
10. Associated with feelings of self-confidence, trust, and security	10. Feelings of guilt, insecurity, and frustration are frequent
11. Accompanied by kindlier feelings toward other people generally	11. Tends to be self-centered and restricted
12. Joy in many common interests and in ongoing sense of being alive when together precludes boredom	12. Boredom is frequent when there is no sexual excitement or social amusement

13. Relationship changes and grows with ongoing association, developing interests, and deepening feelings	13. Little change in the relationship with the passing of time
14. Accompanied by willingness to face reality and to tackle problems realistically	14. Problems and barriers are often disregarded; idealization may have little regard for reality

Impulse marriages are often just as unprofitable as impulse buying, and if a commitment to marriage is made too early, the future marriage relationships may be jeopardized. There have been many studies on the relationship of age and success in marriage, and while it is agreed that this is not the most important single factor in a marriage relationship, it is significantly related to marital success. One investigator found that for the man the best age for marriage is twenty-two or over, and for the woman, twenty and over.

Religion is involved in marriage. Confessors' manuals of the Middle Ages tell of the regulations, not only of the degree of permanence, but also the details of marriage relationships, even to the intimacies of the sex life. However, religion is not only restrictive. It also has a constructive role in marriage. It strengthens and supports an altruistic view of love by showing that true love is not earned but is best manifested in an attitude of giving. Conflicts within marriage are helped by showing that all are sinners and need forgiveness. Religion helps with the budget by putting first things first. A sense of community is engendered by the fellowship of the church with its social life and pastoral assistance. The church and the family stand as two basic institutions whose destinies are tied together.

Little Hands Reach Out

Although many young people do not seem to realize it, one of the logical outcomes of marriage is parenthood. In their preoccupation with each other they sometimes feel that their love life has reached its climax. Pregnancy and children are viewed as intrusions into the idealistic stage, and they make no preparation for commencing a family. Human nature being what it is, their plans sometimes go astray.

It certainly seems wise for a young couple to go for a year or so before commencing their family. They then have opportunity to adjust to each other and to get on their feet before the wife is faced with pregnancy and some of its possible accompaniments. A financial factor enters, and the working wife can help get the home under way.

However, if the commencement of the family is delayed too long, it becomes more difficult to get it started. Very often in later years there are feelings of remorse and regret that the family was not commenced earlier. One of the causes of unhappiness in marriage is voluntary childlessness. With the advent of a baby into the home, a new love experience is opened up before the couple. In the nurturing of little lives and the making of the sacrifices necessary to enable them to come to maturity, some of the noblest aspects of love are realized.

A baby in the family is, of course, no sure guarantee of happiness. Sometimes the mother, preoccupied with the child, neglects her husband, and relationships worsen. A cartoon showed a baby in his diaper, sitting and looking around, stating, "I'm tired of being the only thing that keeps our family together." He will not necessarily do this. There are at least two values which come from parenthood. This experience very often binds the parents together in a common task. It also turns life outward, away from themselves, and happiness which is generally a by-product comes from their interest in this new little life.

Love for children goes in cycles in normal family development. Statistics show that today the average American woman has her last child at twenty-six years of age and becomes a grandmother at forty-four. After this, the couple goes through the complete cycle again with their grandchildren. To watch the delight on the face of a grandfather is to sense something of the experience which grandparents are passing through as they relive their own children's childhood days. Strangely enough, people are very often much better grandparents than they were parents.

Humanity Offers Its Challenge

If love is restricted just to one of the opposite sex or one's children or one's grandchildren, it has not yet developed in the way it should. In any case, sociologists are speaking much these days about the period in married life which they call "the empty nest." Data from the 1950 census indicates that a family's life can be split into two sections, with about twenty-nine years to go after the departure of the children from the home as against twenty-eight and one-half years prior to the empty nest period. The twenty-nine years that lie out ahead can be very bleak if there is not some love object to be focused upon by the couple.

For love to be adequately developed, an individual must be aware of his relationship to humanity. John Donne well stated it in his writing in the year 1624:

No man is an island, entire of itself; every man is a piece of the continent, a part of the main; if a clod be washed away by the sea, Europe is the less, as well as if a promontory were, as well as if a manor of thy friends or of thine own were; any man's death diminishes me, because I am involved in mankind; and therefore never send to know for whom the bell tolls; it tolls for thee.

This type of concern is not natural to men and women, and the passing of the years sometimes brings a certain cynicism which divides man even further from his fellows.

Religious motivations become of the greatest significance here. Commenting on Adler's emphasis, Weatherhead (**184**, p. 275) says:

Adler goes one better. The patient *must* love his neighbor. Yet, that "must" is hard to fulfil. One wonders, indeed, whether its fulfilment is possible apart from religion. In my view, only as man sees his neighbour as his brother, because both are equally loved of God, can he, relying on divine grace, show that unbreakable goodwill to his brother which the word "love" connotes.

The New Testament is full of audacious challenges to love. It teaches that having loved God one will naturally have love for his fellowman. The two are inextricably tied, as the Bible says, "We know that we have passed from death unto life, because we love the brethren" (1 John 3:14).

God's Love and Our Response

"God is love," writes the apostle John. He confronts us with the Christian interpretation that the love of God is the motivating force of divine activity, the dynamic for all human altruism, and the standard by which all other forms of love are measured and evaluated. However, when we come to the specifics and distinctives of God's love for men, and men's love for God, it is like making an analysis of a musical masterpiece. After the impact of the mood of the music, the emotional responses, and the spell of the performance, analysis seems anti-climactic. But the insight into the music will probably increase and heighten the subjective pleasure of the listener at the next performance. Therefore, in much the same way, a more thorough knowledge of the elements of divine love will certainly enrich any religious experience.

In his monumental study of the love of God, Nygren uses the musical metaphor and sees two "motifs" which have come to the front whenever men have grappled with the idea of divine love. These two motifs are the concepts involved in the Greek words *eros* and *agape*. Nygren traces the words back to their earliest usage to show that although both are translated with the English word "love," they had two entirely different meanings in their origin. But like the twin themes of a great symphony, there have been periods in history when the two motifs have been united, intermingled, and almost indistinguishable. At other times the motifs emerged clear-cut, conspicuous, and unmistakably different. So, in his discussion of two periods of history Nygren (**140**, p. 669) says, "The Renascence takes up the Eros motif, the Reformation the Agape motif."

For the ancient Greeks, *eros* was the way to God. The gods themselves had no needs, but man was, in the words of Maslow (**126**, p. 69), "a wanting animal." Becoming conscious of his need, he reached out for his god. The metaphors of the older writers showed the emphasis. Aristotle used the figure of the ladder to describe the process of the individual's ascent to God. Gregory of Nyssa described finding God as being like climbing a mountain, or like the human soul shot as an arrow towards the heavenly mark. In each instance it is the *eros* love's longing which lifts man up to heaven.

Agape love, by contrast, is the love which comes from God and moves downward to man. Nygren (**140**, p. 75) says, "Christian fellowship with God is distinguished from all other kinds by the fact that it depends exclusively on God's *Agape*. He highlights four distinctives: (1) *agape* is spontaneous and unmotivated; (2) *agape* is indifferent to values in the object of love; (3) *agape* is creative; (4) *agape* is the initiator of fellowship with God. Above everything else, *agape* is God's way to man.

Agape and *eros* run in two different directions as is seen in Nygren's (**140**, p. 219) chart of the contrast between *eros* and *agape* in the four dimensions of love, which follows below.

AGAPE		DIMENSION	EROS	
DIRECTION	VALUE		VALUE	DIRECTION
(DOWNWARD MOVEMENT) ↓	3 2 1 0	God's Love Neighborly Love Love for God Self-Love	0 1 2 3	*(UPWARD MOVEMENT)* ↑

Nygren starts with man's self-love which is pre-eminently *eros*, having no *agape* value. Man only loves for what he can ultimately get, and love toward God is for his own gain.

In the dimension of love for God, *eros* has a legitimate place. A man strives upward towards God because he has a need and seeks satisfaction in the divine fulness. *Agape* is also concerned with loving God: "Thou shalt love the Lord thy God with all thy heart, and with all thy soul, and with all thy mind. This is the first and great commandment" (Matt. 22:37-38). However in *agape* the motivation is that the individual becomes conscious of the overwhelming, unmotivated love of God and responds with a grateful love for God.

Love of one's neighbor, in the *eros* sense, means that the neighbor may become useful to the *eros* lover, who will use him as a stepping-stone. *Agape* love for a neighbor, on the other hand, represents the divinely motivated love felt towards an unlovely object. This love is given without any hope of reward or gain. It might be expressed in the commonly used phrase, "loving the unlovely."

The most noticeable of all the contrasts is seen in the love of God. The *eros* motif is a tendency upward towards God. It was, as we have seen, the way in which the Greeks described the experience of coming to know the love of God. But in Christian formulations man cannot find his way to God unaided. So Nygren gives a zero value to *eros* in regard to the love of God. In the *agape* motif the tendency is a downward move from God, and Nygren sees it as having the highest value of 3 in the scale.

In no other discussions of love have the reciprocal aspects of love been so evidently presented. Man loves and is loved. Which comes first, loving or being loved? The obvious answer is that in *agape* love God loves man first, and man reciprocates in his love for God. The distinctive Christian concept is that of *agape,* the unselfish, giving love.

A legend of ancient Rome told the story of Cupid and Psyche. Psyche was a beautiful woman, and the goddess Venus, resentful of Psyche's attractiveness, commissioned her son Cupid to fire one of his darts into Psyche, causing her to fall in love with some despicable creature. Unfortunate for Venus, Cupid himself came under the spell of Psyche's beauty and fell in love with her. After a long and difficult relationship Venus finally accepted Psyche, bringing her into the palace of the gods where she was given the embrace that made her immortal. Thus Psyche (soul) and Cupid (love) found each other. Psychology in its search for a soul discovers, like the writer of the legend, that soul and love belong together.

8

The Difficult Process of Growing

Within the body the processes of growth take place automatically. Almost too automatically for some people, for they look with dismay at their expanding waistline or shrink from the telltale bathroom scales. The processes of maturation by which the organism passes through the orderly stages of development indicate the teleological wisdom of the human frame. As the word maturation describes physical growth, so maturity tells of the processes of emotional growth. But unfortunately, emotional development is not nearly as inevitable as physical.

Growth and religion are intertwined, but the history of religion is replete with instances of attempts by individuals or groups to attain a static condition of holiness. Much of the impetus for these "perfectionist groups" has come from a literal interpretation of Jesus' statement in the Sermon on the Mount, when he said, "Be ye therefore perfect" (Matt. 5:48). Attainment of the state of sinless perfection has been self-righteously claimed by some religious people and despaired of by many others. The apostle Paul stated his conviction, "Not as though I had already attained, either were already perfect: but I follow after, if that I may apprehend that for which also I am apprehended of Christ Jesus" (Phil 3:12). The clue to the meaning of the word translated "perfect" in the Sermon on the Mount is to be found in the writings of Epictetus, who used it to describe a man setting his feet on a path and still advancing. Accordingly, some of the modern translations have rendered the phrase, "Be ye mature."

Maturity has important psychological as well as theological meanings. The Latin root of the term "mature" is a word which means "fully grown" or "ripe." The small boy who steals fruit from an orchard discovers its sourness, and the resultant stomach-ache indicates that fruit needs to be ripe to be enjoyed. Immature personalities, like unripened fruit, can be very sour. But like fruit left to grow, there is always the possibility that they can be ripened.

Psychological Insights Involved in the Maturity Concept

One of the popular books on maturity is H. A. Overstreet's (**143,** pp. 16-41) *The Mature Mind* which claims that there are psychological insights leading to the acceptance of the "maturity concept." Most of these are associated with personalities of the psychological world.

Psychological age.—The great figure in formulating the concept of psychological age was Binet, the Frenchman, who devised the now-famous Binet Intelligence Test. It had long been known that some children were brighter than others, but the problem was to devise a technique whereby the relative brightness or dullness of the children might be related to their chronological age. Binet formulated the proposition that an individual had a mental age as well as a chronological age. After examining thousands of children, he devised norms of skills and the ideas of children at specific age levels. The main insight of Binet was that people have a psychological age which does not necessarily correspond with their physical age. Overstreet (**143,** p. 17) says, "A boy ten years old by the solar calendar may be only five years old by his psychological calendar; or he may be fifteen."

The notion became a concern for educators. All the implications have not yet been absorbed into our educational system, but there has come a healthier respect for difference and an acknowledgment that children of the same chronological age are not necessarily ready to do the same standard of school work. Binet's main concern was with mental age, intelligence, or the capacity to solve problems. Psychologists extended their investigation and concluded that the same principle obtained in the emotional and social areas of the individual's life. A woman of forty-five years of age could have an emotional response of twelve years, while a man thirty-six years old might have the egocentric outlook of a child five years old. Not all adults are adult. Though they have grown chronologically, they may not have developed socially or emotionally.

Conditioned responses.—The Russian physiologist, Ivan Pavlov, is an all-time great in the psychological world. He began his work as a physiologist and in experiments with dogs succeeded in establishing what came to be known as "conditioned reflexes." A dog was placed in a laboratory and kept in harness with its surroundings carefully controlled. A tube inserted into its mouth made it possible to measure the amount of its salivation. As the dog was fed, it was at the same time given a stimulus. The commonly used stimulus was the sound of a buzzer. When the dog was later given a stimulus without the food, it responded physiologically as if it had ingested food. It was thus said to have been conditioned.

In 1914 an experimenter named Shanger Drestovnikova, a student of Pavlov's, experimented with dogs by using visual stimuli. As discrimination became increasingly difficult, the dog's behavior underwent a change. Animals which had previously been docile now became antagonistic and snapped at the harness holding them in position. Afterwards, it was postulated that the equivalent of a nervous breakdown had been induced in the dog. Similar results were later obtained with sheep, pigs, and monkeys. In 1925 an experimenter named Krasnogorski began conditioning processes with children. As he progressed he found that it was possible to change aspects of the child's personality.

Conditioning processes have been applied in such diverse areas as conditioned reflex therapy in the treatment of emotional illnesses, learning theory for educational theorists, and the psychological formulations of behaviorism. One frightening aspect of the whole procedure is that the brainwashing techniques of communism are thought by many to be the direct outcome of applying Pavlov's principles to conditioning the minds of men and women.

The most important implication of Pavlov's work for the consideration of maturity is that human nature is not fixed. To salivate while being given food was natural to a dog, but now it had been taught to salivate at the sound of a bell. Obviously a dog's nature was not fixed and unalterable. It could be conditioned and changed. A newspaper cartoon showed a man sitting in a chair reading a newspaper. Nearby stood his son with a friend. With his finger on the switch of the vacuum cleaner, the son was saying, "You see, every time I press the switch his legs go up." The man had been conditioned for the appropriate response to his wife's cleaning activities. But it all goes much deeper. Humans have the capacity to grow and change, and can be conditioned to new and different responses from what might be called "natural."

Individual uniquenss.—It has long been known that individuals differ from each other, but only in fairly recent days have psychologists shown that individuals have distinctive skills and capacities. The development of psychological tests made it possible to determine aspects of individual uniqueness. It is difficult to discover just who was the pioneer, but early Carl Stumpf began measuring musical ability. Thorndike played a large part with his celebrated dictum, "Whatever exists, exists in some amount, and can be measured."

A towering giant who believed in applying the principle of individual uniqueness to the choice of a vocation was Frank Parsons, who wrote the pioneering book, *Choosing a Vocation,* and is largely responsible for the vocational guidance movement as we know it today. Application of these principles has been made to many areas of life. Today, psychological tests have been multiplied many times over.

For the maturity concept it means that because each individual is unique, his growth potential will be greatest along the line of his peculiar ability. One of the tragedies of our age of automation lies in the fact that many people see their work as a means of gaining income rather than as a source of personal satisfaction. A person will have more maturity potential when his life work is in line with his special abilities, skills, or aptitudes.

Adult ability to learn.—Edward Thorndike published a book called *Adult Learning* in 1928 and challenged the long-held notion that childhood is the time of learning and that in adulthood the capacity to learn has been lost. It had long been accepted that an old dog could not be taught new tricks, but Thorndike emphatically declared that this was wrong. Failure to learn was rarely, if ever, due to age.

F. W. Boreham was haunted by a fear of being "too old at forty." He had an interest in writing and spasmodically contributed to religious and secular periodicals, but a conversation with a layman stirred a renewed interest in the writer's craft and a prospect of a shortened writing career. Mr. Soundy, a layman some years older than he, one day asked him his age. Learning that Boreham was in his late thirties, the layman uttered a warning, "If you take my advice you will make the most of the next few years. You will have precious few ideas after you are forty (**41**, p. 135). Boreham was overshadowed by the specter of "being too old at forty." He gave his every energy to gathering material and laboriously struggled to improve his literary style by writing and constantly revising. The feeling of being "too old at forty" was reflected in his essay *Forty,* which perpetuated his fears, apprehensions, and hopes. By the time of his fortieth birthday he had completed two books. In the following years the grand total swelled to forty-six books. His creative abilities only reached their zenith after his fortieth year. Experience had shown that no man need ever be "too old at forty."

Adults rarely fail to learn because of factors within themselves or their culture. They generally lack motivation. It has become increasingly obvious that not only can adults learn but they must learn. To become a mature person the adult has to realize that he is in the school of life with no point of graduation, only doors opening to new spheres of opportunity.

Fixation and regression.—Two other psychological insights play a large part in the maturity concept. At an Australian pleasure resort called Terrigal, there is an unusual headland called "The Skillion" because of its resemblance to what Australians call a "skillion" roof. It projects out into the sea, rising from the level land behind and sloping up until it reaches its highest point where its cliff face abruptly falls away. It looks deceptively easy to climb, and on a pretty day many people set out to conquer the slope and view the beautiful seascape below. With the majority of them one of two things happens. Some climb only a short distance before realizing the slope is too steep, and they sit down to take it easy. Others continue to climb and may even get three-quarter ways up the incline before despairing of ever making the top, and they turn around to go back.

The illustration dramatizes two psychological mechanisms which are the enemies of growth. The first is *fixation*. This means that the growth processes of the individual have been halted. He concludes that it is easier for him to live at the safe, protected, infantile level than to venture out on the road to adulthood. The second mechanism is *regression*. Like the sightseers who climbed three-quarter ways up the hill and gave up to return, so there are people who seriously attempt to face life's challenges. Then, when they are hurt by life or experience they have difficulty in continuing to live at this level and turn to regress to a less demanding, infantile level of living.

The Growth of the Self

No one knows what a newborn infant thinks, and it is generally agreed that it is highly improbable that he thinks anything. Many psychologists do not see the ego as standard equipment for the infant. His basic needs are animal, and around him is the big, booming, buzzing world. Growing awareness of the surrounding environment and differentiation within that environment leads to ego development. The ego is governed by the *reality principle,* and as reality emerges from the nebulous mistiness of infantile surroundings, ego development is facilitated.

There comes a day when the infant begins to use the pronouns *I, me,* and *you,* and the process marks the dawning of an ability to distinguish self from others. As the process continues, he discovers what other people think of him. He proudly proclaims that he is "mother's good boy" in a big forward step in the development of the self.

Bonner (**23,** p. 459) feels that the body has been neglected in considering the ego. He thus speaks of the "bodily" self. The body is the first object the child knows, and so it occupies the first place in his world of perception. At some stages of growth the body is more important than at others.

Irving Stone (**171,** p. 11) portrays the thirteen-year-old Michelangelo as sitting before his mirror and gazing at his reflected image. He says to himself, "I'm not well designed. My head is out of rule, with the forehead overweighing my mouth and chin. Someone should have used a plumb line." Bodily and facial proportions are often a consuming interest for the adolescent. Later in life, an erstwhile friend turned on Michelangelo in a jealous rage and smashed his nose, so humiliating him that he withdrew from life, showing the psychological blow to be worse then the physical.

Adler noted the body's place in ego perception in his idea of "organ inferiority." The whole concept of psychosomatic medicine is founded on the close association of emotions and the body, as the latter often expresses the individual's emotional conflicts. Some go as far as to call functional illnesses "organ language."

With the development of the sense of reality the infant learns to tolerate delay. He discovers that he cannot have satisfaction the moment he wants it and that he must adjust himself to the demands of his environment. Learning to substitute future gratification for immediate satisfaction is a part of the development of the ego. It is a principle which will remain with him for the rest of his life. This will be discussed further later in this chapter.

The emerging capacity for speech enables the individual to communicate with others and to know the world of reality. Communication is of consequence for a number of reasons. There is a special sense in which the individual is born alone. Through the growth of speech skills he comes to know the world around him and breaks out of his peculiar isolation. Helen Keller offers an example. Deaf, dumb, and blind, cut off from the world around her, she seemed more like an animal than a human being. Then the devoted teacher worked with her, managing at last to tap out a word on her hand. With the act of communication the hidden splendor gets out, and she becomes one of the great figures of our day. Through speech we enter into the community of knowledge and come to know the world about us.

As the child becomes a participant in the drama of life, ego development progresses. In play he builds blocks, smashes houses, takes various roles. Roles may be readily interchanged but become more meaningful in the game of life. As an adult he will later learn of life's roles, and his capacity to fulfil these roles will be a decisive factor as he becomes a husband, employer, father, or executive.

Speech also allows an individual to clarify his own thought processes. Man is sometimes said to be different from the animals because of his capacity to imagine. However, if he resorts too frequently to imagining he may get lost in the unrealities of fantasy. One of the best tests of thoughts is to verbalize them. Through the act of expression the individual externalizes his thought processes and is able to see the fallacy of his thinking. One writer has called the procedure "the test of verbalization" (49, p. 35).

Self-identity is linked with an individual's name. Shakespeare says that a person's good name is his most treasured possession: "Who steals my purse steals trash; but he that filches from me my good name . . . makes me poor indeed." One study showed that people who dislike their names often find difficulty in accepting themselves.

Among the Communists there has been a readiness to change names. Trotsky's original name was Lev Bronstein. While escaping from Siberia he used fake identification papers inscribed with the name of his jailor, Leon Trotsky, and so he took the name by which he is known to history. So it was with many other revolutionary leaders.

Joseph Vissarionovich Djugashvili was known at various times as J. Besoshvili, Chizhikov, David, Ivanov, Ivanovich, K. Kato, Ko. Koba (after hero Georgian legend), K. St., Nizheradze, Ryaboil (police nickname meaning pockmarked), Soso (diminutive of Joseph in

Georgian), Stalin (meaning steel man), Oganess Vartanovich Toto-
myants, Vassily, Vassilyev (**178**, p. 475). The changing of names by
these revolutionaries might only have been a symptom of the inner
turmoil and hostility which they experienced. A man's name is associated with his religion. In British countries it is still the custom to
refer to a man's "given" name as his "Christian" name. The name
becomes a symbol of the new Christian allegiance. Self-identity is
facilitated with an individual's acceptance of his name.

The ego is governed by the "reality principle" and is the executive
force in the systems of personality. Consequently, the individual
learns not only to delay pleasures but also to deny many of his impulses. All areas of self-denial may well represent the indication of
the growth and strength of the ego.

Characteristics of the Maturing Person

Ira Progoff claims that the basic conclusion reached independently
by Adler, Jung, and Rank was that neurotic people were emotionally
ill because their potentiality for growth of one kind or another had
been blocked. A basic problem is to establish adequate criteria for
the evaluation of growth processes. Numerous attempts have been
made, and a consideration of the concepts of trends, description, and
areas may help to set a backdrop for our own conclusions.

Coleman (**38**, p. 81) suggests seven broad trends as characterizing
a healthy personality development in any culture. They are trends

from (1) dependence to self-direction, (2) pleasure to reality, (3) ignorance to knowledge (4) incompetence to competence, (5) diffuse sexuality to heterosexuality, (6) amorality to morality, and (7) self-centeredness to other-centeredness.

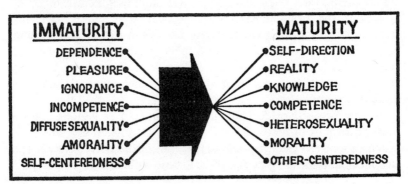

IMMATURITY — MATURITY

DEPENDENCE → SELF-DIRECTION
PLEASURE → REALITY
IGNORANCE → KNOWLEDGE
INCOMPETENCE → COMPETENCE
DIFFUSE SEXUALITY → HETEROSEXUALITY
AMORALITY → MORALITY
SELF-CENTEREDNESS → OTHER-CENTEREDNESS

The above figure shows Coleman's concept of trends in adjustment. The movement and development may be blocked by fixation or regression. It will be seen that *development*, *direction*, and *discipline* of the self all stand out.

Allport (**7**, p. 307) prefers a descriptive approach and sees the mature individual as distinguished by at least six features: (1) having a widely extended sense of self; (2) being able to relate himself warmly to others in both intimate and non-intimate contacts; (3) possessing a fundamental emotional security and accepting himself; (4) able to perceive, think, and act with zest in accordance with outer reality; (5) capable of self-objectification with insight and humor; (6) living in harmony with a unifying philosophy of life.

Areas of maturity concern English and English (**57**, p. 308), who see three realms of growth. (1) *Intellectual maturity*. An individual should have intelligence commensurate with his age or an adult level. Associated, also, is the thought of practical wisdom as contrasted with intelligence alone. (2) *Emotional maturity*. Mature emotional behavior is steady and socially acceptable. Sometimes this refers to the degree to which a person has departed from behavior appropriate to childhood and manifests that of adulthood. (3) *Social maturity*. The socially mature person has mastered effective social techniques for adequate and satisfying relationships with his fellows.

In the three foregoing formulations the emphasis is on trends in personality, a description of the mature person, and the areas of maturity within personality. The very diversity of maturity criteria complicates the process, but our present attempt will be descriptive, with the resultant maturing person necessarily hypothetical.

The maturing person is a creature of emotions but not their slave.— Even though modern man has made tremendous progress in his intellectual discoveries, he is constantly confronted with the fact that although a rational animal he is not *altogether* rational. Most of his personal problems are in the areas of his emotions.

Emotions are primitive mechanisms which were necessary for early man in facing his rugged life. Living in primeval days, an individual had to be prepared for any eventuality—for an enemy tribesman, or a ferocious animal that might leap upon him and tear his frail frame apart. Faced with these situations, primitive man had two alternatives: he could fight, or flee, with either alternative calling for a tremendous burst of energy.

Emotional reaction includes a triggering of the body's emergency system. An individual in a state of fear, not only feels a certain way, but has a total physiological reaction. Adrenaline is poured into his body from the ductless glands; his heart beats more rapidly; the pupils of his eyes are dilated; the whole body is prepared for action, so that he can fight his enemy or flee from the situation.

Investigations have shown the effectiveness of the body's emergency system, and at least three effects of strong emotion have been shown. (1) A person in the grip of an emotion can exert himself over a long period of time, and the normal processes of fatigue do not seem to prevail. Men in combat or other types of emergencies can go for long periods without sleep. (2) A second effect of emotional upheaval is to give a tremendous burst of strength. During a fire a man in a state of fear picked up a safe and carried it outside. Later it took three men to carry it back. (3) A third effect may be to make an individual insensitive to pain. An injured football player may go on in the excitement of the game unaware of his injury.

However, in a modern civilization emotions are more frequently a liability than an asset. Civilized society does not allow the individual to give physical expression to his hostility, and he has to learn to handle it in other ways. Hostility can be expressed openly and in a verbal manner against the source of frustration. The adolescent boy damages his father's car, and the father fumes at him in a manifestation of *direct hostility*. A person may direct hostility towards himself. The clerk makes a foolish mistake and knows that there will be trouble. He develops a sick headache and may be said to be a case of *repressed hostility*. Another way of dealing with hostility is to express it in some way such as chopping wood, playing golf, talking to an understanding friend, or having a session of counseling. *Expressed hostility* describes these activities.

Possibly the most troublesome method of handling hostility is to express it openly but not against the original source of frustration. The man in trouble at work goes home and takes it out on his wife and children, thus showing *displaced hostility*. Displaced hostility occurs under a number of circumstances. If the source of frustration constitutes a danger to the individual, as with the boss who has the power to dismiss him, or if the individual has ambivalent feelings toward the person who thwarted him, as when a dependent wife vents her hostility on the children rather than her inconsiderate spouse, hostility is displaced. Displacement may also occur when the source of frustration is unknown or inaccessible. For the frustrated individual a single cause, like the government, becomes a target.

Investigating the way in which communism is perceived by those affiliating with it, Almond (11) shows that people joining the Communist party have an image of a militant organization on the attack. An analysis of Communist literature shows very little emphasis on the "constructive" side of life, the main drive being against the "wrongs" of society. Hostility is also a central factor in most maladjusted individuals, and many who join the party show resentment, antagonism, rebelliousness, and hatred. The party provides an opportunity for the expression of their hostilities. Communism being an outlawed organization, the very act of joining is a defiant gesture. Becoming part of a protest against society provides expression for the hostility of maladjustment.

An individual must continue to grow emotionally, but fixations and conditioning processes thwart emotional growth. Wayne Oates uses the term "dated emotions." Early in life a child learns to dominate the situation by screaming, kicking, or holding his breath until he is blue in the face. So comes the evolution of techniques of manipulating others. Faced with conflicts in later life, emotions blaze and dominate, with rationality rapidly receding.

The maturing person is guided by long term purposes rather than immediate desires.—A popular definition of maturity is, "the capacity to postpone pleasure." Like many popular sayings it has more than a grain of truth in it. The maturing person looks ahead and plans for the future. Allport (9, p. 219) puts it succinctly: "Every mature personality may be said to travel toward a port of destination, selected in advance, or to several related ports in succession."

Dr. C. Bühler, in her study of outstanding personalities, concluded that each life was definitely ordered and steered toward a selected goal. These lives were characterized by aim and ambition. On the other hand, would-be suicides indicated that life had become intolerable because there was no goal to seek. Directionality and discipline are two essential ingredients of growth.

The psychopathic or sociopathic personality is a difficult type of individual, who bedevils our society and fills our jails. Writing in his fascinating *Rebel Without a Cause*, Robert M. Lindner (119, pp. 2-4) sees the psychopathic personality as an individual in an essentially infantile condition. The psycopath either will not or cannot grow beyond the infantile perspective to adult attitudes toward life.

Whereas an adult is able to postpone the intake of food, the infant must satisfy his hunger immediately. If satisfaction is delayed, frustration is expressed by crying or other aggressive behavior. Like the infant, the psychopath must have immediate gratification. He cannot wait for the normal preliminaries that lead to sexual gratification; he must rape. To gradually build up a reputation that would gain the applause of society would take too long; he must perform some daring act to focus all attention upon himself.

Another infantile characteristic of the psychopath, seen by Lindner, is his inability to achieve goals in a socially acceptable order. A well-balanced adult has clearly defined goals ahead, and these are reached by planned, orderly, logical procedures. Perseverance in pursuing these goals and objectives characterizes the adult.

I have to go to the electric company to pay my bill. On the way I may meet a friend and converse briefly, stop to look in a shop window, focus my attention on the dilemma of the driver in a stalled car, and pause to observe the construction of a new building, but ultimately I make the electric company and pay my overdue bill.

However, the psychopath, like the infant, is aimless and lives in the area of immediacy. For him the side attraction becomes the central feature. Watching the progress of the building, he decides to remain there for the afternoon and neglects the overdue light bill, and its nonpayment brings an inevitable consequence. He lives by fits and starts.

As with the infant, the psychopath has little frustration tolerance. Living in the world where gradualness and persuasiveness are highly prized, he faces constant frustration. He either attacks the cause of frustration with intensity, or he flees on his nomadic way without regard to the practical outcome of either line of action.

The Christian religion is frequently criticized because of its emphasis on the future. It calls upon its followers to set up goals, to work towards objectives, and to sacrifice immediate pleasures for future satisfaction. However, all of these are factors in growth, for as Allport (9, p. 220) says, "Without some sustained goals somewhere a personality remains childish."

The maturing person has a perspective of life beyond his own self-interests.—At birth man is fundamentally self-centered. The Freudians say the newborn child is mainly *id* and consequently motivated by the pleasure principle. With the dawning of reality the individual realizes that the world does not exist for him alone. At some point in time he comes to the realization, "I am incomplete." A large part of the process of maturing is involved in the psychological journey from self-centeredness to other-centeredness.

Allport calls the development "an extension of self." He sees the experience of falling in love as an illustration. The lover discovers that all his personal urges and drives are focused on another person. Things of interest to the other person become of interest to him. Hitherto he felt self-sufficient, but now he discovers that he needs another. This other person's welfare becomes paramount in his thinking, and his self is extended.

Empathy is a word used by psychologists to describe the process of understanding another individual's feelings and concerns. Empathy and sympathy are often confused, but English and English (57, p. 178) make a distinction:

> While the empathic process is primarily intellectual, emotion is not precluded, but it is not the same emotion as that of the person with whom one empathizes. The parent may empathize with the child's puny rage, feeling pity or amusement, whereas in sympathy he would feel rage along with the child. The attitude in empathy is one of acceptance and understanding, of an implicit "I see how you feel."

As described, empathy is a hallmark of the mature person.

The Christian faith lays great emphasis upon community. The natural correlate of loving God is to love one's neighbor as oneself, and the celebrated Golden Rule bids Christians to think in terms of others. Overstreet (143, p. 63) says: "A person is not mature until he has both an ability and a willingness to see himself as one among others and to do unto those others as he would have them do to him."

The maturing person develops the capacity of self-objectification.— Socrates asserted, "I must first know myself." The whole process of maturing is wrapped up with developing self-knowledge. Self-knowledge is not easy to gain. Allport quotes a study in which, in a psychology class, 96 per cent of the students thought they possessed better than average insight into their own personalities, with only 4 per cent of them admitting a possible deficiency. It would be highly improbable that this was true to the facts of the case, but in humans vanity often beclouds a sense of judgment.

The psychological term for self-objectification is insight, which has been defined by English and English (57, p. 264) as "reasonable understanding and evaluation of one's own mental processes, reactions, abilities; self-knowledge." The counselor looks upon insight as a desirable objective for his counselee. Rogers describes it as involving perception of relationships, acceptance of self, and the element of choice. In each of these self-objectification plays a large part.

Psychological investigation has shown a number of correlates of insight. People with insight are much less likely to project their thoughts into their estimates of other people and are also generally more intelligent than the average. One of the less expected correlates is that people with insight have a very good sense of humor.

The maturing person is constantly developing the capacity to be able to stand off and look at himself, know himself, and be prepared to laugh at himself when necessary. The classical illustration is of Socrates attending a performance of Aristophanes' *The Clouds*. The play had in it a character wearing a mask meant to ridicule Socrates. At the appropriate moment, when the audience was enjoying the caricature, Socrates stood and turned his head side-on, so the audience could compare his profile with the mask worn by the actor on the stage. Socrates was indicating his capacity to join with the people who were laughing at him.

The Christian religion has always been concerned with people gaining self-knowledge. A great proportion of the Bible is given over to teaching or showing examples of people who were unable to face themselves for what they really were. The older but still relevant phrase, "conviction of sin," has behind it the implication of an individual giving up his elaborate rationalizations and defences and realistically acknowledging his own nature for what it really is.

The maturing person has a unifying philosophy of life.—Immature individuals are generally at conflict within themselves. If the conflict becomes serious enough, one becomes neurotic. Should deterioration continue, psychosis may ensue. The term "schizophrenia," one form of psychosis, literally means "split personality." The previously closely related elements of personality are no longer as closely integrated as they were but have been fragmented. Integration and unification of personality are a part of the maturing process.

Religious experience enters the maturing process at many points, but it is nowhere of greater moment than here. Major Mayer (**127**, p. 59), the army psychiatrist who interviewed many victims of brainwashing, described in a copyrighted interview in *U. S. News and World Report* the person who resisted best of all.

Q How about the man who had a strong religious faith?

A This touches on one of the great deficiencies in our knowledge. Some intensive studies must be made of those people who resisted from the beginning to the end, who remained unshakable in their convictions, and, incidentally, who survived in larger numbers and came home in better shape, because it was the group of resisters, by and large, who can be described this way. A number of people told us that they had resisted every overture of the enemy by invoking abstract, sometimes theological, convictions which has long been a part of their lives—

Q Religious convictions, you mean?

A Yes. Our findings here were the same as our findings among combat soldiers who are faced with the constant problem of defense against battle fear. A really convinced religious person, be he a devout Catholic, or devout Orthodox Jew, or a member of a fundamentalist Protestant sect—whatever his religion, if it had been part of his whole life, if his family were organized along lines of religious training and the moral and ethical precepts of such training—such a man often was able to defend himself and his principles with this armament. The new convert, the "foxhole religion" type of individual, is not defended by that kind of abstract idea.

The challenge of unscrupulous brainwashing processes calls for mature personalities, and the maturing process is inextricably associated with religion.

A Mature Religion

But not all religion is within itself mature. Clark (**34**, pp. 256-57) has suggested criteria by which to evaluate the maturity of religion.

1. *Is it primary?* Does the religion derive from a sense of compelling individual need, or is it a piece of pious, imitative playacting? This will not always distinguish it from immature religion, but it will from dead religion. Whatever else it is, mature religion must always be alive.

2. *Is it fresh?* Has it, like religion in childhood, a fresh sense of curiosity and cosmic wonder?

3. *Is it self-critical?* Can the individual see weaknesses in his religious position at the same time that he remains loyal to it?

4. *Is it free from magic?* Does the individual sense a source of ideal power to which he gives free obedience in his attempt to harmonize his life with the divine? In other words, is his a genuine religion as we have defined it or merely a magical substitute conceived of by the individual as a means of securing favors from a cosmic source?

5. *Is it meaningfully dynamic?* Does his religion give meaning to life in such a way as to enlist and motivate his total energies so that it is capable of becoming a satisfaction for its own sake?

6. *Is it integrating?* Does it relate itself to all of his experience, thus integrating his life and demonstrating moral results consistent with his own aims, as well as those of a wholesome society?

7. *Is it socially effective?* Does the individual's religion strengthen his sense of community with others in such a way as to be ultimately creative of a more wholesome society?

8. *Does it demonstrate humility?*

9. *Is it growing?* Is his faith an expanding one, both in his search for deeper truths and in his progressively wider, willing identification of the interests of others with his own?

10. *Is it creative?* Does the religious life of the individual contain elements and show characteristics of its own, or is it in every respect a mere repetition of the religion of others? In a sense this is the supreme test of the mature religious life.

Clark's ninth question highlights growth in religion. As Jesus looked upon the people of his day and watched their reactions to the religious challenges, he characterized them, "This generation . . . is like unto children" (Matt. 11:16). Peter says that the believers are to grow in grace and in the knowledge of our Lord Jesus Christ (2 Peter 3:18). The obvious reference is to growth in knowledge and in attitude. The climatic statement in Paul's hymn of love is, "When I was a child, I spake as a child, I understood as a child, I thought as a child: but when I became a man, I put away childish things" (1 Cor. 13:11). The Bible abounds in exhortations concerning growth, and it is legitimate to conclude that religion is an important ingredient in the maturing processes of personality.

9

Religion and Mental Health

The mental hygiene movement is of comparatively recent origin and in a large measure is built on the work of Clifford Beers. Beers had been an inmate in a mental hospital on several occasions, and was exposed to the cruelties and indignities of the institutions of his day. He wrote of his experiences in a book called *The Mind That Found Itself.* Solomon said, "Of making many books there is no end" (Eccl. 12:12). Manuscripts often gather dust as the author's early optimism gradually fades, and another book dies in its birth. So it might have been with Beer's contribution except for a fortuitous circumstance.

Seeking the imprimatur of a great name, he took the manuscript to William James to ask his evaluation. Already besieged by a multitude of would-be authors, James rapidly thumbed through the newest submission but was immediately fascinated by Beer's story. He gave the book his endorsement, writing an introduction, and its success was assured.

The book worked wonders, creating a widespread interest which grew until Beers felt compelled to leave his employment and launch the new Mental Hygiene Movement. He served as its first secretary, a position which he occupied until the day of his death. Thus, the writer of *The Varieties of Religious Experience,* William James, who had done so much for the study of psychology of religion, gave impetus to the new mental health movement. In at least this sense they can both be said to have common grounds.

Beers became the crusader for a new approach to mental illness in the succession of Philippe Pinel in France, and Dorothea Dix in America. As secretary of the new movement, Beers directed its affairs with vigor, but the mental hygiene movement had a separate existence from the church, although there were always ministers who were in-

147

terested. Of more recent days there has been a steady growth in the relationship of religion and mental hygiene. In the light of the early relationship of religion and mental health, a new evaluation is far overdue.

Since the dawn of history, religion and medicine have had a close association, with an emphasis on the mental aspects of life's difficulties. Even physical illnesses were treated through what might now be called psychotherapy. Hygeia, the Greek goddess of health, was worshiped in temples where incubation was practiced. Incubation involved the patient sleeping in the sanctuary of the temple, where the deity was supposed to effect cures or prescribe remedies in dreams. Weatherhead (**184**, p. 21) says:

> Actually, patients stayed all night and slept in the precincts of the temple, while priest-physicians, having prepared the minds of patients by lectures and talks, whispered suggestions in the name of the god into their ears. Reading of this in modern days, we can realize the effectiveness of this method. The patient may have been asleep or awake or between the two states. The priest was, in any case, *acting for the god,* and the patient was in a highly suggestible state.

Mental disorders were thought of in terms of primitive demonology, and various techniques were used to exorcise the troublesome demons. Coleman (**37**, p. 23) says:

> Such treatment was originally in the hands of medicine men or shamans, but was eventually taken over in Greece, China, and Egypt by the priests, who were apparently a curious mixture of priest, physician, psychologist and magician. Although these priests were dominated in the main by belief in demonology and established exocistic practices, they did make a beginning in the more humane and scientific treatment of the mentally ill.

Although both religion and medicine were primitive, crude, and elementary, they were inextricably woven together in ministering to the physical, mental, and religious needs of these individuals.

Passing time brought the development of scientific investigation which lead to the inevitable conflict between science and religion. In his presidential address to the American Psychiatric Association in 1956, R. Finley Gayle, Jr. (**72**, p. 29) gave a new slant to Freud's "scientific insults" and developed the provocative idea that the war between science and religion had been based on three successive fronts.

1. *With regard to the world around man.*—The discoveries of Copernicus and Galileo challenged the Ptolemaic system of astronomy. Many theologians felt threatened because of the implication that the earth was not a place at the center of the universe especially prepared by God for his people. Some religious leaders refused to look into a telescope for fear that it would threaten their view of the design of the universe, and thus eliminate the necessity for a Designer.

2. *With regard to the world of man.*—The conflict shifted from the firmament above to man himself, as the theory of organic evolution challenged the fondly held view that man was a special creation apart from all other forms of animal life. Evolutionary theory seemed to many sincere people to challenge their faith. Just as the new system of astronomy appeared to eliminate a Designer, now the Creator was dispatched.

3. *With regard to the world within man.*—As scientific investigation approached closer to the citadel of self, new conflicts emerged in the latest chapter of the conflict between science and religion. The new set of antagonists are psychiatry and religion. Psychiatry came under suspicion and attack by some ministers of religion who felt that science was trying to do away with a Saviour. But there was a mutual fear. Some psychiatrists were apprehensive about clergymen "doing therapy," while ministers were concerned about psychiatrists "forgiving sins." However, while religion has had its battles, so has psychiatry. Many of the struggles of psychiatry have been with various segments of society apart altogether from any religious affiliation. As Dr. Zilboorg makes clear in his *History of Medical Psychology,* one of psychiatry's most acrimonious antagonists over the centuries has been the medical profession itself. Only recently have psychiatrists begun to enjoy the approbation of most of their colleagues.

Far more serious than the conflict over areas of responsibility is the criticism of Freud, as he attacks the very nature of religion. Freud's (**66**, p. 79) stature in the psychological world makes his attack the more devastating, as he draws an analogy between the obsessional neurosis and religion:

The true believer is in a high degree protected against the danger of certain neurotic afflictions; by accepting the universal neurosis (religion) he is spared the task of performing a personal neurosis. [His religious dogmas are] "neurotic survivals."

Freud's exposition of his ideas are found in two books, *Totem and Taboo* and *The Future of Illusion,* with the latter containing his main onslaught on religion. He maintains that primitive man was constantly appalled by natural forces and the riddle of death. To get closer to the forces of nature, he personified them and sought to placate them by worshiping and building shrines.

Modern man finds it difficult to advance from the level of his primitive counterpart. The child grows into a man only to discover that he is destined to remain a child forever. He takes over the personification of natural forces, investing them with the traits of a father, and trusts this father figure to protect him. Ernest Jones (**101,** III, 354) says that Freud stated unequivocally his conclusions about religious beliefs and made his main contribution to psychology of religion when he said:

> Psycho-analysis has made us aware of the intimate connection between the father complex and the belief in God, and has taught us that the personal God is psychologically nothing other than a magnified father; it shows us every day how young people can lose their religious faith as soon as the father's authority collapses. We thus recognize the root of religious need as lying in the parental complex.

Moral values developed as society realized that life was unworkable without some restraints on man's aggressive nature. Thus, the moral restrictions were projected onto the father-god image.

Leslie D. Weatherhead (**184,** pp. 399-406) springs to challenge Freud and is peculiarly fitted for the task. A Methodist minister, he has done outstanding work in the psychological field. As an admirer of Freud, he has helped reconcile Freud's views with liberal Christianity. In answering Freud he makes three fundamental assertions.

1. *To desire a father does not invalidate the fact that one may exist.*—Freud's fundamental error was in beginning with the assumption that God does not and cannot exist. To explain religion he then claimed that man had made God in his father's image. Actually, there is nothing to prove this. If it were asserted that a physical hunger—a desire for food—showed that food is a figment of man's imagination, it would be ludicrous. A better assertion would be that the only way that God could reveal himself was through man's needs.

2. *Christianity is a historical religion, not a religion invented to fill a need.*—The historicity of the founder of Christianity is well enough established. Apart from the Bible it is vouched for by the younger Pliny (A.D. 61-114), Tacitus (A.D. 55-120), Suetonius (A.D. 75-150), and Josephus (A.D. 37-100). It is as well authenticated as the historicity of Plato. Along with numerous other facts, there is almost incontrovertible evidence of the historicity of the Christian faith.

3. *Christianity is too austere in its demands to be the kind of illusion that men invent.*—Freud talks as though Christianity were an invention of men who wanted to calm their fears and escape from the realities of life. However, for the truth of Christianity men and women have been willing to suffer torture, disgrace, banishment, imprisonment, and death.

This answer to Freud by Weatherhead, who espouses many Freudian concepts but rejects his atheism, may be symbolic of the rapprochement taking place between religion and psychiatry.

Mowrer ever awaiting an opening in Freud's argument, springs to the attack at the point of reality. He refers to the onslaught on psychoanalysis from so many fronts, contrasting the psychoanalyst's difficulty with the ever-increasing church attendance in the United States. Mowrer (**132**, p. 10) says, "In other words, Freud's 'reality principle' appears to be doing less well than the 'illusion' with such an unpromising future." Moreover, the continued vitality of religion fascinates Mowrer, who criticizes Freud's idea that religion developing in primitive man's mind has been perpetuated like a congenital weakness. Mowrer shows that religion has survived because it has unique psychological survival value for the individual. Often the individual with strong religious convictions has emerged victorious from experiences of peculiar pressure. Mowrer also takes up the question of the mental health of churchgoers. It is often asserted that there are more neurotic people among churchgoers than in the normal population of nonchurchgoers. The assertion would be difficult to prove without a carefully controlled study. Even if the facts were as stated, Mowrer says that one obvious conclusion would be that the fact that the church offers salvation means that it should attract neurotic people. It would be absurd to condemn hospitals because they have sick people in them. The church with its call to the sick, sorry, and needy folks will always attract certain neurotic personalities.

Experimental evidence regarding the place of religion in mental illness has been presented by Wayne E. Oates (**142**, pp. 5-10) in his book, *Religious Factors in Mental Illness*. At the time of writing, Oates was the chaplain of the Kentucky State Hospital at Danville, Kentucky. Working with a group of ten students under his supervision, the team studied the religious experiences of 68 mentally ill persons. The study was a search for "leads" as to the role that religion played in the psychotic conditions of the patients.

One group of 17.2 per cent of the cases showed a conflict of long-standing rebellion or submission on the part of the individual toward the religion of his home. In many cases the religion was not an inner spiritual discernment but an experience tied up with the individual's anxious rebellion toward his parents.

In the second group, representing 10.3 per cent of the cases, religion was taken as a "last straw" attempt to solve otherwise unmanageable problems and to justify failures in personal relationships and loss of self-control. The religious responsiveness of these patients was viewed by both the psychiatrists and chaplains as a sort of counsel of despair, setting off the crisis stage of the illnesses which were already in motion before the individual was influenced by a religious individual or group. Then an individual or group would suggest religious ideas or practices that in themselves became a problem to the patient.

A third group of the patients, comprising 20.5 per cent of the total, showed psychotic conditions simply "clothed" with religious ideas. They often picked up their ideas from other patients, or talked to the chaplains with religious "chatter" simply because they were ministers, or used religious expressions as a means of getting attention, approval, or favors. Little or no religious concern appeared in the pre-psychotic history of these persons. In about half of these cases the chaplains were able to develop a real religious interest. Apparently, patients who were this conscious of how the chaplains felt about them had gone a long way toward recovery.

A fourth group of 51.5 per cent of the patients showed no evidence of religious interest or past religious concerns. This is true even though they came from rural communities in southeastern Kentucky, which is supposed to be a very active "Bible belt" area, and which is highly productive of independent religious sects of an ecstatic nature. Whereas much has been written about the repressive effect of religious teachings, these theories are inadequate to explain how over half of the patients were suffering from essentially the same kind of diseases as were their more religious fellow patients.

Combining his studies with those of Samuel Southard, done with a group of patients at Lakeland, Kentucky, Oates (**142**, p. 10) concludes with regard to the role and function of religion among mentally ill persons:

1. Religious affiliation with this or that group has little or no correlation with mental illness, neither in terms of the particular denomination of the patient nor in terms of the fact of church membership.

2. However, *the way in which religious teachings* are presented to the person has much to do with the way he accepts, rejects, or falls into interminable conflict over these teachings.

3. Particularly important in this experience of communication of religious teaching are the mother and father of the individual (or the persons who fill the role of the parents in the event of their death or defection). The concept of God and the concept of parents can easily develop obstructive "adhesians" to each other in the religious perceptions of the patient.

Boisen's investigation of the "Holy Roller" sects led him to investigate the alleged damage to emotional stability which followed from contact with the group. In one community he followed through with an examination of the new admissions of a local mental hospital and was amazed at the small number of "Holy Roller" admissions. Boisen (**22**, p. 88) says, "I have seen hundreds of cases brought before psychiatric staffs but I have yet to see anyone committed because of peculiar beliefs whenever these beliefs were shared by two or three others." Boisen concludes that the amount of mental disturbance coming even in this most extreme religious manifestation has been greatly exaggerated.

Nothing is gained by overstating the case. It must frankly be acknowledged that not all religion is good, and there are expressions of religion which are not conducive to mental health. Weatherhead (**184**, pp. 414-20) gives a good summary of some of the possibilities of the perversion of religion. (1) It can be misused to cover a flight from reality. (2) It can be misused to provide a false security. (3) It can be misused to buy an escape from the results of misdemeanors. (4) It can be misused to give a halo of holiness which is narcissistic and self-centered.

Similarly, in a writing which is very sympathetic toward religion as a whole, Thorpe (175, p. 506) sums up a number of the problems associated with an immature religion and its effects on mental health.

Another aspect of the last named problem is that of utilizing religion as a means of escape from reality, or as a dependency mechanism which encourages the individual to "cast his burdens on the Lord"—and cease to do anything about them himself.

A ready answer to the situation would be to refer to the biblical teaching about burdens, as Paul says, "Every man shall bear his own burden" (Gal. 6:5). The problem lies not in the biblical teaching but in the individual's lack of knowledge.

The Religion of the Neuroses

Another aspect of the relationship of neurosis to religion is the neurotic manifestations which have a similarity to primitive or perverted forms of religion. In many ways these primitive forms periodically reappear, like some peculiar, shabbily dressed and socially unacceptable aunt who persistently visits her sophisticated relatives, blissfully unaware of the embarrassment she causes.

A number of investigations have noted the points of resemblance between the neuroses and primitive religious forms. Fromm mentions ancestor worship, ritualism, and totemism as representing the neurotic reactions of modern man. Sigmund Freud was fascinated by the same subject and wrote about it in his book, *Totem and Taboo*.

Ancestor worship is a neurotic fixation on father or mother, with the individual unable to break loose from parental relationships and spending all his days under the overshadowing father or mother figure. The dependency can endure with undiminished intensity even after the parent's death, crippling the patient's judgment, rendering him unable to love, and causing him to live in a constant state of insecurity. This centering of an individual's life around an ancestor, spending most of one's energies in his worship, is not very different from a religious cult.

Primitive ritual is seen in many of the compulsive types of neurosis. The guilty person may constantly wash his hands or perform some other irrational act. Ritual may also take a mental form, causing the subject to think or say certain formulas. In each instance the symptoms resemble a religious ritual.

In *Webster's New International Dictionary*, *totemism* has been defined as "a class of natural phenomena or material objects—most commonly a species of animals or plants—between which and himself the savage believes that a certain intimate relation exists." Fromm sees totemism in the person whose exclusive devotion is to the state or his political party or a similar organization. The only criteria of truth and value is the interest of the state or the party or the organization. Good examples of this are seen in nazism or communism.

Freud (**69**, pp. 37-39) has also noted the similarity of neurotic manifestations and the primitive religious notion of *taboo*. Taboo is a complex concept which may be said to have two opposing, yet related, ideas. On the one hand, it means sacred or consecrated, but on the other, it signifies uncanny, dangerous, forbidden, and unclean, and generally expresses itself in prohibitions and restrictions. Freud sees three points of correspondence between the compulsions of neurotics and taboo: (1) Both feel that they must obey certain prohibitions and are unaware of why this should be. They have an inner certainty that violation of the prohibition will be followed by unbearable disaster. (2) As in taboo there is often a neurotic prohibition against touching, known as "touching phobia." The prohibition extends, not only to direct contact, but also the figurative use of the phrase "to come into contact." So certain thoughts are prohibited. (3) Both taboo and compulsions have a remarkable capacity for displacement from one object to another.

A thought-provoking aspect of religion and mental health is the relationship between morals and neuroses. A number of investigators have noted that neurotic drives may often cause infidelity in marriage. Behind the contention lies the theory that love develops from infantile self-centeredness towards a maturity willing to give and think of others. One study done by Morton Hunt (**90**, p. 378), comparing a group of female psychiatric patients with a matched group of normal women, showed six times as many of the abnormal group had extra-marital affairs. Marriage counselors' reports show that extra-marital affairs generally involve inappropriate love objects, and therapy often leads to a decrease in the attractiveness of the illicit affair, with a renewal of love and interest in the legitimate marriage partner. We may infer that neurotic drives are often associated with immoral attitudes and that well-formed moral standards could indicate a good psychological adjustment to life and its values.

156 PSYCHOLOGY IN SEARCH OF A SOUL

The New Co-operation

It has been said that after all the conflict between theology and psychiatry, the present situation is one of "peaceful coexistence." Another step is needed from coexistence to active co-operation.

Among psychologists themselves, there has been a shift in the evaluation of religion. Jung was one of the pioneers in such an attitude. This onetime disciple of Freud was the son of a Swiss clergyman, and in addition to parting company with his teacher on the emphasis on sex, he realized the influential role of religion in the emotional life. Jung (**103**, p. 77) says, "A religious attitude is an element in the psychic life whose importance can hardly be overrated." He also said, "The psychologist must remember that certain religious convictions not founded on reason are a necessity of life for many persons." (**103**, p. 224). In yet another instance, Jung indicates that "the physician's recognition of the spiritual factors in their true light is vitally important" (**103**, p. 224). Possibly the strongest of all the statements made by Jung (**103**, pp. 228-29) was that in which he made a plea for more co-operation between psychology and religion:

It is coincident with the general exodus from the Church. Quoting a Protestant minister, I may say: "Nowadays people go to the psychotherapist rather than to the clergyman." . . . I should like to call attention to the following facts. During the past thirty years, people from all the civilized countries of the earth have consulted me. I have treated many hundreds of patients, the larger number being Protestants, a smaller number Jews, and not more than five or six believing Catholics. Among all my patients in the second half of life—that is to say, over thirty-five —there has not been one whose problem in the last resort was not that of finding a religious outlook on life. It is safe to say that every one of them fell ill because he had lost that which the living religions of every age have given to their followers, and none of them has been really healed who did not regain his religious outlook. This of course has nothing whatever to do with a particular creed or membership of a church.

Again, Jung (**103**, pp. 229-31) says:

It is indeed high time for the clergyman and the psychotherapist to join forces to meet this great spiritual task. . . . It seems to me, that, side by side with the decline of religious life, the neuroses grow noticeably more frequent.

Another indication of religion and psychiatry getting together is to be found in the statement made and passed by the entire membership of the Group for the Advancement of Psychiatry in July, 1947. This statement reads:

> For centuries, religion and medicine have been closely related. Psychiatry as a branch of medicine has been so closely related to religion that at times the two were almost inseparable. As science developed, however, medicine and religion assumed distinctive roles in society, but they continue to share the common aim of human betterment. This also holds for that method of psychiatry known as psychoanalysis.
>
> We as the Group for the Advancement of Psychiatry believe in the dignity and the integrity of the individual. We believe that a major goal of treatment is the progressive attainment of social responsibility. We recognize as of crucial significance, the influence of the home upon the individual and the importance of ethical training in the home. We also recognize the important role religion can play in bringing about an improved emotional and moral state.
>
> The methods of psychiatry aim to help patients achieve health in their emotional lives so that they may live in harmony with society and with its standards. We believe there is no conflict between psychiatry and religion. In the practice of his profession the competent psychiatrist will therefore always be guided by this belief. (153, p. 254).

From the perspective of religion, there has been a movement toward the wedding of psychology and religion. Following the phenomenal success of the book, *Peace of Mind,* by the young Boston rabbi, Joshua L. Liebman, there came a spate of books leading to the best sellers by Norman Vincent Peale. Preceding this, however, there was the move by theological seminaries to do something about training ministers in psychology. The first of such courses was introduced in 1890 in the Hartford Theological Seminary. Interest has continued to grow, and most seminaries now offer courses in pastoral psychology, pastoral counseling, and introduction to clinical training and allied fields. Many of these institutions offer graduate programs of study and clinical experience leading to master's degrees or the doctorate in pastoral theology, pastoral counseling, clinical psychology, and guidance.

Moreover, there are institutions across the nation which take religious workers for an internship in clinical training. Some churches have set up clinics within their own buildings, with a team consisting of psychiatrist, psychologist, social worker, and minister. In other instances, one of the members of the staff has been given the title,

"Minister of Counseling." A recent book has come out with a plan to train Sunday school teachers and other leaders to be lay counselors.

Some of this work has tended to be superficial, and there have been critics of the "cult of reassurance." However, the minister often has unusual opportunities to help people with the milder psychological problems. One survey showed that 42 per cent of all people who sought help for their emotional problems turned first to the minister. The minister is in a unique position to be of help to troubled persons. Frequently, he is on the scene before the problem has developed beyond the incipient stage; he is a welcome visitor in the homes of his church members. His knowledge of the total setting of the individual's life enables him to detect personal problems as they begin to manifest themselves. If he has some psychological training he can make a referral at an opportune time and help to save the deteriorating situation.

Religion's Distinctive Contribution

Ridenour, commenting on the developments in the relationship of religion and psychiatry over the past twenty-five years, says that the assumption underlying the numerous conferences on the subject is that they will explore the common ground of both religion and psychiatry. What actually happens, however, is that most of the time is spent trying to show what the clergyman can learn from the psychiatrist to help him in his contacts with people. Ridenour (**154,** p. 91) comments, "Yet curiously enough they never get around to discussing what religion has to offer psychiatry—surely a strange omission."

Is there a distinctive contribution which religion makes to mental health? The extensive survey contained in *Americans View Their Mental Health* (**76,** p. 319) showed that of the people who went to visit a psychiatrist, less than half (46 per cent) felt that it was worthwhile. On the other hand, 65 per cent of those turning to their minister for assistance said they were helped. In all probability the psychiatrist had far more serious cases than the minister, and this may account in part for the smaller number of good reports. But the help gained from this counseling surely indicates that the minister of religion has a special contribution to make.

An examination of some of the ways in which religion fosters mental health will form the basis for the remaining portion of this chapter.

1. *Religion can give a sense of cosmic security.*—There is a sense in which modern man has an awful loneliness in his heart and needs spiritual reassurance to make him feel at home in the universe. If he does not find this sense of oneness through religion, he will search frantically for assurance from somewhere else. The obsessive, compulsive neurotic is trying frantically to establish an orderly world in which there will be no fear of any untoward event to break the routine of life.

Maslow's theory of a hierarchy of needs lists physiological needs as basic. The starving individual feels that he only needs food, but as soon as his physical needs are satisfied his safety needs call for attention. He is now conscious of the importance of an orderly world in which to live.

The psalmist used two names for God: "the Lord of hosts" and "the God of Jacob," the first referring to God's sovereign power and the second calling attention to his care for the individual. Christians see their God as sovereign, ruling the destinies of man. Some of the old-time preachers had sermon topics like "Every Man's Life—a Plan of God," and showed the Creator God as interested in individual men and women. Such a faith gives cosmic security.

2. *Religion can provide motivations for life.*—The frequently used argument against religion is that granted that the believer feels a sense of cosmic security, one of the unfortunate results is that he loses his motivations for living, is willing to leave everything in the hands of God, and does nothing about his own responsibilities. The question has already been discussed in chapter 5, but some new light comes from an unusual source. DeKoster (**45**, p. 120) shows that Trotsky, a Marxist, spent time in his later life comparing Calvinism and communism as dynamic forces. Both the Calvinists and the Communists have a strong assurance in a power far higher than that of any human. Calvinism sees this power as residing in a sovereign God, and the Communists believe in the dialectical forces of history. Yet, despite this belief in the inexorable forces, both Calvinism and communism, Trotsky noted, gave their followers a tremendous impetus for action.

There is a thinly drawn line of distinction between fatalism and Calvinism. When William Carey made his plea for the Baptist missionary enterprise, the older Ryland showed a fatalism when he said, "Young man, sit down, when God pleases to convert the heathen he will do it without your help or mine." Carey, a Calvinist, spent all of

his days promoting and laboring in the missionary cause and brought
a new insight to the Christian church as it launched out on a new era
of missionary activity. It has been shown that very frequently the most
"other worldly" individuals will labor fervently for the propagation of
their message in "this" world.

3. *Religion helps an individual to accept himself.*—The neurotic
person cannot face reality and spends much of his time putting up
defenses. It is often claimed that religious people put on a "holier
than thou" attitude. If they do, they are flying in the face of the
teachings of the Bible which has much to say about the sinfulness of
man. Jesus constantly warned about the religious smoke screens people
erect and said, "Not everyone that saith unto me, Lord, Lord, shall
enter into the kingdom of heaven; but he that doeth the will of my
Father which is in heaven" (Matt. 7:21). The whole point of Jesus'
story about the publican and the sinner was that the self-righteous
Pharisee was trusting in his outward show and deceiving himself,
while the penitent publican could not even look up but said, "God
be merciful to me a sinner" (Luke 18:13). The penitent publican's
religion, in which he accepted his own shortcomings, gained the com-
mendation of Jesus.

Some studies in psychotherapy have shown that as subjects progressed in therapy, they took a more realistic view of themselves and
shortened some of their unreal objectives. Realism became the hallmark of their lives; pretense was dropped. The word "hypocrite," frequently used by Jesus, literally means an actor. Possibly the most
threatening thing the authentically religious person faces is his own
admission of unworthiness, but it must surely come if he is to have a
satisfactory religious experience.

4. *Religion makes confessional experiences available.*—One result
of misdemeanors in life is the awful feeling of isolation. We try to
keep the whole matter private, but in so doing we put ourselves into a
position of isolation, so that we no longer feel at one with our fellows.
The church has intuitively known this down through the years and has
made confessional experiences available. Catharsis is a well-known
technique in psychotherapy. It involves the purging of the emotions
as the story is poured out and release gained. As Jung (**103**, p. 35)
says it: "I still continue in my state of isolation. It is only with the
help of confession that I am able to throw myself into the arms of
humanity freed at last from the burden of moral exile."

This does not constitute an advocacy of the Roman Catholic practice of confession. Mowrer (**132**, pp. 194-95) sums up some of the objections to it from a psychological viewpoint: (1) Catholic confession is often little more than an empty, perfunctory formality. A Catholic chaplain offered the information that confessions last from forty seconds to three minutes, while an observer averaged the confessional time at sixty seconds. (2) The penance assigned is not psychologically adequate. Apparently, not only the Mikado had difficulty in making "the punishment fit the crime." (3) Absolution and forgiveness are questionable procedures.

In each of Mowrer's criticisms it will be noted that they are related to the ecclesiastical setting, rather than the act of confession. Bainton (**13**, p. 106), in his life of Martin Luther, notes, "He looked upon confession as useful, providing it was not institutionalized."

Confession takes other forms within Protestant churches, and the current emphasis on pastoral counseling provides a vehicle for the experience. The clinical pastoral training movement probably has been influenced more by Carl Rogers' *Client-Centered Therapy* than any other school of thought. Although not always in agreement with the movement, Mowrer (**132**, p. 137) admits, "Pastoral counseling is a mere euphemism for a voluntary nonprescriptive form of confession; and this, if handled rightly, can unquestionably be helpful."

Weatherhead (**183**, pp. 70-76) suggests three benefits which can come from confession: (1) It cleanses the mind. (2) It relieves the conscience. People will say, "If I have been able to talk to someone about this thing, and he has been able to show me God's forgiveness, then certainly, I can go to God and I can tell him about it." (3) It ends the loneliness of pretense. Within confession the facade of defenses can be pulled down, and channels can be opened so that the isolation pretense is broken through.

Distinctly a part of the religious tradition, confession may be of great psychological value for the individual.

5. *Religion stabilizes in time of crisis.*—Boisen, in his study, *Religion in Crisis and Custom,* shows that crisis periods are characteristic of normal growth. Even in the routine development of life experiences, coming of age, getting married, birth of children, old age, bereavement, and death are all crises. Significantly enough, most of these crisis experiences have some associated religious ceremonials, and religion and crisis somehow or other go together.

Crisis periods tend to have an associated religious quickening. In normal periods men may not bother to think too seriously, but times of crisis bring a new intensity. Crisis periods have the twofold possibility of making or breaking an individual. Religious convictions help in the constructive use of crisis.

Boisen notes the relationship of religious fervor to the difficulties of life. During the depression years following 1929, it was anticipated that there would be an increase in the number of people admitted to mental hospitals, but the only rise came from the economic factors which prevented people from supporting the mentally ill and thus necessitated their returning them to the hospital. On the other hand, "holiness" sects grew with great rapidity, and the number of people associated with radical groups trebled. The constituencies of these churches were generally drawn from the underprivileged classes, and the churches made no effort to change the economic system by launching social crusades but focused on the healing of the individual.

6. *Religion provides a therapeutic fellowship.*—Johnson (**99**, pp. 232-58) has developed his idea of dimensions of personality and speaks of the I-me relationship of mind and body, the I-it relationship of the individual to his environment, the I-we relationship of group life, and the I-Thou relationship of a man and his God. Life is a bundle of relationships, and the I-we relationship of group life is a manifestation of man's need for community.

Group life helps the individual. It gives him a sense of belonging; it offers protection from real or fancied threats; it causes him to curb his self-centered desires, while at the same time enhancing his self-esteem. In the give and take with the group the individual discovers himself.

But modern man easily loses his sense of relatedness, and may wander through the crowded streets filled with an awful sense of loneliness. Jung sees repression as the mechanism whereby the individual has a psychic secret which isolates him from his fellows. Religion comes with its message of community and fellowship. After the day of Pentecost, the Christians "continued stedfastly in the apostles' doctrine and fellowship, and in breaking of bread, and in prayers" (Acts 2:42). And alongside these vital religious experiences the writer puts "fellowship." The Greek word, *koinonia,* literally means "having in common" or "going shares." The modern church with its emphasis on small groups in its educational organization serves to draw people close to each other, giving the individual both a sense of significance and an opportunity for service.

Understanding

Sigmund Freud was in many ways a turbulent spirit, not only critical of religion, but belligerent toward any fellow worker who disagreed with him, as is shown in his conflicts with former colleagues like Adler and Jung. Yet, there was one friendship of which very little is heard, and concerning which Jones (101, II, 46) says, "It lasted without a cloud to the end of his life." The partner in this friendship was a Swiss clergyman named Oskar Pfister. Freud addressed him as "Dear man of God" and carried on an intensive correspondence with him.

Some of the letters show another side to Freud's attitude towards religion, as when he said,

In itself psychoanalysis is neither religious nor the opposite, but an impartial instrument which can serve the clergy as well as the laity when it is used only to free suffering people. I have been very struck at realizing how I had never thought of the extraordinary help the psychoanalytic method can be in pastoral work, probably because wicked heretics like us are so far away from the circle (101, II, 440).

There is even a wistful note in Freud's statement, "From a therapeutic point of view I can only envy your opportunity of bringing about sublimation into religion" (101, II, 458).

The friendship of these two men might be a parable of rapprochement. Pfister's spirit and understanding drew Freud to him, and from their divergent backgrounds they moved to a position of mutual respect and achieved an excellent working relationship. Religion and the psychological disciplines belong together. As they learn to respect each other, they can join hands for the betterment of mankind.

10
Personality's Checks and Balances

In chapter 4 it was seen that man's preoccupation with the stars was of more concern to him than the workings of his own personality, and that attention was only focused on personality in an effort to discover the reason for the differences in the reaction time of astronomical observers. Even when man looked within his own personality, he became absorbed in the questions of stimulus response reactions rather than with his own nature.

In the last two decades of the nineteenth century, psychologists could speak of the ego, the self, and even the soul. Then came the attack on the word "soul," causing the term to fall into disuse. Allport (8, p. 71) says: "One of the oddest events in the history of modern psychology is the manner in which the ego (or self) became sidetracked and lost to view." It was not until the rising interest in psychoanalysis developed that ego again emerged as a respectable term, and of more recent days there has been a renewed interest in the ego concept.

To understand the place of the ego in the assumptions of personality theory, it is necessary to see that it involves a concept of systems, within which there are drives as well as checks and balances. The systems may be categorized as: (1) the unregulated urges, (2) the value system, and (3) the ego or self.

The Unregulated Urges

Montagu (131) uses the phrase "unregulated urges" to describe the primary system of personality, and it has merit because it describes as it designates. Other efforts to delineate the system have involved the use of such words as impulses, unlearned motives, drives, instinctual and basic needs. Typically, Freud favored his own word, "id." Freud's tendency to coin words has, in part, been responsible for the definition of psychology as "the study of the id by the odd."

The "unregulated urges" are the raw material of personality and are governed by the *pleasure principle,* which is their standard of judgment. Karl Menninger sees the unregulated urges as having a twofold drive to love and hate: by the gratification of the sexual drive, and the venting of the destructive tendencies.

Psychologists are not all agreed about the unregulated urges. What lies at the core of personality? Is it a devil, an angel, or something between the two? Freud and Carl Rogers have both spent much time examining the naked psyche, divested of its Sunday clothes, and many feel that Rogers' client-centered therapy is indebted to, and influenced by, Freudian psychoanalysis. But the formulations of the two schools unwittingly become embroiled with theology as they consider the nature of man.

Donald E. Walker (**181,** p. 89) states the case by showing Carl Rogers to be the successor of Rousseau, who began his presentation of *Emile* with the observation that every man is a perfect being as he comes from the hands of his Maker. Unfortunately, an imperfect society corrupts the pristine splendor. Walker claims that Rogers comes close to this assumption of the "great golden beast," which slumbers beneath the surface of neurotic man but is hidden by the facade of tensions, symptoms, and antagonisms. Discussing the character of his counseling technique, Rogers (**156,** p. 29) says:

In the first place, it relies much more heavily on the individual drive toward growth, health, and adjustment. Therapy is not a matter of doing something *to* the individual, or of inducing him to do something about himself. It is instead a matter of freeing him for normal growth and development, of removing obstacles so that he can again move forward.

The troubled person has forces within him which need to be set free, so that he can become what he has the capacity to be.

Rogers originally planned to become a minister, spending two years studying in a seminary. He is very sympathetic towards religious beliefs, currently serving on the advisory board of *Pastoral Psychology,* the psychological periodical for ministers. On the other hand, Freud is opposed to religion, which he sees as a "neurotic survival." But Walker claims that in Freud's view of the nature of man he inherits the tradition of Augustine, that man is basically and fundamentally hostile, antisocial, and carnal. So, in *The Future of an Illusion,* Freud (**66,** p. 6) says:

SYSTEMS OF PERSONALITY

System	Freudian Term	How Develops	Principle	Functions	Origin	Scriptural Term	Conscious?
Unregulated Urges	Id (it)	Instinctive strivings	Pleasure	Pleasure seeking Love (Sex) Hate (Aggression)	Biological inheritance	"Flesh" Gal. 5:24 "Old man" Col. 3:9 "Heart" Mark 7:21	Unconscious
Value System Sub-systems Ego-ideal Conscience	Superego (Greater I)	Influence of parents teachers, etc.	"You ought" "Thou shalt not"	*Moral or Judicial* 1. Inhibits unregulated urges. 2. Persuades ego to accept moralistic goals. 3. Strives for perfection.	Social inheritance	"Conscience" Acts 23:1	Partly conscious and partly unconscious
Ego or Self	Ego (I)	Contact with reality. Development of speech. Learning to tolerate delay.	Reality	*Executive* Deciding between (1) strivings of unregulated urges. (2) demands of value system. (3) reality of situation	Dawning of consciousness	"Inner man" Eph. 3:16	Conscious

One has, I think, to reckon with the fact that there are present in all men destructive and therefore anti-social and anti-cultural tendencies and with a great number of people these are strong enough to determine their behavior in human society.

Freud (**69**, p. 94) comes out even more frankly in his *Totem and Taboo* when he states, "Psychoanalysis here confirms what the pious were wont to say, that we are all miserable sinners." If we accept the Freudian view of man, the ultimate problem of psychotherapy becomes reconciliation, in some workable fashion, of the conflicting demands of a hostile antisocial human nature with the needs of the society.

The student of psychology of religion finishes up with strange bedfellows. Freud, seen as antagonistic towards religion, enunciates a view of human nature portrayed in the New Testament. Paul tells of his struggle with his own unregulated urges. "I do not understand my own actions. For I do not do what I want, but I do the very thing I hate" (Rom. 7:15, RSV). His use of the word "flesh" coincides with the idea that the unregulated urges have a close contact with bodily processes, from which they derive their energy, so he says, "In me [my flesh] dwelleth no good thing" (v. 18). Similarly, in the ministry of Jesus he had reference to something akin to the unregulated urges when he said, "For it is from inside, from men's hearts and minds, that evil thoughts arise—lust, theft, murder, adultery, greed, wickedness, deceit, sensuality, envy, slander, arrogance and folly" (Mark 7:21-22, Phillips).

The Value System

Among the descriptive terms applied to human beings, we cannot afford to overlook that stated by Kluckhohn when he says man is an "evaluating animal." Man is always choosing between alternatives, setting up goals, and deciding something is good or bad, better or worse, lower or higher. A value system, often unacknowledged or even consciously unknown, plays a large part in all of these experiences.

An individual's value system stands at the opposite extreme to the unregulated urges in the systems of personality. Freud gave it the name of Superego or "greater I." The value system is sometimes called the judicial system, while others refer to it as the moral arm of personality. Freudians see the value system's functions as being threefold: (1) to inhibit the impulses of the unregulated urges, particularly those of an aggressive or sexual nature; (2) to persuade the ego to accept moralistic goals for realistic ones; (3) to strive for perfection.

The growth of a value system is a devious process. A child's concept of telling the truth, for example, evolves with passing years. At four years the child distinguishes between fact and fiction; at five he exaggerates and tells fanciful tales but begins to know when he is fooling. By the time he has reached six years of age, he can distinguish between truth and fiction, but he may continue to lie in spite of telltale evidence. The seventh birthday brings less lying, and the child becomes concerned about wrongdoing, particularly other people's. At the dawning of the eighth year, the child begins to become essentially truthful but still boasts and tells tales. A parent, watching a child pass through these stages, will sometimes wonder if the child will ever develop a well-formed value system.

The value system grows and develops as the individual responds to the rewards and punishments of parents, teachers, and other authority figures. It is sometimes described as an "interiorizing" of the external voice of authority. It may be thought of as having two subsystems: (1) the *conscience,* characterized by the principle of "Thou shalt not," and (2) the *ego ideal,* which has the "You ought" principle.

Allport (4, p. 73) prefers the simple term "conscience" and sees a process of conscience development in the growing individual. He theorizes that as the conscience develops, it grows from a *must conscious* to an *ought conscience,* and three things take place:

1. External sanctions give way to internal . . . 2. Experiences of prohibition, fear, and "must" give way to experiences of preference, self-respect, and "ought." . . . 3. Specific habits of obedience give way to generic self-guidance . . . [as the individual develops] broad schemata of values [which give direction to his conduct.]

Whether we accept the idea of subsystems of a value system, or Allport's idea of conscience, it still remains primarily the way an individual feels about his conduct. The fear of punishment, of the "you must," and the feeling of obligation, of the "I ought," form a value system's emotional basis.

Value systems are not standardized. They come in different sizes and shapes as is seen in the following drawing of a continuum of a value system. A value system can be thought of as fitting on a continuum which stretches all the way from scrupulosity to the psychopathic or sociopathic personality. Each individual fits somewhere on

SCRUPULOSITY   SOCIOPATHIC
                                                               PERSONALITY

the continuum. The well-balanced personality would be somewhere between the two extremes.

Persons characterized by scrupulosity have morbid guilt reactions. An individual may feel that he has committed the unpardonable sin or be overwhelmed by his failure to fulfil some trivial religious obligation. Some of the great saints have been characterized by scrupulosity. Martin Luther offers an illustration of scrupulosity as is seen in Bainton's (13, p. 41) portrayal of the guilt-ridden monk:

> Luther would repeat a confession and, to be sure of including everything, would review this entire life until the confessor grew weary and exclaimed, "Man, God is not angry with you. You are angry with God. Don't you know that God commands you to hope?"
> This assiduous confessing certainly succeeded in clearing up any major transgressions. The left-overs with which Luther kept trotting in appeared to Staupitz to be only the scruples of a sick soul. "Look here," said he, "if you expect Christ to forgive you, come in with something to forgive—parricide, blasphemy, adultery—instead of all these peccadilloes."
> But Luther's question was not whether his sins were big or little, but whether they had been confessed. The great difficulty which he encountered was to be sure that everything has been recalled. He learned from experience the cleverness of memory in protecting the ego, and he was frightened when after six hours of confessing he could still go out and think of something else which had eluded his most conscientious scrutiny.

Significantly enough, Luther later entered into a deeper religious experience in which the undue concern for guilt was lost.

Psychiatrists often fear that religious leaders see the rousing of guilt feelings as their primary activity. It is necessary to distinguish between the words "sin" and "guilt." For the Christian, "sin" represents the act, and "guilt" is the word used to describe the way the individual feels about it. If he is emotionally disturbed, his condition may have no relationship to reality. It may simply be an abnormal reaction, such as he would have in any other area of life irrespective of religious convictions.

As bad as scrupulosity may seem, it is not as damaging to the individual, or to society, as is the psychopathic or sociopathic personality. The place of a value system is seen, in the categorization of the sociopaths, under the heading of "character disorders." The sociopath or psychopath is characterized by an inability to understand or accept moral values, a marked discrepancy between his level of intelligence and the development of his conscience, an inability to profit from mistakes and ordinary experiences, and a lack of the capacity to forego immediate pleasure for future gains and long-range plans. He is not able to maintain a steady loyalty to another person, has a low tolerance for stress, and rejects constituted authority and discipline. However, he has the capacity to put up a good front to impress others and is frequently a facile liar. The quality of the emotional life is the central consideration.

We often speak about a "well-balanced" personality, and the phrase is particularly pertinent to value systems.

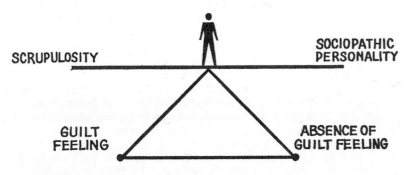

The above figure shows the value system as a balancing mechanism, which can tip the scales of the individual's emotional life and determine the quality of his feeling tone in reaction to life's experiences.

Most psychotherapists are pessimistic about the prognosis of therapy with the sociopath. The main line of action must be preventive and aim at ameliorating the causes. Family realtionships apparently play a large part in the development of a sociopathic personality.

Coville, Costello, and Rouke (40, p. 127) mention three parent-child relationship patterns which are frequently seen in the background of the sociopath. (1) *Rejection.* The individual comes from an emotionally cold home in which he feels unwanted, and his anti-social behavior may spring from an unconscious desire to punish his rejecting parents, or a self-punishment for his feeling of hostility towards them. (2) *Overindulgence.* The overindulged child never learns to restrain impulses or postpone gratification. (3) *Lack of identification.* The growing child learns through identifying with an adult who may become his model. Many sociopaths come from broken homes or those in which there were prolonged parental absence, where they were rejected by parents or had inferior fathers and mothers.

Working with delinquents, Abrahamsen (1, p. 155) noted a similar pattern in the character disorders and says, "This lack of object relationship has made it difficult if not impossible for them to develop a Super Ego." Lack of good relationships with parents was obvious. As slow as it may seem, the best work with antisocial personalities will be done in the preventive activity of building better homes, where there is a concern for the development of better formed value systems.

An immediate question is, "What is a value?" Though we feel we know what a value is, it is difficult to define. Clyde Kluckhohn (111, p. 395) gives his definition: "A value is a conception, explicit or implicit, distinctive of an individual or characteristic of a group of the desirable which influences the selection from available modes, means, and ends of action." Values can be subdivided into the groups of *conceived* and *operative.* Many individuals have conceived ideals but do not bother to implement them. Operative values are the ones we work on.

An individual's *real* values may be better understood by applying four tests. (1) *The choice test.* What does this person do in situations involving a choice? (2) *The time test.* How much time and energy is the individual willing to spend in following the value? (3) *The sacrificial test.* What satisfactions is he willing to forego on behalf of the value? (4) *The emotion test.* How much satisfaction or guilt does the individual experience when he is true to his value or violates it?

The emotional test of an individual's values recalls the essential emotional nature of conscience. Conscience is like an electronic computer. It can give wonderful guidance to life and help the individual feel right or wrong about what he does or fails to do. With the conscience as with the computer, much depends upon the factual information fed into it. If the wrong facts are given to the computer, the wrong answer will emerge. Similarly, the validity of the feelings of the conscience depends upon the values accepted by the individual.

An incident related by J. Edgar Hoover in his book, *Master of Deceit*, illustrates the emotional test. Hoover (**87**, p. 120) tells of a young woman who was a dedicated Communist. Watching the fluctuations of the Communist line, she finally became convinced that communism was wrong and decided to leave the party. She then experienced the phenomenon Hoover says affects party members withdrawing from communism, which he calls "the counterattack of the unconscious Party discipline." Doubts would suddenly arise, disappear, then reappear. When she seemed to want to slow down in her party work, her old enthusiasm would return. She found, as she explained later, that her process of "mental reorientation was impeded by the study and teaching of Marxist-Leninist works, which is the Communist Party's antidote for such an eventuality."

The long processes of constant discussion, schools, and self-study of the Communists had built up within her a conscience which served to keep her involved in Communist activities. Hoover comments that this is the reason why Communists continually emphasize their schools, the reading of their literature, and self-study. It builds a discipline that automatically attacks doubts, rationalizes contradictions, and guides every decision in the party's favor.

Abrahamsen points to a strange aspect of the value system in which the individual has unconscious guilt. The delinquent or criminal unconsciously wants to be punished and leaves behind clues which will inevitably lead to his apprehension. The case of Leopold and Loeb is an illustration. They tried to commit the perfect crime, but Leopold left his glasses at the scene of the crime. Abrahamsen suggests that these people have unconscious desires; their superego accuses them, and the crime is committed with a clue left behind so that they will be apprehended and punished.

For Mowrer, the value system is the key to the whole matter of anxiety. He takes issue with Freud's view that the individual is anxious because of what he wants to do but does not dare. Mowrer rather claims that the difficulty lies in what the individual has done but wishes he had not. He sees Freud's theory as indicating that repression is directed towards the unregulated urges, while Mowrer says repression has been turned toward the value system.

Commenting on the fact that some two hundred thousand children are born out of wedlock in the United States each year, Clark E. Vincent (180) lays much of the blame on faulty value systems. He says that we have a philosophy of "fun morality," in which children are raised from their earliest days. If a child likes something, even food, it is good for him; teachers are warned that a child will learn faster if he is "having fun." In personal relationships in business, the stress is upon making the employees feel as if they are "just one big happy family."

The idea is carried over to sexual relationships before and outside of marriage. Sex is fun, just don't get caught. This is the idea that is pushed by the entertainment media which has so much access to young people's lives. Thoughtful observers of the contemporary scene are emphasizing the necessity for convictions and a sense of values.

But from whence come the values held by individuals and groups? Coleman (38, pp. 303-7) says that there are three sources of values: (1) science, (2) experience, and (3) religion. After an examination of the first two, he acknowledges that man has traditionally looked to a revelation from God as the ultimate source of values. This is religion's peculiar province. Some sociologists frankly acknowledge that the church is largely responsible for the values of society. Moberg (130, pp. 175-77) sees the church's function in maintaining society's values as being carried on in several areas. (1) The church helps people define goals and purposes. It encourages good will, unselfishness, and kindness, which are in many ways the antithesis of people's natural inclinations. (2) The church is a critic of society. It acts as society's conscience and judges institutions and practices by its ethical standards. Prophetic voices speak out against those who would exploit society for their own benefit. (3) The church influences social standards. Religious institutions have been called "a great social lighthouse," because of the concepts they have brought to the world. (4) The church guards the mores of society. Reinforcement is given to moral ideals, and it conserves customs and habits beneficial to society. These socializing activities are the direct outcome of the consensus of the personal values held by the individual members of the group.

Jung claims that although Freud was against religion and rejected divine revelation and any ideas of immortality, it is necessary to have some standards. He says Freud's idea of the Superego was "a furtive attempt to smuggle in his time-honored image of Jehovah in the dress of psychological theory" (**103**, p. 122).

Mowrer pleads for a new idea of faith in God. People have thought of God for too long as *something out there* rather than as *something in here*. He quotes from the Old Testament:

Behold, the Lord passed by, and a great and strong wind rent the mountains, and brake in pieces the rocks before the Lord; but the Lord was not in the wind: and after the wind an earthquake; but the Lord was not in the earthquake: And after the earthquake a fire; but the Lord was not in the fire: and after the fire a still small voice (1 Kings 19:11-12).

Our problem might well be that we have lost faith in God because we have lost faith in conscience. Unbelieving man is essentially material. To say, "I ought" is no more morally significant than to say "I itch." Religion has much to say about essential inner moral sensitivity. Just to be religious is not a guarantee that life will be lived by the highest values, but it is at least the acceptance of a conceived, if not a practiced, value system, with the ever-present possibility of the conceived values taking on a new significance.

The Ego or Self

From what has been said the reader might think that man is a more or less a helpless pawn of either his nature or his ideals. Anna Russell (**132**, p. 49) in her "Psychiatric Folk Song" sings:

> At three I had a feeling of
> Ambivalence toward my brothers,
> And so it follows naturally
> I poisoned all my lovers.

> But now I'm happy; I have learned
> The lesson this has taught;
> That everything I do that's wrong
> Is someone else's fault.

Rather unfortunately, the singer has minimized the all-important system of personality. For between the crude, primitive, selfish, demanding forces of the unregulated urges, on the one hand, and the standards, ideals, and perfectionist goals of the value system, on the other, there stands the all-important third system called the ego or self.

What is the nature of the self or ego? Descriptive powers are suddenly inadequate, but we are aware of some central core of existence. All around us is change. Our environment changes as does our body, but the essential core of self remains. Sometimes the word "self" is used, sometimes "ego," but for our purposes the expressions will be used interchangeably.

In the previous chapter we noted the developing self or ego, but this essential ego is not to be thought of as a synonym for personality but rather as a part of the totality. Moreover, despite the illustrations, the ego must never be thought of as a little manikin within the individual. There is an essential oneness involved in the realtionship of unregulated urges, value system, and the ego, and it finds its expression in the Freudian statement, "Where id was there shall ego be."

With the dawning of life the infant gradually becomes conscious of himself and other human beings, and the ego becomes the contact region of personality with the external world. Because it is the *contact* region of personality, the ego is also the *conflict* region. The ego is personality's executive force. Although we have followed Freud's main principles so far, we now reach a point of departure. Freud thought that the ego had no energy of its own and that the only source of energy was the id or unregulated urges. The newer emphasis of ego-psychology claims "ego-autonomy," meaning that the ego is not a slave to either the unregulated urges or the environment but has its own energy.

In its executive functions the ego has three would-be masters which it must obey or rule. They are the unregulated urges, the value system, and the external world representing reality. The way in which these three can be organized and related to each other by the ego, in a large measure, determines the growth and successful adjustment of the individual. Whereas, the unregulated urges were dominated by the pleasure principle, the value system by the "Thou shalt not" and the "You ought" principles, the ego is governed by the *reality principle*.

Always remembering the essential unity of the personality systems, an illustration may help to show their relationship. At the rodeo the Brahma bull riding contest is an ever popular event. The bulls are bad tempered and for their size extremely agile. The rider has only a piece of rope around the animal's middle which he can grasp. At a signal the animal is released and begins its mad plunging, pitching, rolling movements in an effort to rid itself of its unwanted burden. Calling on every trick learned by years of experience, the cowboy struggles to control his bovine mount, all the time conscious of the roaring crowd and the struggling beast.

If we add to the picture of the man on the bucking bull, a little person who sits on the rider's shoulder whispering instructions in his ear, we will have something of an illustration of the three factors in operation. The Brahma bull represents the unregulated urges seeking to rid themselves of all control; the little person whispering instructions to the rider represents the value system, while the rider of the bull represents the ego. The ego, like the rider, is trying to live by the ideals of the value system and control the unregulated urges, while being conscious of the external world of reality represented by the excited, cheering, watching crowd.

The thoughts of a young man walking down the street may illustrate. He sees a very attractive and shapely girl approaching. His unregulated urges suggest the possibility of seduction. His value system tells him that she is a woman like his mother, his act might ruin her life, he could get apprehended and arrested, and it would be a violation of his religious principles. His ego recalls him to the reality of the situation. It would be but a momentary satisfaction; if caught and jailed, his future career might be ruined. If he wants the girl, why not become friendly with her and discover if they would be suited for each other, win her love and affection, and finally marry her.

The term "ego-strength" becomes relevant. In popular usage ego-strength is confused with the word egotistical, describing a self-centered and self-sufficient person having no consideration for others. But "ego-strength" is the antithesis of egotistical. The individual with "ego-strength" either resists his own desires or puts them into a correct perspective in life.

Abrahamsen (1, p. 67) has formulated a series of laws with regard to crime. He sees three factors—criminal tendencies (T), the situation (S), and resistance (R)—entering into any criminal act. He thus formulated his law:

A criminal act equals the product of a person's criminalistic tendencies elicited by the momentary situation, all of which results in his mental resistance being so decreased that he carries out the criminal act. This law can be put into a formula:

$$C = \frac{T + S}{R}$$

He also suggests that the formula can be applied to all sorts of human behavior by simply substituting H (human behavior) for C. Thus the formula becomes:

$$H = \frac{T + S}{R}$$

Every individual has impulses and tendencies within. The so-called instinctive forces want immediate satisfaction. When placed in a situation where one can give expression to these, one's consideration of reality and the power of resistance will be an indication of his "ego-strength." Paul speaks about "ego-strength" in his writings and says, "Strengthened with might by his Spirit in the inner man" (Eph 3:16). The Ephesian epistle speaks about the work of the Holy Spirit within the life and personality of the individual, and the inner strengthening seems to be at the heart of the work of the Spirit of God in an individual's life.

The Lost Soul

Has psychology, which lost man's soul amid the brass instruments for measuring reaction time, found it again in the laboratory of life, amid the turmoil resulting from two world wars? At least one psychologist thinks so. Allport says:

I am inclined to believe history will declare that psychoanalysis marked an inter-regnum in psychology between the time when it lost its soul, shortly after the Franco-Prussian War, and the time when it found it again, shortly after World War II (167, p. 141).

The implications of this are broad and wide. The same writer goes on to examine some of these:

It does mean, however, a recognition of the fact that our predecessors who regarded psychology as the science of the soul, were not wrong in setting the problems of unity and personal relevance before us. What they call the soul, we may now, with all good conscience, call the ego. . . . We may safely predict that ego psychology in the twentieth century will flourish increasingly (**167**, p. 158).

Religion is coming into its own as a factor in developing personality. The ego, seen in similar terms to the soul by some psychologists, is assuming a position of greater importance in psychological thought. In the many and varied theoretical formulations regarding personality there are gaps which can be filled only by the motivations peculiar to religious experiences.

PART THREE

Suggestion and the Soul

Suggestion in its most highly developed aspect, hypnosis, has associations of mystery and mumbo jumbo. It is generally regarded as beyond the pale of discussion in religious circles. But the association of religion and suggestion is so obvious that it must be considered.

In the early writings on psychology of religion, suggestion was frequently mentioned. George Albert Coe's work on conversion, for example, utilized hypnosis as an experimental procedure. However, more recently the subject has been ignored. Attention is focused on suggestion in chapter 11, where it will be seen that there are overtones of the phenomenon in all areas of religious experience. Moreover, the techniques of work and method in religion already utilize suggestion and could perhaps become more effective with greater knowledge of the phenomenon.

Possibly the most dramatic of all areas of psychology of religion is to be found in faith healing. Here, suggestion and autosuggestion have their heyday. Historically, "faith healing" has taken place under many different circumstances. Frequently it seems to depend, not so much on the nature of the faith object, as the subjective attitude of the individual who has faith.

Factors involved in faith healing come under the focus of attention in chapter 12. These may be seen in religious practices all the way from the healing campaign to the dignified Episcopalian "laying on of hands" or the Roman Catholic pilgrimage.

11

Suggestion and Religion

A native aborigine in Australia hears that an enemy has sung over a bone and pointed it at him. Despite all of the efforts of doctors with their scientific know-how, he languishes and dies. The President's wife appears in public with a new hairdo, and in the succeeding weeks beauty salons are inundated with patrons who want their hair done "just like the First Lady's." A dignified volunteer from the audience crawls around the stage on his knees and barks like a dog, much to the delight of the onlookers and the embarrassment of his wife and family.

A rabble-rouser harangues a group and easily leads them into a most illogical course of action. The driver on the freeway notices a strange weariness creeping over him, and a moment of unconsciousness warns him of "highway hypnosis." In a religious gathering of an enthusiastic mountain group, a normally timid woman takes up a poisonous snake and handles it without the slightest vestige of fear. The psychotherapist puts his subject into a trance and revivifies a hitherto forgotten childhood incident and helps to free him from a crippling phobia.

As different and diverse as all of these activities are, a psychologist would see one common underlying similarity. They are all examples of the psychological mechanism of suggestion.

Suggestion has had a long association with religion. No only do primitive religions display bountiful evidence for a connection between the two, but even in the more sophisticated developments of religion, there is a remarkable, though unintentional and often unacknowledged, connection. However, as easy as it is for the investigator to shrug off religious phenomenon with the words, "It's only suggestion," it is a far different matter to define the nature of suggestion and its specific relationship to religion.

180

Mesmer was the pioneer in the modern era of suggestive techniques, but Bryan (27, p. 23) claims that Mesmer learned his techniques from a Roman Catholic priest, Father Gassner. Gassner enjoyed a wide reputation as a healer of the mentally ill. His technique was to enter the church clad in impressive robes and carrying a large cross. The subjects had been prepared by assistants, who built up the anticipation that the devils would be cast out as soon as the subjects were touched with Father Gassner's brass cross. Gassner had remarkable success with his technique and attracted the attention, not only of officials of the church, but also visiting medical authorities.

Among those coming to see Gassner's demonstration was Mesmer, a man with training both in theology and medicine. From his observations he at first theorized that Gassner's healing ability lay in the brass cross, but his inquiring mind led him later to postulage that healing took place through "animal magnetism." This magnetism could be conveyed by "passes" or stroking movements of the hand, or to people as they sat around tubs covered with lids and holding bars of iron through which the magnetic fluid allegedly flowed. Water was "magnetized"; people wore magnetized clothes and ate from magnetized plates.

Mesmer was investigated by a Commission of the French Academy of Medicine and the Academy of Science. Incidentally, the Commission included an American, Benjamin Franklin. Though they denounced him as a charlatan, even in their condemnation the investigators declared, "It is impossible not to admit that some great force acts upon and masters the patients and that this force appears to reside in the magnetiser" (184, p. 108).

England was the locale for the next development. James Braid, a Manchester doctor, discovered that he could induce a trance state in his patients. It was he who designated the phenomenon "hypnotism," from the Greek root *hypnos,* meaning sleep. After a wider experience, Braid tried to change the term to "monoideism," a much more accurate word. However, like an indiscretion of youth constantly resurrected to haunt the middle-aged model of respectability, Braid's original, inaccurate designation lived on. Braid was a careful investigator, and his interest meant that at last a man with a scientific turn of mind was able to debunk Mesmer's concept of animal magnetism. Thus began a new era of investigating the nature of suggestion.

In earlier books on psychology a chapter on suggestion was almost inevitable, but the discussion generally raised more questions than it answered. Modern textbooks make very little mention of the subject. Marcuse (**124**, p. 85) comments, "the omission of this topic from current texts is not a sign that the problems have been solved but that they were, and still are, embarrassing."

One of the fundamental problems is the difficulty of definition. A simple and popular viewpoint says that suggestion is "the uncritical acceptance of an idea." Weatherhead's (**184**, p. 111) more complicated definition says, "If the mind really accepts an idea as true, and if the idea is reasonable, it tends by means of unconscious processes to actualise itself or come true." English and English (**57**, p. 535) define suggestion as "the process by which one person, without argument, command, or coercion, directly induces another to act in a given way or to accept a certain belief, opinion, or plan of action." Rather unfortunately, this latter leaves no place for autosuggestion. Like a generous-hearted mother whose house is full of children, grandchildren, and their friends, suggestion is a flexible appellation which includes suggestion , heterosuggestion, autosuggestion, and all the multiple aspects of hypnosis and the depths of hypnotic trance.

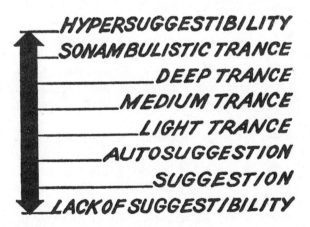

If the suggestion processes were chartered on a continuum, the levels of suggestibility could be something like the above figure. Although it is not possible to be dogmatic about the order, the processes of suggestion range all the way from simple suggestion to the hypnotic somnambulistic state. This wide variety of experiences sometimes confuses the observer's understanding of suggestion.

Tests of suggestion have been devised in an effort to measure the elusive quality, and Chevreul's pendulum illustrates the way in which these work. The subject takes a ring which hangs from a cotton thread over a piece of paper, on which two lines have been drawn and made to cross. The hand is held steadily but without resting the elbow, so that the ring is suspended above the place where the lines bisect. The subject now thinks about the way he would like the ring

THE CHEVREUL PENDULUM DEMONSTRATION

to move, either backward or forward, or from left to right along the lines. As soon as the subject gets the trick of keeping his mind on the direction he wishes the ring to go, the ring will begin to respond. It moves apart from voluntary action and from swinging backwards and forwards; the subject can cause it to go in circles. The paper may have a scale on it, and it is possible to measure the amount of the swing from the scale.

Several other tests have also been devised to measure suggestibility. In the *body sway test* the individual stands with his eyes closed. He is told that he is falling forward or backward, and his score is measured by the degree of his sway. *Press and release tests* involve the subject holding a rubber ball while suggestions are offered that he press or release, with his response measured. The *arm levitation test* is of the same order as the previous two, the response of the outstretched arm being measured after suggestions have been given. Another test is the *depth of hypnotic trance,* with a standardized scale used to measure the depth of the subject's response to hypnotic suggestions. Tests of suggestibility generally fall into two broad categories, with either an idea being translated into action without any voluntary activity by the subject, or the subject accepting a judgment with a minimum of critical mental activity.

Erickson (58, pp. 24-26) has postulated three "psychological principles of suggestion":

1. *The law of concentrated attention.*—The principle is that when mental processes are concentrated on an idea, the idea tends to actualize itself. When the idea involves the use of muscles or other motor activity, it is called *ideomotor activity.* A person sitting in the back seat of a car and feeling that it is traveling too fast discovers that his foot is moving to relax the pressure on an imaginary accelerator or apply a nonexistent brake. If the idea affects the sense organs, it is referred to as *ideosensory activity.* A heating element is applied to the subject's forehead, and he reacts as the temperature is raised. A hidden switch turns off the electricity, and the subject manipulates the control until he indicates the now nonexistent heat.

2. *The law of reversed effort.*—Coué formulated this concept many years ago when he claimed that in any conflict between the will and the imagination, the imagination always emerges victorious. Coué (39, p. 16) further asserted the formula, "In the conflict of the will and the imagination the force of the imagination is in direct ratio to the square of the will." The frequently used illustration is of a man walking along a nine-inch plank laid along the ground and experiencing no difficulty. The plank is later suspended fifty feet above the ground, and the same man cannot now walk across it because of the fear that he will fall. His imagination has suggested the possibility of falling and so defeats his intentions.

3. *The law of dominant effect.*—An emotion attached to a suggestion makes it more effective. Furthermore, a strong emotion tends to repress or eliminate a weak emotion.

As with any other mental mechanism, there are difficulties in describing the nature of suggestion. Earlier investigators assumed that there was a single unitary trait of personality called suggestion, and a suggestible person has been defined as "an individual in whom ideas, actions, beliefs, decisions, etc., could be induced by another through stimulation whether verbal or otherwise but exclusive of argument or command" (114, p. 116). As research techniques improved, the results of tests of suggestion gave evidence of the existence of several specific types of suggestion, rather than just one generalized entity. For convenience we will think of suggestion as it involves aptitude, attitude, prestige, autosuggestion, and direct and indirect aspects of the process.

Aptitude for suggestion.—Most people have the capacity to be hypnotized, with only a small percentage of the population devoid of the capacity. The general picture that the average citizen has in mind is that the hypnotizable individual is deficient in some way, either mentally or emotionally, but evidence does not confirm this evaluation. Some experimental work has indicated that people who can be hypnotized may actually have superior intelligence. Erickson (58, p. 27) states the situation:

When persons say, "I can't be hypnotized," a reasonable response to that statement is, "Well, that's very interesting, but I certainly wouldn't brag about it." Why not brag about it? Because those who make the poorest subjects, generally speaking, are children under the age of six, psychotics, morons, and others of low-grade intelligence. Why should this be? These persons have difficulty with monoideism, concentrating on one idea. The mind of the child wanders, as does the mind of the moron or the psychotic. They can't hold onto just one idea. Thus they find it difficult to cooperate. This is not to intimate that if a person is unable to go into hypnosis, there may not be another reason for the failure. Such reasons will be discussed later. Certainly, however, inability to enter hypnosis is not something in which to take particular pride.

The capacity to translate an idea into action in the muscular or sensory processes is, apparently, part of the innate ability of the particular individual. Commenting on the widespread use of hypnotism by dentists, Marcuse (124, p. 147) says, "Nowadays most dentists are beginning to be aware that in addition to looking into mouths they also have to look into personality." Obviously, some personalities are much more open to the various types of suggestion than are others.

Attitude in suggestion.—The attitude of the subject towards the "suggester" is a determinative factor in the process. Much debate has been focused on the issue of whether a person can or cannot be hypnotized against his will. The concensus of findings is that without resorting to some form of subterfuge, it is almost impossible for an individual to be involuntarily hypnotized.

In the practice of hypnotherapy different attitudes are encountered. The best subjects frequently are those who come on the recommendation of other clients. They sometimes have such a spirit of anticipation that they are easily inducted, and relax into a deep hypnotic trance with an amazing rapidity. On the other hand, one investigator has found that clients with a high score on the paranoid scale of the Minnesota Multiphasic Personality Inventory are not good subjects for hypnotherapy. Their suspicious attitude blocks the process.

The subject's attitude toward the experience generally makes him a "good" or "bad" subject for suggestion processes. The terms "good" and "bad" as used in this setting have no ethical implication but refer to hypnotizability.

Prestige in suggestion.—Possibly the most intensive single investigation carried out on suggestion was that of Hull (**89**), reported in 1933 in his book, *Hypnosis and Suggestibility*. From his investigations he concluded that there were two different types of suggestion: prestige and nonprestige. After examining the results of a variety of suggestion tests, he noted a correlation between responsiveness to the arm levitation, waking postural suggestion tests, and susceptibility to hypnosis. Hull claimed that each of these tests involved what he called "direct prestige heterosuggestion."

This phenomenon has been demonstrated in the simpler forms of suggestion. An experiment was carried out at three street crossings where pedestrians were observed. A person chosen as "stooge" played the part of both a well- and poorly-dressed individual. Before the "stooge" began to function, 99 per cent of the people conformed to the traffic lights. When the experimenter, dressed in a freshly pressed suit with white shirt and tie, stepped out and walked against the light, 14 per cent of the people followed him. After changing clothes and donning scuffed shoes, soiled, patched pants, and an unpressed blue denim shirt, the experimenter again violated the traffic signal, but only 4 per cent of the people followed his lead. The higher the apparent status of the "suggester" the more readily the group followed his suggestions (78, p. 390).

In Mesmer's celebrated work, he operated in a salon hung with mirrors, furnished with beautiful draperies, and filled with the sound of restful music. At the appropriate moment Mesmer entered, clad in a lilac robe of finest silk. Everything was done to build his prestige. Weitzenhoffer (185, p. 300) notes, "If a person has a high to very high suggestibility and feels that you are a 'powerful' hypnotist, a sudden look from you with a firm command of 'sleep' will be sufficient to bring about hypnosis." So the attitude of the subject interacts with the prestige of the operator in suggestion.

Autosuggestion.—One of the older classifications of suggestion was divided into heterosuggestion and autosuggestion. As the name implies, autosuggestion is that suggestion which a person, wittingly or unwittingly, gives himself. Most people are able to offer themselves elementary suggestion but generally need training to go into a full state of autohypnosis. Autosuggestion is seen in every area of life. Historically, it is closely associated with the work of Coué, who popularized it with his celebrated formula, "Every day in every way I am getting better and better."

A television program on Knute Rockne, the celebrated coach of Notre Dame, told the story of Rockne's ability, not only to affect his team with direct suggestion, but also to affect himself. His team was losing a ball game, and with half time in the offing he searched in his mind for some dynamic message to take to the locker room. He told a friend about the problem, and the friend suggested that it might be a good idea to tell the team that the eastern alumni were against him, and if the team lost the match today, it might mean he would lose his job. Rockne readily took up the idea, went into the locker room, exhorted his men with such fervor, and put the case so convincingly that there was a resurgence of a new spirit, and the team went out and won the game. Traveling back with his friend and discussing the game, Rockne suddenly said, "What's more, I'm going to write those eastern alumni and demand an apology from them." He had effectively convinced himself along with the team. This illustrates the power of autosuggestion.

Direct and indirect suggestion.—Investigations of the correlation of tests of suggestion have shown that *direct suggestion*, which is involved in tests like the body sway and hand levitation, has a positive correlation with the susceptibility of an individual to hypnosis. The suggestion is directly given and accepted. *Indirect suggestion* is what we normally think of as suggestion. It involves some form of deception or misleading cues. A professor may walk into a class and tell his students that he is going to show how quickly an odor can spread through a room. He uncorks a bottle of odorless water, then asks them to indicate when they can smell it. Generally hands begin to raise as an indication of the effectiveness of the teacher's suggestions. Interestingly enough, this type of suggestion apparently has no correlation with hypnosis. If an individual has previously seen an indirect suggestion experiment performed, he is unaffected by it. Whereas in hypnosis, the susceptibility is heightened by witnessing the hypnotism of another person.

This somewhat piecemeal presentation of the elements involved in suggestion may serve to highlight the complexity of the situation. Nevertheless, with these concepts in mind the way is prepared for a consideration of the ways in which suggestion can be seen in many facets of religious belief and practice.

Religious Aspects of Suggestion

The word hypnosis conjures up strange visions in many minds. It has elements of mystery and hocus-pocus, strange stage performances in which the subject eats candles or is rigidly suspended between chairs while six men sit on his body. Or worse still, it has sinister connotations of the strange control which one unscrupulous individual can have over another weaker personality, using him as a dupe and a pawn in some foul plot.

All sensible investigators are agreed that hypnosis should not be used for entertainment and that untold damage may result from the practice. In England an act of Parliament was passed in 1952 which stated, "No person shall give an exhibition, demonstrational performance of hypnotism on any living person at or in connection with any entertainment to which the public are admitted" (**44**, p. 168). The very fact of the existence of such legislation and the periodic agitation for similar law in the United States indicate something of the fears and apprehensions of competent professional people about the indiscriminate use of hypnosis.

Discussions of this order may account for the suspicion with which religious leaders look upon the consideration of suggestion and its relation to religion. There is also the false idea lurking in some minds that a suggestible person must be feeble-minded or moronic, and if religious individuals are suggestible, the implication is that they are of a lesser mold.

Most serious investigators are agreed that suggestion plays a large part in religion, but when it comes to pinpointing the specifics, there are multiple difficulties. Rabbi Glasner (27, p. 18) suggests areas of rapprochement between religion and hypnosis. (1) There is a natural connection between the two phenomena. (2) In some investigations research into the nature of religion has been facilitated by the use of hypnosis. In the pioneer work of Coe into the relationship of conversion and suggestibility, he used hypnosis as a research tool. (3) Religious healing has a lot in common with hypnotic techniques. A reading of the chapter on religious healing will reveal some of these. (4) Some clergymen utilize hypnosis in their pastoral counseling. A recently published book was called *The Pastoral Use of Hypnotic Technique* (187). However, the reception of the book was by no means warm, and many critics raised their voices in protest.

One of the pioneers in the medical use of hypnosis was James Esdaile, a surgeon who worked in India in the late nineteenth century. He performed thousands of minor operations and some three hundred major surgical procedures with the patient hypnotically anesthetized. Esdaile became an apologist for hypnosis and maintained three propositions: (1) Hypnosis was a natural God-given method of healing. (2) The power produced by the unconscious mind while an individual is in a hypnotic trance is similar to the power of the Creator. (3) All men have within them special power given by God, and the power of hypnotizability is a special gift of God. Bryan (27, p. 21) concludes that Esdaile's premise is that hypnosis is natural, powerful, and universal.

Aspects of both religion and hypnosis in which there are parallels offer a fertile field for investigation. We will examine anticipation, concentration, dependence, autonomy, prestige, confidence, repetition, imagery, group influences, autosuggestion, ability to withstand physical pain, euphoria, and delayed suggestion response. In each instance hypnotic aspects will first be examined, and then the religious parallel will be considered.

Anticipation.—Individuals who are the most responsive to suggestion generally have an optimistic attitude about the outcome. A person who is critical, skeptical, or censorious is generally a poor subject. Writing on induction techniques in hypnosis, Christenson (**114**, p. 33) says that a suitable subject must have both an interest in the process and a willingness to co-operate. If he lacks confidence in the operator, or feels antagonism toward him, a hypnotic induction will be highly improbable.

Expectation probably overshadows any other single consideration in suggestion. The widespread use of hypnosis by dentists was probably hastened by the anticipation of patients. An early dental report told of a dentist who placed an anesthetic gas mask on his patient's face. The patient relaxed and developed analgesia. Dental work was carried out without gas being used. Anticipation was the primary factor in the experience. Just as the sight of the bewildering array of the dentist's tools of trade suggests fear, so it is obviously possible to offer other types of suggestion to patients.

Without anticipation there is no religious experience. It has its genesis in faith. "He that cometh to God must believe that he is, and that he is a rewarder of them that diligently seek him" (Heb. 11:6). The story is often jokingly told of an individual in the rural area who can only "get religion" during a revival held in the summer under a brush arbor. The story often has a closer correspondence to facts than we realize. The type of religious experience, whether gradual or sudden, calm or emotional, during tender years or later in life, generally follows the pattern anticipated by the subject, and for which he is consequently prepared.

Concentration.—What takes place in the mental processes of the individual responding to suggestion? Mention was made earlier of Erickson's insistence that a suggestible person must be able to focus his attention on one thought, then continue to concentrate on it. Van Pelt (**27**, p. 8) sees the process of suggestion as set out in the figure below.

Even though Van Pelt's idea of "units of mind power" is somewhat doubtful, and the scheme does not pay enough attention to the unconscious factors, it does highlight concentration as a vital part of the process. This theory goes in the face of those who see hypnosis as a form of sleep. Braid, who coined the term "hypnosis," literally meaning sleep, later preferred the term "monoideism," emphasizing the focal point of a single idea.

As the subject goes more deeply into hypnosis, all other stimuli but

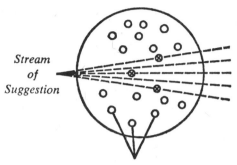

Stream of Suggestion

Ordinary State
Only a few "units" affected
by suggestion, therefore
effect is weak.

Units of Mind Power
Scattered units of mind power
untouched by suggestion.

Hypnosis
Units of mind power concentrated
and all affected by suggestion,
therefore strong effect.
No mind power left to take notice
of anything apart from the hypnotic suggestion, therefore even
pain is ignored.

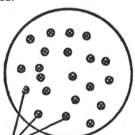

After Hypnosis
Units of mind power
scattered again but
now each carries a
dose of suggestion.

*Units of Mind Power
with a Dose of Suggestion*

THE NATURE OF HYPNOSIS

the operator's voice are gradually rejected. An individual was being
hypnotized, and from a nearby room came the clatter of a typewriter
and the sound of conversation. The subject later recounted that the
noises annoyed him and caused him to feel that it would be impossible
to enter into a hypnotic trance under these conditions, but the sounds

were gradually excluded from his consciousness. As the session progressed a carpenter began to hammer on the wall, but the subject was completely oblivious to it all. Later he revealed that he was unaware of the carpenter's noise.

Religion is, in one sense, the concentration of an individual's powers on a single object. Paul's assertion, "This one thing I do," might well be the motto of the sincerely religious person. Wittkofski (187, p. 35) maintains that Christians believe that man has been created for the eternal contemplation of deity and that "from one particular vantage point, contemplation can be defined as a form of meditation that employs a very deep degree of concentration."

The same author feels that training in hypnosis can be seen as "a splendid form of training in pursuit of man's everlasting destiny" (187, p. 35). The biblical command is, "Thou shalt love the Lord thy God with all thine heart, and with all thy soul" (Deut. 6:5). Jeremiah expressed a similar idea, "Ye shall seek me, and find me, when ye shall search for me with all your heart" (29:13). The psalmist's response to God is, "Bless the Lord, O my soul: and all that is within me, bless his holy name" (Psalm 103:1).

The Jewish term "Kavanah," meaning "concentration," as used in the Talmud had a peculiar significance for the act of prayer. Bowers and Glasner (25, p. 4) comment, "Bachya denied all value to the outward acts of religion if devoid of Kavanah. And Maimonides declared that a prayer without Kavanah is no prayer at all." In the practice of Kavanah there were two main objectives: (1) bringing about a state of religious ecstasy and (2) inducing a greater awareness of God. To bring to pass these states, the worshiper focused all his attention on combinations of Hebrew letters, developed techniques of breathing, and utilized bodily postures and movements. Bowers and Glasner believe that this helped to bring about a state akin to autohypnosis, leading to the objective of Kavanah, or "concentration."

Early investigators into religious experience spoke about the person before conversion as having a divided self. Conversion brought about the unification of personality's powers by focusing on one object. Failure at this point has constantly tormented believers. Christopher Robin's problem in saying his prayers while reminiscing over the day's adventures is paralleled in later life by Studdert-Kennedy's soldier, whose fantasy life is so rich that he cannot concentrate his thoughts and pray to God because of "the color of her hair."

Dependence.—The person offering suggestion becomes an authority figure in the mind of the subject, who often seems to regress to a dependency relationship. The types of relationships between operator and subject in hypnosis have been put into two categories: the "mother type" and the "father type." The "father type" is the more authoritative relationship in which the suggester orders his subject to follow his suggestions. Stage hypnotists are frequently of this type.

A "mother type" relationship in hypnosis is on the more permissive order and characteristic of the clinical use of hypnosis. In hypnotherapy more emphasis is laid on the co-operation of the subject. Erickson's hand levitation induction technique is developed on the basic idea that the subject is able to determine the speed of induction, timing its progress or halting it if need be. However, in either case there is a certain element of dependency. With the "father type" this is particularly so.

An early writer declared that no one could have God for his father who did not have the church for his mother. Without going as far as this declaration, the believer is still conscious of the dependency on the deity whom he worships. The convert after an experience of grace often relates the story of his former days of self-sufficiency, which ended when he came to himself and threw himself upon the grace of God. The evangelical crisis demands that an individual acknowledge that he is a sinner and find himself utterly dependent upon the merits of God's son on the cross. Devotional literature emphasizes the dependency of the believer, as do many of the best-loved hymns.

Autonomy.—To overstress the dependency aspect of suggestion is to overlook the apparently contradictory aspect of the individual's autonomy. Even in a hypnotic trance, a person will generally not transgress his normally accepted moral standards. Stage hypnotists have made this discovery, and Polgar (**147**, pp. 145-46) tells of his experience:

When I demonstrated at Columbia University, I hypnotized a group of about fifteen persons. "I have some champagne here," I announced, as I poured water from a pitcher into cups. Under the hypnotic spell the group became quite hilarious as they imbibed the plain water.

But when I tried the same experiment with the deeply religious Mennonites in Freeman, South Dakota, I failed utterly. Even under the deep trance of hypnosis, the members of this religious group refused to accept what was offered them under the guise of liquor. Nor would they smoke when I commanded them to do so, thus proving again that even under hypnosis, no one will do anything which he believes is immoral, dishonest or contrary to his innermost convictions. The Mennonites were highly pleased with the moral strength of their group. This was no surprise to me. But to complete my experiment I asked another person—not a Mennonite—to come on the stage. He was young and a very good hypnotic subject. I gave him a glass of wine and told him it was water. He believed me and drank it, saying, "We have good water here in South Dakota." You can mislead your subjects easily if you are an unscrupulous hypnotist.

Three of the Mennonites were so shocked by my order to drink non-existing liquor that they revolted and woke up, and I could not put them to sleep again. The faith-prestige relation between hypnotist and medium was gone. Nothing could touch their religious faith—it was stronger than my suggestion.

I could tell hundreds of similar examples. For instance no Orthodox Jew under hypnosis will eat ham. But any unethical hypnotist could delude him as I could have duped the Mennonites of South Dakota.

Polgar's mentioning the necessity of employing subterfuge highlights the autonomy of the subject in suggestion, particularly with reference to his moral standards.

Prestige.—Stage hypnotists are aware of the place of prestige in suggestion. A good hypnotist must have unbounded confidence in his ability. So Polgar (**147**, p. 160) says:

Most important at the beginning of any hypnotic experiment is the outward appearance of absolute confidence and authority on the part of the hypnotist. It is the previously mentioned faith-prestige relation. Any indication of weakness or uncertainty, timidity, or shyness on my part will destroy this faith-prestige relation and will result in resistance against hypnosis and myself.

Gassner's robes and brass cross, Mesmer's lilac robe, the doctor's white gown, and the carefully planted press publicity of the stage hypnotist all aim at something of the same prestige factor.

The Orson Welles broadcast, *War of the Worlds,* was responsible for one of America's worst panics. Looking back on the event, investigators noted the prestige element. Although they were fictitious, titles such as Professor Farrell of the Mount Jennings Observatory, Chicago, apparently affected people's perception of the situation. One person said, "I believed the broadcast as soon as I heard the professor from Princeton and the officials from Washington."

In religious circles prestige plays an elemental role. Time magazine recently reported that ministers were the only professional group who used honorary degrees as titles. A preacher who has never been to college but has a degree conferred by a college which does not have a doctoral program will proudly display the degree, letting it be known that he expects from henceforth to be addressed as "Doctor." Preachers wear robes and distinctive clothing. Ecclesiastical pomp and ceremony utilizes the prestige element in impressing its followers and building their suggestibility.

Confidence.—Any lack of confidence in the operator rapidly reveals itself in suggestion experiments and hypnotic procedures. Uncertainty is conveyed to the subject without a word being spoken, and the negative nonverbal communication is enough to hinder the process. Erickson (**58**, p. 53) illustrates:

Recently a doctor was asked to hypnotize a subject. Everything went well until the operator asked the subject to review a book on chemistry. The operator did not believe that it would be possible for the subject, who was in a very deep trance, to review a book on chemistry. The operator manifested the lack of confidence immediately and the subject awakened from the deep trance, asked, "What's wrong with you?"

The religious leader intuitively knows that he must declare, "Thus saith the Lord." Paul says, "If the trumpet give an uncertain sound, who shall prepare himself to the battle?" (1 Cor. 14:8). Banks's (**15**, pp. 32-34) advice to preachers follows the same line:

Revival preaching to be effective must be positive. The doubter never has revivals. . . . A revival is a revolution in many important respects, and revolutions are never brought about by timid, fearful or deprecatory addresses. They are awakened by men who are cocksure of their ground, and who speak with authority. . . . Revival preaching must be directed toward the heart and not the head. . . . Get hold of the heart and the head yields easily.

The thought is not new or novel, for it was said of Jesus that he spoke with authority (Matt 7:29).

Repetition.—Ericson (**58**, p. 20) sees repetition as being a fundamental consideration in hypnosis and says, "If asked for a capsule definition of hypnosis, one might say: suggestion and repetition." Suggestion more specifically refers to the nature of the subject, and repetition to the technique utilized, thus implying that in suggestion repetition is the first and foremost technique.

One authority gives a sample of the language used in an induction procedure in hypnosis. An examination of it reveals that in the space of one page the word "relax" or a synonym for it is used 101 times. It has long been acknowledged that "repetition breeds retention," but it is often maintained that monotony causes a loss of attention. However, it is now realized that the constant repeating of an idea, even to the point of monotony, helps the suggestion process.

Le Bon's (113, p. 121) celebrated work on crowds reveals his familiarity with a similar factor operative in groups.

It was Napoleon, I believe, who said that there is only one figure in rhetoric of serious importance, namely repetition. The thing affirmed comes by repetition to fix itself in the mind in such a way that it is accepted in the end as a demonstrated truth.

Hypnotists have noted the same repetitive element in religious processes.

Much that is conducive to self-hypnosis in religious practice will similarly pass unnoticed. Consider the darkened interior of the church, the hush, the brightly illuminated altar as point of fixation, the nature of the music —these and the ofttimes monotonous chant of the priest or minister, together with other factors, furnish ideal conditions for the trance. It may even be revelant to recall the tendency of many to "sleep" during religious observances! (114, p. 5).

Spurgeon's sermon to street preachers offers an example of the use of repetition in religious oratory.

Go on with your preaching. Cobbler, stick to your last; preacher, stick to your preaching. In the great day when the muster roll shall be read, of all those who are converted through fine music, and church decoration, and religious exhibitions and entertainments, they will amount to the tenth part of nothing; but it will always please God by the foolishness of preaching to save them that believe. Keep to your preaching; and if you do anything beside, do not let it throw your preaching into the background. In the first place preach and in the second place preach and in the third place preach.

Believe in preaching the love of Christ, believe in preaching the atoning sacrifice, believe in preaching the new birth, believe in preaching the whole counsel of God. The old hammer of the Gospel will still break the rock in pieces; the ancient fire of Pentecost will still burn among the multitude. Try nothing new, but go on with the preaching, and if we all preach with the Holy Ghost sent down from heaven, the results of preaching will astound us. Why, there is no end, after all to the power of the tongue! Look at the power of a bad tongue, what great mischief it can do; and shall not God put more power into a good tongue, if we will but use it aright? Look at the power of fire, a single spark might give a city to the flames, even so, the Spirit of God being with us, we need not calculate how much, or what we can do; there is no calculating the potentialities of a flame and there is no end to the possibilities of divine truth spoken with the enthusiasm which is born of the Spirit of God. . . . Go on! Go on! Go on! In God's name, go on! For if the preaching of the gospel does not save men, nothing will. (**176a**, p. 150).

Either directly or by some allusion, the same suggestion has been repeated thirty-one times in the course of thirteen sentences. Spurgeon is seeking for a response, and he uses repetition. The adage that "repetition breeds retention" may have to be extended to say that it also paves the way for action.

Imagery.—The primitive unconscious is adept at functioning at a symbolic level, and its processes are apparently amenable to imagery. Most suggestion procedures make frequent use of imagery. Sometimes such suggestion procedures employ quite a bewildering array of figures of speech.

Although hypnosis is not really sleep, a subject is frequently told that he is going into a deep, deep sleep. He may be asked to imagine himself stretched out beneath a pine tree on a beautiful summer day. The blue sky above is flecked with fluffy white clouds, the lazy drone of the bees comes to his ears, and a feeling of peace is stealing over his body as he gradually sinks into restful sleep.

Or he may be told that he is drifting down a stream in a canoe, hearing the sound of the lapping water, conscious of the slow, even movement of the craft with the warm sun making him feel pleasantly tired. The induction "patter" generally majors on the restful and relaxing, as the subject is projected into a symbolic situation.

Stressing the values of similes or illustrations, Ericson (**58**, p. 369) says:

Phrases vivid with simple imagery such as, "your arm as straight and still as an iron bar," "your arm is floating through the air like a feather on a breeze," "limp as a wet dishcloth," "limp as a piece of tired lettuce," are of great value in trance introduction.

Descent into the trance is encouraged by the use of responses which involve asking the subject to feel as if balloons are lifting his arm, or weights holding it down. He may be told that a vice is clamping his hands together so that they cannot be released. One operator found the test unsuccessful, but later inquiry revealed that the subject did not know what a vice was and was consequently unable to visualize as requested. As the state is deepened, the subject visualizes a bucket of boiling water into which he plunges his hand and makes it sensitive, or creates a mental image that the doctor has injected a hypodermic needle into his wrist and caused his hand to become numb. He may be asked to see his body shrink or his surroundings become those of another day, as he is regressed to an earlier age level.

A skilful operator uses imagery familiar to the subject. If the client has told of his interest in farming, farming metaphors dominate the suggestions offered. This is a *feedback* procedure, utilizing familiar associations in the word picture painted by the operator. Some operators spend time with the subject, not only building rapport, but also finding the subject's interests and ideas so that the feedback is more effective.

Shakespeare's Mark Anthony demonstrates an orator's intuitive awareness of the value of imagery.

> If you have tears, prepare to shed them now.
> You all do know this mantle: I remember
> The first time ever Caesar put it on;
> 'Twas on a summer's evening, in his tent
> That day he overcame the Nervii:
> Look, in this place ran Cassius' dagger through:
> See what a rent the envious Casca made:

Anthony's reference to tears, the summer evening, the tent, Caesar's mantle, and the dagger slash, all build the suggestive impact.

In a more modern setting Governor Orval Faubus, during the Little Rock integration crisis, demonstrated the use of imagery:

Today we find the members of the famed division, which I helped rescue, in Little Rock, Arkansas, bludgeoning innocent bystanders, with bayonets in the backs of schoolgirls, and the warm, red blood of patriotic American citizens staining the cold, naked, unsheathed knives. In the name of God, whom we all revere, in the name of liberty we hold so dear, which we all cherish, what is happening in America?

With a fine turn of phrase Clement of Tennessee revealed his apprehension: "Is the bayonet going to become the bookmark of southern education?"

Symbolism permeates religious forms and practices. The apocalyptic literature of the Bible is a wide screen for an infinite variety of pictorial projections. Prophetic preaching is a panorama of the vivid color and strange images of an Ezekiel, or of Jonathan Edwards' puny mortal dangled like a spider over the molten pit, or the more homely metaphors of the frontier preacher.

The more sophisticated religious leader is repelled by the primitive imagery used by his uneducated fellow religionists, and pleads for dignity and decorum. However, it is highly probable that he conducts his own worship service in a building in which every knob, arch, and corner has some symbolic meaning. His

> Storied windows richly dight
> Casting in their dim religious light,

are probably ornamented with a large number of mystic shapes, as incomprehensible to the simple worshiper as the hieroglyphics of a Pharaoh's tomb. Periodically changing his vestments to spread their nonverbal message, he listens reverently to the choir's anthem, shot through and through with simile and metaphor.

All religious forms and practices utilize imagery and symbolism. If these are going to have an effective influence, feedback procedures must be borne in mind. Symbols will be most effective, however, when they strike a familiar note in the individual imaging process of the subject.

Emotion.—The unconscious does not function at the rational intellectual level but responds more readily to an emotional approach. Subjects who have been hitherto unable to express their feelings will frequently be able to abreact and pour out their pent up emotions while in a hypnotic trance. The emotion repressed into the unconscious was provided with a way of escape; similarly, emotion may provide access to the unconscious.

Ericson's *law of dominant effect* is a statement of the way in which emotion strengthens suggestion. The use of emotion as a suggestive power in a social issue is seen in Governor Handley's prohibition speech in 1916:

I bear no malice toward those engaged in the liquor business but I hate the traffic.

I hate its every phase.

I hate it for its intolerance.

I hate it for its arrogance.

I hate it for its hypocrisy, for its cant, and graft and false pretense.

I hate it for its commercialism: for its greed and avarice; for its sordid love of gain at any price.

I hate it for its domination of politics; for its corrupting influence in civic affairs; for its incessant effort to debauch the suffrage of the country, for the cowards it makes of public men.

I hate it for its utter disregard of the law, for its ruthless trampling of the solemn compacts of state constitutions.

I hate it for the load it straps to labor's back; for the palsied hands it gives to toil; for its wounds to genius; for the tragedies of its might-have-beens.

I hate it for the human wrecks it has caused.

I hate it for the almshouses it peoples; for the prisons it fills; for the insanity it begets; for its countless graves in potter's fields; I hate it for the mental ruin it imposes on its victims; for its spiritual blight; for its moral degradation.

I hate it for the crimes it commits; for the homes it destroys; for the hearts it breaks.

I hate it for the malice it plants in the hearts of men; for its poison; for its bitterness: for the dead sea fruit with which it starves their souls.

I hate it for the grief it causes womanhood—the scalding tears, the hopes deferred, the strangled aspirations, its burden of want and care.

I hate it for its heartless cruelty to the aged, the infirm, the helpless; for the shadow it throws upon the lives of children; for its monstrous injustice to blameless little ones (179a, p. 280).

It will be noted that the speaker uses imagery and repetition. The vital aspect is the emotional overtone, guaranteed to strike a response in the listeners.

The influence of the group.—Suggestion most typically involves the influence of at least one person over another, with the operator offering suggestion and the subject responding. Hypnotic processes are sometimes aided by having the subject see another person put into a trance. One investigator tells of a depressed trainee nurse who badly needed hypnoanalytic treatment but refused to even meet the physician. Her help was enlisted on the pretext that her friend needed someone with her while undergoing therapy. Watching her friend being inducted, she herself went into a trance and proceeded with therapy.

Religion is essentially a group phenomenon, and the influence of one person on his fellows is a factor in religious gatherings. The more ecstatic groups highlight the worshipers' responses which inspire the preacher, who in turn excites the worshipers and furthers the circular stimulation. I was introduced in a Negro church where the elderly minister noted complaints about not enough fire in the pulpit and speculated that the main trouble was not enough kindling in the pews. He then exhorted the congregation, "Give him some kindling, brethren." In the midst of the congregation's enthusiastic responses the preacher would have a heart of stone if he were not moved to a more fervent presentation.

One revivalist preacher has a technique of planting "decoys" in his congregation. When he gives the invitation for seekers to come to the front of the meeting, the "decoys" move forward to give the impression that people are responding. Even before a single individual has come he will announce, "Here they come, they are coming now." People are encouraged to "jump on the band wagon."

Responses by the group are also utilized in the more dignified and liturgical church groups. "Acts of faith" involving bodily movements, responses to the minister or priest joined in by the congregation, the singing of the group, the congregational movements of standing, sitting, and kneeling in unison all play a part in raising suggestibility.

Autosuggestion.—Despite the influence of others on the individual, suggestibility in the final analysis is an internal quality of the individual's personality make-up. Autosuggestion was discussed earlier in the chapter, where it was seen that an individual can offer his own unconscious a potent idea which may be a powerful influence on his attitudes or behavior. In many ways the simplest form of suggestion, it is most effective when prepared for with training and posthypnotic suggestion. When this condition has been attained, it is usual to refer to it as autohypnosis.

Indian holy men use autohypnosis in their religious practices. In Van Pelt's investigation of the control of the heart beat by hypnosis, he refers to the holy men who by autohypnosis slow down their circulation and appear to be dead. While in this state they may be buried and then later have a complete recovery (**114**, p. 268).

Karl Menninger has suggested possible scientific aspects of prayer, saying, "The effect of prayer upon God is scarcely subject to investigation, but the effect of prayer upon those who offer it could well be made a matter of scientific research" (**25**, p. 3). In any such research, prayer and worship activities will probably provide the best examples of autosuggestion in religion. Bryan notices that prayer generally involves some preparation in which the individual takes a special pose of kneeling, sitting, or lying, generally with the head bowed. The palms of the hands may be placed together, at the side, or on the ground. Bryan further notes that no religious group prays with fists clenched. The typical posture is a relaxed position with all conscious tension at least temporarily abandoned, and most religious persons close their eyes in prayer and so exclude all other stimuli while focusing their thoughts on God.

Most inquirers have seen suggestion as operative in the healing miracles of the New Testament. Bryan also notices autosuggestion and refers to the woman healed of the issue of blood. Although faith was a vital part of the process, Bryan calls attention to the phrase, "She said within herself." He concludes that autosuggestion had at least a preparatory role in the healing.

Acts of faith, such as kneeling, crossing oneself, taking up different positions, repeating prayers, creeds, or statements of faith, have autosuggestive powers. Coué's techniques of autosuggestion involved having his patients count off knots on a piece of string. He had apparently noted the efficacy of counting the rosary beads as a means of autosuggestion.

The constantly recurring "power of positive thinking" cult in Protestantism seems to be a thinly disguised reaffirmation of the power of autosuggestion.

Euphoria.—For most people clinical hypnosis is a relaxing experience. Hadfield (**77**, p. 75) quotes one of his subjects as reporting after hypnosis,

When I came, I thought I was going to be doped; that you were going to put something in me, perhaps something I did not like. Now I know that I have lived for years in a cellar; you have lifted me out and liberated what was in me.

A large proportion of subjects, upon coming out of a trance, will remark, "I never felt so relaxed in all my life," or something of this order. A feeling of well-being is a typical reaction.

It has also been noted that people in a hypnotic trance may be characterized by heightened sensory activity, improved memory, or increased muscular strength. Early investigators sometimes concluded too readily that hitherto unpossessed powers could be made available in hypnosis. But even though Marcuse (**24**, pp. 96-100) seriously challenges many of these conclusions, nevertheless, he acknowledges that emotional inhibitions may be removed, allowing the individual to utilize powers and strengths he already had but could not normally mobilize.

Vital religious experience most typically has an associated euphoria. Reporting their conversions, the most frequently used description of postconversion reaction was "a feeling of release and happiness." The "peace of mind cult" has the euphoric emphasis. Rather unfortunately, in hypnosis as in religion, euphoria has a tendency to wear off, and wise ministers warn against the "letdown" which may later come. Religious experience must involve more than the emotional returns.

Ability to withstand physical pain.—Modern doctors and dentists have been able to utilize the anesthetic aspects of hypnosis in their procedures. Esdaile called attention to this use of hypnosis way back in the nineteenth century in India, and some authorities believe that his techniques would have had a much wider use if it had not been for the introduction of modern chemicals and anesthesias. By a strange turn of the wheel, doctors and dentists are going back to this earlier technique. Induction of anesthesia is a relatively simple procedure in a good subject. The glove anesthesia, in which the whole hand becomes numb and loses its feeling, is often used as a test in the depth of hypnotic trance which is induced. It may be that there is some relationship between the anesthesia produced by suggestion and the capacity of religious martyrs to suffer.

The practice of Thai Pusam, carried on among devotees in Malaya, is built on Hindu mythology. The worshipers push daggers through their arms, pierce their cheeks with metal rods, hang fishhooks on their bodies, walk through burning coals, pull carriages by hooks on their backs, or carry "kavidas." A pamphlet issued by a temple in Malaya describes the event:

The devotees, to prove their sincerity and to make some sacrifice for the sake of God, carry "kavida" (a semi-circular thing with bars attached in the bottom to support on the shoulders, and the same is decorated with flowers and feathers of peacock, the vehicle of Lord Subramania). Some devotees walk on sandals embedded with iron nails and poke silver pins through their cheeks, tongues and over the body. During the process of poking silver pins the devotees do *not feel any pain or hardship as their minds are concentrated and exalted on the thought of God. God alone and nothing else occupies their minds.*

A similar phenomenon has been noticed among the medieval Jews as they prepared for martyrdom. Bowers and Glasner (**25**, p. 19) quote Scholem:

In a powerful speech of the great mystic Abraham ben Eliezer Halevi of Jerusalem (died about 1530) we find a recommendation to those who face martyrdom. He advises them to concentrate, in the hour of their last ordeal, on the Great Name of God; to imagine its radiant letters between their eyes and to fix all their attention on it. Whoever will do that, will not feel the burning flames or the tortures to which he will be subjected. "And although this may seem improbable to human reason, it has been experienced and transmitted by the holy martyrs."

Many similar instances could be found in the Christian tradition. The unhealthy seeking for martyrdom, which has periodically appeared in Christian history, has been looked upon with suspicion by scholars who have pondered whether it really represented the suffering and sacrifice as was alleged, or brought some sort of ecstatic joy to the "sufferer."

Delayed suggestion response.—Posthypnotic suggestion is one of the most dramatic aspects of hypnosis. A suggestion is given to a person that after he comes out of the trance he will perform an act, such as taking off his shoes or opening an umbrella when the operator taps on the desk. After the trance, the subject hears the operator tap on the desk and feels an irresistible urge to take off his shoes or open an umbrella, although he has no conscious recollection of ever having been told to perform the act. Sometimes there is a time lapse, as in the situation when the subject is given the suggestion that ten days later he will carry out an act. If he is a good subject, there is an excellent chance that he will follow through on the designated day. One record shows that a man followed a suggestion in exactly the manner stated and at the designated time, a year after it was given.

In religious circles there is a concern about the lack of relationship between theology and ethics, and that Christian living is not of the quality which might be expected. Religious educators have long puzzled over the low quality of Christian living and have sought the reason. One of the ready answers has been that religious teaching is too "material-centered", and there has been a call for more "activity" in church teaching programs.

Planners of religious activity programs have had their heyday, and the children have certainly enjoyed religious education more, but has there been a better development of character? Until some more reliable techniques of measurement have been developed, it is difficult to make an evaluation, but it would be a brave man who would say that the character of the products our religious education processes is much higher than it used to be.

If suggestion has something to teach us, we may have to reconsider jettisoning our "material-centered" concept in education. The process of communication may become our focal point as we endeavor to discover where it can be improved. One outstanding American clergyman has a powerful sermon on the subject, "Ideas That Use Us." Suggestion teaches us the potency of an idea planted in the individual's thought processes.

Attention may have to be paid to the teacher as communicator and the student as responder. The communicator must be aware of the value of prestige and confidence in the responder, and the use of imagery, repetition, and emotion in the communication techniques. This does not mean elimination of activity but, rather, making it purposeful and the vehicle for passing on an idea that will become dynamic in the student's life.

Jesus frequently alluded to that part of man which he called the heart. For example: "Thou shalt love the Lord thy God with all thy heart" (Matt. 22:37). "Out of the heart [of man] proceed evil thoughts, murders, adulteries, fornications" (Matt. 15:19). If, as some writers maintain, Jesus used the word "heart" in much the same way as we refer to unconscious aspects of personality, suggestion techniques which give us the most ready access to the unconscious may have to be used more frequently than they have been heretofore.

Rather unfortunately, to use the broad term "suggestion" or, worse still, the narrower word "hypnosis" is to jar the composure of religious leaders. The concern is understandable, with the waters muddied by stage hypnotists and other unscrupulous people who will use the individual's innate capacities to "make a fast buck."

If the words have sinister associations, the situation may call for new terminology to describe the old phenomenon. For, whether we like it or not, we are continually using suggestion techniques in our work. In the wide range of religious activities, from the simple bed-side prayer to the evangelistic invitation in which the congregation monotonously sings, "Have Thine Own Way, Lord," for twenty-five minutes, church activities utilize suggestion.

Wittkofski (**187**, p. 17) comments on one strange aspect of the opposition to hypnotism:

> The clerical use of hypnotic techniques can hardly escape the vociferous opposition to hypnotism that some fringe religious groups proclaim. Actually, many of these variant religions denounce hypnotism because they do not wish to have their own techniques copied or to have their particular feats duplicated. The Christian Science reader widely employs a splendid technique for the induction of the hypnoidal and often the hypnotic stage. The sick person is told to deny the illness, believe that he is totally well, and then the reader begins to read with a monotonous voice from the rather dull writings of Mary Baker Eddy. Among the practitioners, those who can most easily read in a monotonous manner are the better readers. The easy "Christian Science technique" can be employed almost anywhere by the orthodox minister. The clergyman who enters a hospital with obvious hypnotic paraphernalia may find himself in very serious difficulty, but no one will dare to interfere with the sympathetic cleric who strives to console the sick and takes the time to read to such a one from a "holy book." But such a book should never be too interesting!

It might be relevant to recall that Mrs. Eddy learned her techniques from Quimby, who was well known as a hypnotist.

Suggestion is as much a normal mechanism of personality as is sublimation. It can be used by the advertiser to sell his goods. Gill and Brenman (**74**, pp. 281-93), in a thought-provoking analysis of brainwashing, show the remarkable parallels between brainwashing and hypnosis. The interference with the avenues of intake, inhibiting of the processes of output, absorption of attention, automatization, and the capitalizing transference potentials are all elements found in both brainwashing and hypnosis.

Does not religion, with its respect for the individual and its motivating forces, have a sense of responsibility to understand suggestion more clearly and use it for the blessing of man and the glory of God? If all the time spent studying educational and organizational principles is justified on the ground of greater efficiency in propagating the gospel, no greater motivation is needed for a study of suggestibility, for this concept underlies all the techniques of our work.

12

Religious Healing

For many years chaplains in the Australian Army wore a Maltese cross as the insignia on their uniform. The insignia dated back to the day of the Crusades, when the Knights Templars established hospitals on the island of Malta to minister to the pilgrims falling ill or wounded while making their way to Palestine. The religious convictions of these soldier monks manifested themselves in their care of the sick. Religion has always had a close association with the sick, as is seen in the establishment of hospitals by the church, a practice which continues to this day.

It is impossible to read the Bible without becoming aware of the healing processes associated with the teaching of religion. Healing was practiced in a restricted way in the Old Testament. However, some of the most dramatic healing miracles are to be found within its pages. With the dawn of New Testament times and the ministry of Jesus there came a blaze of healing activity.

Psychosomatic is a word of fairly recent origin. Literally, it means "soul and body," referring to the close relationship of body and spirit. The soul affects the body, and the health of the soul may be an indication of the health of the body. Way back in Bible times John wished for his friend Gauis, "above all things . . . thou mayest prosper and be in health, even as thy soul prospereth" (3 John 2). This was an anticipation of the emphasis of psychosomatic medicine. Man is a unity; body and soul cannot be separated. Religion and health are inextricably intertwined.

It is also possible to see psychological laws in the healing activity of Jesus. Weatherhead has classified the miracles of Jesus into the following categories: (1) those miracles in which suggestion seems to be the main mechanism concerned; (2) the miracles in which Christ used a more complicated technique; (3) healings in which the mental attitude of friends or bystanders produced a psychic atmosphere in which Christ could more powerfully work. Weatherhead does not claim to explain the healing miracles of Christ but only shows that they may be seen as illustrations of psychological laws. The very existence of such a listing and its wide acceptance is an indication of the rapprochement of psychology and religion on such a sensitive matter.

Suggestion

Faced with the claims of faith healers reporting miraculous cures, the American Medical Association suggests that they may be due to suggestion, spontaneous remission, or improper diagnosis. Although the term suggestion is frequently used in the discussion of all areas of religious experience, it is nowhere more relevant than in religious healing. Sometimes suggestion is classified into (1) heterosuggestion, suggestion given by another, (2) contrasuggestion, a response opposite to that suggested, and (3) autosuggestion. Autosuggestion is frequently associated with healing processes.

Autosuggestion has been defined as "suggestion arising from oneself." Coué (1857-1926) was the outstanding exponent of autosuggestion. He gave his subjects the instruction, "Say every morning and evening, 'Every day, in every way I am getting better and better,' " adding with unconscious humor, "Don't think of what you are saying. Say it as you would say the litany at church." The phrase could be modified to suit individuals, but there were some stipulations. There must be no negatives; the disease must not be mentioned, for the unconscious would snatch at the name; no future tenses were to be used as it was to happen immediately. The will was not to be called into action. After twenty years of work, Coué (**39**, p. 16) made a summary of four laws:

1. When the will and the imagination are antagonistic, it is always the imagination which wins, *without exception*.
2. In the conflict between the will and the imagination, the force of the imagination is in *direct ratio to the square of the will*.
3. When the will and the imagination are in agreement, one does not add to the other, but one is multiplied by the other.
4. The imagination can be directed.

Coué (**39**, p. 22-23) gives further instruction:

Before sending away your patient, you must tell him that he carries within him the instrument by which he can cure himself, and that you are, as it were, only a professor teaching him to use this instrument, and that he must help you in your task. Thus every morning before rising, and every night on getting into bed, he must shut his eyes and in thought transport himself into your presence, and then repeat twenty times consecutively in a monotonous voice, counting by means of a string with twenty knots in it, this little phrase: *"Every day, in every respect, I am getting better and better."* In his mind he should emphasize the words, *"in every respect,"* which apply to every need, mental or physical.

An onlooker describes Coué (**39**, p. 31) at work in his clinic:

The whilom blacksmith with the disabled arm, when told to think "I should like to open my hands but I cannot," proceeded without difficulty to open them.

"You see," said Coué, with a smile, "it depends not on what I say but on what you think. What were you thinking then?"

He hesitated. "I thought perhaps I could open them after all."

"Exactly. And therefore you could. Now clasp your hands again. Press them together."

When the right degree of pressure had been reached, Coué told him to repeat the word, "I cannot, I cannot . . ."

As he repeated this phrase the contracture increased and all his efforts failed to release his grip.

"Voila," said Coué, "Now listen. For ten years you have been thinking you could not lift your arm above your shoulder, consequently you have not been able to do so, for whatever we think becomes true for us. Now think 'I can lift it.' "

The patient looked at him doubtfully.

"Quick!" Coué said in a tone of authority. "Think 'I can, I can!' "

"I can," said the man. He made a half-hearted attempt and complained of a pain in his shoulder.

"Bon," said Coué. "Don't lower your arm. Close your eyes and repeat with me as fast as you can, 'Ca passe, ca passe.' "

For half a minute they repeated this phrase together, speaking so fast as to produce a sound like the whirr of a rapidly revolving machine. Meanwhile Coué quickly stroked the man's shoulder. At the end of that time the patient admitted that his pain had left him.

"Now think well that you can lift your arm," Coué said.

The departure of the pain had given the patient faith. His face, which before had been perplexed and incredulous, brightened as the thought of power took possession of him. "I can," he said in a tone of finality, and without effort he calmly lifted his arm to its full height above his head. He held it there triumphantly for a moment while the whole company applauded and encouraged him.

Coué reached for his hand and shook it.

"My friend, you are cured."

"C'est merveilleux," the man answered. "I believe I am."

"Prove it," said Coué. "Hit me on the shoulder." The patient laughed, and dealt him a gentle rap.

"Harder," Coué encouraged him. "Hit me harder—as hard as you can." His arm began to rise and fall in regular blows, increasing in force until Coué was compelled to call on him to stop.

"Voila, mon ami, you can go back to your anvil."

The man resumed his seat, still hardly able to comprehend what had occurred. Now and then he lifted his arm as if to reassure himself, whispering to himself in an awed voice, "I can, I can."

There were no conscious attempts to use religion, but the twenty knots in the string that had to be counted obviously had some religious connotations. Coué's disciple, Brooks, discusses the variations of Coué's formula. Apparently a literal translation of the formula reads, "Every day in every respect I am getting better and better." Brooks said that Coué considered the best English translation to be, "Day by day, in every way, I am getting better and better." Brooks went on to add an adaptation for those subjects with religious convictions and suggested, "Day by day, in every way, by the help of God, I'm getting better and better." He says, "It is possible that the attention of the unconscious will thus be turned to moral and spiritual improvements to a greater extent than by the ordinary formula" (39, pp. 90-91).

We note in Couéism several factors. (1) The recognition, in fact almost the deification, of the unconscious. (2) The emphasis on the "power of positive thinking" which has periodically reappeared in both psychological and religious circles. (3) The close association with hypnotic procedures. In the process of teaching his patients autosuggestion, Coué used exactly the same series of tests as a hypnotist does. (4) The whole process could be readily adapted to a religious emphasis. (5) The remarkable similarity between Coué's methods and those used in the modern healing mission.

In its modern therapeutic applications the use of suggestion is called hypnotherapy. It may be utilized to deal with conflicts underlying symptoms, to explore the unconscious by such methods as automatic writing, to regress the subject to earlier stages of development, and to allow the expression of emotion. Some therapists have combined the technique with the insights of psychoanalysis and by hypnoanalytic procedures shortened the treatment process.

Rather unfortunately, suggestion has often been used to deal with symptoms which can be dramatically removed without doing anything about the underlying cause. Wolberg (**188**, II, 19-20) describes a case in which his subject could not face the fundamental emotional difficulty, and so he obliged him by moving the symptom to another part of his body.

A thirty year old man who had developed a spastic paralysis of his left leg with a peculiar gait that interfered with ambulation. Function was restored in one session. The patient had no desire to inquire more deeply into his problems, and was satisfied with mere symptom removal. It was impossible, in the one session, to gain understanding of the dynamic significance of his symptom. In this case I was able to demonstrate to the patient quite conclusively that his paralysis could be shifted from his leg into his arm. He was then able to walk, but his arm was paralyzed. Then the arm paralysis was shifted to his shoulder.

Later, the paralysis was moved to one of the man's toes, but he still had a paralysis, because the fundamental cause was untouched.

Some personalities are more suggestible than others. A doctor once said, "It is sometimes more important to know what kind of a fellow has the germ, than what kind of germ has the fellow." Children are more suggestible than adults, and Lederer's (**115**, pp. 41-49) formulations about personality changes in illness become relevant. In chapter 8 it was noted that all of life was a maturing or growing process and that fixation and regression were constantly encountered roadblocks in the growth process.

A life experience may be diagrammed as in the figure below dealing with the effect of illness on developmental processes. The maturing person continues to grow, but the crises of illness may cause the individual to regress and function at an infantile level. A number of factors help to create the situation. The sick person loses his independence. He is not expected to have opinions of his own about treatment and medicine but to obey the commands of the surrounding medical "experts." All of his attention is focused on his body, and the constant concern with pulse, temperature, bowel movements, and so on, helps to return him to his earliest and most infantile stage of development. Separated at least temporarily from his employment, he may be cut off from his income and lose his sense of status as the breadwinner of the family. An experience of pain, pure and simple,

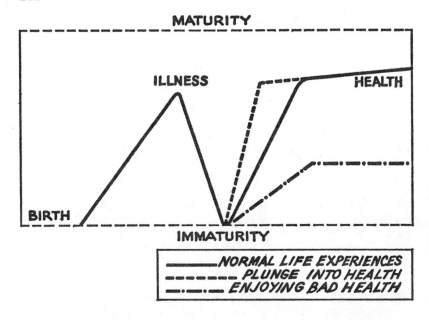

can easily bring a break with the world and cause a withdrawal from its stark reality. Regression offers the most obvious way out of it all.

The situation is further complicated in the process of recovery, generally called convalescence. If it is accepted that illness frequently results in regression to an infantile outlook, the process of convalescence may be conceived of as a "growing up" process. Convalescence has been likened to adolescence, and in an abbreviated form all of the difficulties faced by the adolescent may be encountered by the convalescent. Like the adolescent, the convalescent may try to recover too quickly and in his "plunge into health" damage himself.

On the other hand, the convalescent, as indicated in the figure above, may "enjoy bad health" and have some good reasons, even though unconscious, for not recovering. William P. Williamson, (186, pp. 13-21) professor of surgery at the University of Kansas School of Medicine, says that the average rate of recovery from surgery on ruptured discs across the country is about 85 per cent. However, in compensation cases where the patient is eligible for payment for medical care, time off from work, and medical disability, the same neurosurgeons using the same technique only have a 35 per cent recovery rate. As a neuro-surgeon, Williamson also treats patients' "whiplash," injuries caused when a cat is hit from behind and the individual's head snaps back resulting in muscle spasm, pain in the neck, and headache. Williamson says that he has yet to see a patient with a "whiplash" injury who did not have a lawyer behind him, and was suing the man who ran into his car.

Studies on placeboes have shown how medicine's effectiveness may be altered by the patient's faith in the doctor or the medicine. Dr. Beecher, (186, pp. 13-21) in his carefully controlled studies, showed that of one hundred average type people suffering pain after surgery, thirty-five of them will get prompt relief from an injection of plain saline. With neurotic individuals the effectiveness rises to 60 per cent of those injected. Making the opposite approach, it was noted that if an injection were given with the inference that it would not do much good, 25 per cent of the patients got no help from morphine.

Suggestion is obviously an important factor in any type of healing and frequently overshadows medical aspects. It is only logical to expect that an examination of religion and healing will have to be carried on with an open mind and a willingness to see the part played by suggestion in the process.

Methods of Religious Healing

The minister of a church is on the horns of a dilemma. Jesus Christ carried on a ministry of healing, as also did the Christians of the early church. Many times over, Christ exhorted his followers to "heal the sick." The problem comes in trying to decide just how the healing processes should be carried out.

The National Council of Churches has had a Commission on Religion and Health since 1938. Serving on it are representatives of the healing professions, who join with religious leaders in considering the interrelationship of health and spiritual resources. In 1948 a Committee on Spiritual Healing was established. It, in turn, commissioned Charles S. Braden (26, pp. 9-15) of Northwestern University to investigate the healing practices of pastors in Protestant churches. Of the 460 replies received in answer to the question, "Have you ever as a minister attempted to perform a spiritual healing?" 160, or 34.5 per cent, indicated that they had had such an experience at least once. If the qualified "no's" were taken into consideration, some 206, or about 45 per cent, of the pastors reported some use of spiritual healing in one way or another.

Of the 123 pastors who reported both healings and denominational affiliations, there were 46 Methodists, 19 Episcopalians, 18 Presbyterians, 14 Lutherans, 7 Baptists, 5 Disciples, 3 United Brethren, 2 Congregationalists, 2 Evangelical Reformed, and 2 Nazarenes. Five other denominations reported one each. Percentagewise, the Episcopalians rated highest in the number of healings in proportion to the number reporting, with 65 per cent of them engaging in healing by spiritual means. Significantly enough, Braden's study shows that none of the churches reporting fell into the upper-class group.

An examination of this listing shows that they were all Protestants, with no Roman Catholics reporting. Two groups which come at either end of the class structure, and both of whom major on healing, are noticeably absent. In the upper-class grouping are the Christian Scientists, and in the lower-class are the Pentecostal sects which major on healing. One of the most significant findings might well be that amongst the lower-middle group, there are so many churches whose pastors have a belief in religious healing.

The methods of healing reported by Protestant ministers in twenty-five cities (160 cases) and used in Braden's study are set out below (**100**, p. 240). Settling on the methods to use constitutes the heart of the problem.

	Total Organic Illness	Per Cent Using Each	Total Mental Illness	Per Cent Using Each	Total Cases
Prayer	98	70	19	95	117
Forgiveness	44	31.4	13	65	57
Affirmation	35	25	14	70	49
Laying on hands	33	23.6	4	20	37
Anointing	24	17.1	2	10	26
Rituals	14	10	4	20	18
Others	18	12.8	6	31.6	24

Most Christians believe in healing through faith, but trying to decide what techniques are scriptural, decorous, and psychologically helpful confuses the believer. Moreover, the various techniques used by different groups show fascinating psychological aspects of the healing process. An examination of the strengths and weaknesses of the various approaches should lead to some insight.

Healing Objects

A story is told about an early experience in the use of the clinical thermometer with a patient who had never previously seen such a "gadget." The doctor sat the patient down and placed the thermometer in his mouth. When he later returned to remove the instrument, the patient told the doctor how much the new treatment had helped him and how that he could already feel an improvement in his condition.

A modern display at a medical convention of the strange objects sold by "quacks," for use by their patients, is only the extension of an age-old practice of having faith in the therapeutic powers of articles, as widely removed from each other as red flannel and electric machines. Modern day veterinarians tell of the widespread belief in the healing virtue of Chihuahua dogs. The commonly accepted version is that if a Chihuahua is given to a child suffering with asthma, the asthma will be transferred to the dog and the child will be cured, with the unfortunate dog left to suffer his asthmatic miseries. It is small wonder that religion became involved with objects along the way.

The Roman Catholic Church has placed its blessing upon many healing shrines in various parts of the world. Probably the most distinguished and widely known is Lourdes in France. It was founded when a French girl, Bernadette Soubirous, at the age of fourteen, claimed in 1858 to have seen the virgin Mary on eighteen different occasions. She was told by the heavenly visitor to tell the priests to build a chapel and arrange processions of people to drink and bathe in the stream which came from Bernadette, making a hole in the ground. Lourdes has become known throughout Christendom, and millions of people have made the journey there to pray, bathe, and drink the waters. Great care is taken in recognizing "cures," and exhaustive inquiries are made before a "cure" is announced. A total of fifty-four miracles have been claimed as divine healings at Lourdes and accepted by the Medical Commission.

Nevertheless, after a very careful sympathetic examination of Lourdes and participation in a pilgrimage, Leslie D. Weatherhead (184, p. 153) finally concludes:

There is probably no stream in Britain which could not boast as high a proportion of cures as the stream at Lourdes if patients came in the same numbers and in the same psychological state of expectant excitement.

Other types of shrines and relics have been frequently used by the Roman Catholic Church. Relics include "toes of St. Peter, finger nails and toe nails were common, hair, nails of the cross, pieces of wood supposedly from the cross, blood, tears, milk from the virgin Mary." Located at Palermo are the bones of St. Ralia, "credited with effecting cures and warding off epidemics for many years," and even "when an eminent osteologist, Professor Buckland, revealed the fact that they were the bones of a goat it apparently had little effect on their healing power (108, p. 158).

The healing objects used by "healers" among the holiness groups fall into the same category. One well-known healer holds up his hand before the television screen and calls upon his viewers to place their hands on the TV set and "make contact" with the healing power. When on radio he asks those who would be healed to touch the radio set. Apparently, both radio and TV sets have power as healing objects. Quite a few radio preachers ask their listeners to send in a request for a "healing cloth," plus a small donation of course. They claim that the cloth will bring healing to the listener.

It should be noted that the intrinsic value of the object in which the individual has faith is not nearly as important as the attitude of the seeker of healing. The intensity of his expectancy is often the determinative factor in the experience.

Laying on of Hands

The laying on of hands is one of the oldest methods of healing. Used by Christ in his ministry, the practice has become a part of the various ceremonies of the Christian church. Roman Catholics and Episcopalians see in it the symbol of apostolic succession. Some non-liturgical churches use the laying on of hands in ordaining ministers and deacons.

Belief in the healing power of the touch goes back to the dawn of history. An ancient Egyptian papyrus earlier than 1500 B.C tells of healing ceremonies which involved the laying on of hands. In England it was touching by the king, a practice which started with Edward the Confessor. The sick kneeled before the king, who touched them while his chaplain intoned, "He put his hands on them and healed them." The custom was passed on by the royal line. King Charles II is said to have touched nearly a hundred thousand people. Queen Anne was the last of the British rulers to practice the "king's touch." One of the celebrated people she touched was the infant Samuel Johnson in 1712. Boswell tells us that Johnson's mother took him to be "touched" on the advice of the family physician, but it was all to no avail as he was not healed.

The custom spread to the continent and was practiced by many of the French kings. Not all rulers were convinced, however, and it is recorded that William of Orange considered the practice a mere superstition, and he only touched one person. During the process he muttered, "May God give you better health and more sense."

Of more recent days, the laying on of hands generally takes place in a liturgical setting, and a number of Episcopalian groups have used this method. A national magazine gives a description of this type of service.

"Those who would desire the ancient and Biblical sacramental rite of the laying on of hands will please now come reverently to the Lord's altar rail."

Slowly about 20 people moved into the aisle and started toward the altar. Some shuffled feebly. One moved on crutches.

The minister dipped his thumb in a thimble of olive oil. He passed in front of the kneeling men and women. He made the sign of the cross in oil on each forehead and said, "In the name of Jesus Christ I beseech that all pain be put to flight and the blessings of health restored to thee."

This was not a primitive wooden church on a rural back road or a gospel shouter's tent or a storefront temple. It was the chapel of the Episcopal Church of the Heavenly Rest in New York's exclusive Upper East Side. And the man who conducted the healing service was a highly respected, conservative clergyman, Dr. John Ellis Large.

Among the sufferers he has anointed are a well-known Hollywood actor, a steel executive, the wife of a Wall Street financier, the president of a charitable organization, a much-photographed debutante. These people did not come out of curiosity. They were sick and wanted to be healed (155, pp. 38-39).

And this is by no means an isolated example. Similar services have sprung up in many parts of the country. A flourishing organization among the more liturgical types of Protestant churches is the predominantly Episcopalian Order of St. Luke the Physician, which has a magazine called *Sharing*. By recent report the number of churches involved in the order and conducting special healing services has grown steadily from 14 in 1947 to 460, with about 95 per cent of them Episcopalian. The order claims to have 4,200 members in 85 countries. In comparing their techniques with those of other practitioners in the religious field, *Time* magazine calls them the "quiet healers." (**150**, p. 53).

The laying on of hands is also used in nonreligious settings. A layman, Ambrose Worrall, an aircraft engineer, has attracted attention by his work, for which he charges no fees. He lays hands on people and says, describing his experience, "But from then on, whenever I felt this strange weight in my arms I found I could heal people, or at least help them to feel a lot better" (**155**, p. 82).

Faith healers who specialize in the healing campaigns generally lay hands on their subjects. They frequently boast about their "healing right arm" and the feeling, like an electric shock, which comes from it.

I once served as the chaplain of a large army hospital where we had a fine dermatologist of Polish origin and training. While on rounds with him one day we stopped before a bad case of dermatitis. The nurse removed the dressings to show the badly infected skin. Without a moment's hesitation the dedicated doctor leaned over and began to rub his fingers over the infected spots. The onlookers were amazed, as was the patient. Smiling into the patient's face, the dermatologist assured him that everything was going to be all right. Back in his office later, I asked the doctor if it was his usual practice to touch the infected spots. He replied that in his medical training he had been taught never to show fear in the presence of infection. It was claimed that a confident attitude helped to quell the apprehensions of the patient. It could be that the contact of laying on hands has a value of breaking down the isolation which sickness sometimes brings.

Weatherhead (**184**, pp. 134-35) gives a limited endorsement to the practice of laying on of hands but suggests precautions which should be observed. (1) The laying on of hands should take place in private. (2) It should not be indicated that this can replace adequate medical diagnosis and treatment. (3) The minister should be a dedicated person who sees himself as representing the whole church in his action.

The Healing Campaign

A large hall is packed with people, and the song leader directs in the swinging, stirring songs, now and then referring to Brother Jones who will later bring the message of the evening. At a climactic moment, Brother Jones appears on the platform. In appearance more like a wrestler than a preacher, he is snappily dressed and begins to preach in a rapid-fire manner. He tells how an angel appeared to him in a dream with the news that he was to receive the gift of healing, and from that moment on God had performed miraculous healings through him. He explains what happens within him. A feeling comes in the pit of his stomach, then rises through his body and into his arms. It is happening now. It is just like electricity tingling in his right arm. When you come forward and he lays hands on you, you will feel the tingling sensation. Of course, you may not feel it, but it will happen just the same.

The speaker takes some time to carefully explain there are two things that can happen. It will be either a healing or a miracle. If it is a miracle it will take place immediately, but if it is a healing it may take longer, as a slow, gradual process. He is also careful to point out that it is faith that does it. Only a lack of faith will prevent a healing.

A healing line is formed. Only those who have been previously interviewed and given cards are allowed to queue up. Critics say that it is a screening process to make sure that only those with functional illnesses come. A man leads the line across the platform. Brother Jones asks if he believes Jesus can heal him, and when he responds in the affirmative, the preacher smears some oil on his forehead, presses his hands down on his head, and prays in a loud voice, "Lord, remove this demon from this man, heal, heal, in the name of Jesus of Nazareth, come out of him thou deaf demon, come out of him!" Jones makes a strange hissing noise, "Sh . . . . . sh," and exclaims, "There it goes, it has gone." Turning to the bewildered subject, he says, "You are healed now, aren't you?" The man nods.

"Say 'thank you, Jesus.' "

The subject stutters, "Thank you, Jesus."

The healer turns to the crowd and says, "Give Jesus a big hand," and the audience joins in the applause.

After a few dramatic healings, the healer begins to tire. He announces that he is feeling in his body all the ailments of those who come to him, and it will not be possible for him to continue any longer. A murmur of disappointment goes down the healing line as Brother Jones disappears from the platform and is spirited away so that no one can talk with him.

We have been eyewitnesses to a meeting in connection with a healing campaign which is a common occurrence across the nation. Often with enormous tents and a strange assortment of electronic gear, the healers move in on a town and become the spotlight of attention. Claims go to ridiculous extremes. One pamphlet distributed by a healer shows a boy with a plastic eye in his hand. The boy had lost his eye and now wore an artificial one. After attending a healing service, he was able to see through the plastic eye. Such claims attract a large following, and one healer is reported to have programs on 233 radio and 95 television stations.

Healers claim to be fulfilling the command of Jesus to heal, and many people give testimony to the veracity of their assertions. Can it be that this is the authentic healing activity of which the New Testament speaks? An examination of the situation leads the impartial observer to reject the claims for a number of reasons (20, pp. 20-35).

Although testimonies to healing are often heard, there is very little evidence produced to verify the fact. Cases reported are not accompanied by case histories which a medical examiner would require. The Roman Catholic shrine at Lourdes requires a medical examination before the sick person visits the shrine, another after the healing is claimed, a further medical report from the home doctor twelve months later, and then on returning to the shrine, a re-examination by three doctors. Even with all this care, there have been some fraudulent claims. Most leaders of healing campaigns are not willing to have their cases investigated and will frequently become very hostile if an investigation is attempted. Consequently, the possibility of deception is great.

Suggestion can produce dramatic results, particularly when the subject is put into a hypnotic trance, but it generally deals only with symptoms, apart from the root of the trouble. Symptom removal is relatively easy with suggestion. The humorous story is told of the doctor whose patient had the delusion that he was a dog. The medico used suggestion and cured the patient of his difficulty but significantly added, "Rather unfortunately, he now believes he is a water rat." The symptom may be removed, while the real illness remains untouched.

Everything in the healing campaign is geared to raise suggestibility. The careful build-up of the reputation of the healer, the highly emotionalized responses of the crowds, the emphasis on the subject having faith, the apparent "miracles" taking place, all create the climate of anticipation. One psychiatrist noted the glassy eyes of the subjects and saw evidence of a hypnotic trance. In the suggestible atmosphere the symptom is removed, and the crowd is informed that the subject is healed. One can well imagine the awful disappointment when later the symptom reappears or is replaced by another. One observer noted the number of "repeaters" who were to be found in the healing line. Apparently addicted to it, they had to come periodically to have their symptoms removed.

There is religious as well as psychological confusion in the healing campaign. The healers claim that they are carrying on the healing activity of Jesus, but there is no biblical sanction for the healing campaign in which everything is done with an eye to publicity. One healer stated, "There is no such thing as bad publicity; even when it is bad, it is good." Contrast this with Jesus who urged those who were healed to "tell no man."

The nature of faith is misrepresented. It is claimed that if the subject has faith he will be healed and that if he is not healed it will be because of lack of faith. Very often stable, well-balanced people are not healed, while neurotic, shallow individuals with a very immature faith have miraculous experiences. Possibly the worse aspect of it is the impression that God is a means to man's end. Bosworth says, "Our faith makes God act." This statement shows his belief in magic rather than a mature faith. No well-informed Christian would dare to make God a means to man's end. Man must always be a means to God's end.

Pastoral Counseling

Its ministry to the sick has not been forgotten by the church. Hospitals were originally almost exclusively operated by churches. Wherever Christian missionaries have gone, they have taken a ministry of healing. From the place where the church persecuted scientists, it has moved to the view that God has led scientists into discoveries about the nature of the human body and disease. Improvement in health has come from scientific discoveries.

However, Christian ministries to the sick have become more significant of recent days. In church life ministries are carried on and prayer is offered for the sick. But unfortunately, the perfunctory manner in which intercession is engaged in gives little evidence of a vital belief in the efficacy for healing.

In some churches special emphasis is quietly given to healing. A church member with a tumor diagnosed as malignant went to see her pastor. Together they agreed that she should get the best surgeon available and arranged to have the recommended surgery. A group of Christians from the church gathered at her home and prayed earnestly that healing might come to their fellow church member's body, but always it was with the proviso, "If it be thy will." Surgery was successful, and the woman is still hale and hearty. Surgery? Prayer? Or both? No one will ever know because of the impossibility of the separation of the psyche and the soma.

The new pastoral counseling movement is emphasizing the uniting of psychological and religious insights. This puts a pastor into a clinical setting where he learns to work with a team of doctors, nurses, social workers, dietitians and others. He learns to respect their work and has an opportunity to demonstrate his own.

The training in clinical pastoral education takes consideration of a number of factors: (1) The work of the medical profession is recognized and respected while an effort is made to interpret religion to these people. (2) The value of person-to-person relationships is emphasized as the minister learns to relate to people in his crisis ministry. (3) Special religious contributions are made in the form of the minister's role, prayer, and the Bible, which are all brought to bear on the individual.

The church is responsible for a ministry to the whole man and cannot ignore the frailties of the individual's body. Christians must discover ways to bring their unique religious resources to bear on the situation while co-operating with the healing profession. The situation is portrayed in the imaginary conversation of the minister with the doctor as depicted by Kelley Barnett:

Across the patient's bed we face each other; you in your white coat, a stethoscope in your hand; I in my black coat with a prayerbook in my hand. At the beginning we were one, since the beginning we have always been together, unavoidably related, and when you are true to the oath of medicine and I true to the ordination vows, the center of interest has been, is and must always be in the man on the bed, your patient, my parishioner, God's creation. And if we work in unity together, the patient will come to see, to know, to love the Father God who through us, in us, by us, and in *spite* of us, remains, the Ultimate One Who ". . . healeth all our diseases and forgiveth all our iniquities" (**189**, p. 163).

PART FOUR

The Individual Discovering
His Own Soul

Modern Man in Search of a Soul is the provocative title of Carl Jung's well-known book. Every man makes a pilgrimage in life, searching for the meaning of his existence and struggling to understand one's relationships to his fellowman and his God. But above all man seeks to discover himself. The place of suggestion in religious experience and faith healing was noted in Part Three. Now we turn to observe man in his quest to discover himself.

Three stages will be discussed. The search for faith takes the pilgrim along a highway beset with doubts. The intellectual capacities of man are sometimes challenged before he can come to a quest of faith, but it may not be as much an intellectual process as we so often feel. Instead of a struggle and wrestle with reasoning processes, it may represent an easy surrender to the automatic reactions of an attitude or mental set. Alternatively, doubt may be the emotionalized product of a life experience which is the very antithesis of intellectual processes.

A man's commitment to God is at the heart of his quest for his own soul. Conversion is possibly the oldest of all the areas of study in psychology of religion. Psychology finds it a fruitful field. In a remarkable way, even physiology enters the drama as Sargant's devastating attack is launched on conversion.

Vocation follows as a natural result of soul discovery. The investigator passes through deep waters in trying to distinguish the complexities of a call and the individual's response. A layman's sense of calling constitutes a fertile field for discussion.

13

The Dilemma of Doubt

The process of an individual finding his soul is the quest for a faith, which gives the individual a sense of security and oneness with God. It is only natural that in the search for faith doubt, its opposite, also demands attention.

There are at least two ways of evaluating doubt. One is to condemn it and dismiss it as evil. In some instances this is true, and much of the unbelief in the world is devilish. The other approach is to see doubt as a necessary ingredient in a developing faith. The poet Tennyson puts it in this frame of reference:

> There lives more faith in honest doubt,
> believe me
> Than in half your creeds.

In another of his poems he says:

> He fought his doubts and gathered strength,
> He would not make his judgments blind;
> He faced the specters of the mind
> And laid them: thus he came at length
> To find a stronger faith his own
> And power was with him.

Most thoughtful Christians would agree that doubt has a part to play in religion. Like a ship which once sailed gracefully through the seas but now is slowed down by the barnacles and weeds growing on it, so our faith is clarified, strengthened, and cleared of some of the excrescences by the experiences of doubt. Bainton (13, p. 38) tells of Martin Luther, in his growing experience when the young monk was climbing the twenty-eight steps upon which Christ was supposed to have stood outside of Pilate's palace, repeating a paternoster for each step and then kissing the step for good measure. When at last he reached the top, Luther exclaimed, "Who knows whether it is so?" So came the clarification of the issues of the Reformation. Clark (34, p. 256) discusses a mature religion, and one of his vital criteria is, "Is it self-critical? Can the individual see weaknesses in his religious position at the same time as he remains loyal to it?" Questioning processes have a part in a developing faith.

It must again be emphasized that few of the issues of life are decided on an intellectual basis. One of the influential books of the last generation was by Henry C. Link. Link was agnostic, but after leaving college and studying psychology he finally made his move back to the church. The result was his book, *The Return to Religion*. Link (121) says that the West has deified the mind and reason as ends in themselves, but reason cannot solve the problems of birth, life, or death. His writing is a call for an awakening to what he calls "this great fallacy" by the "fools of reason." In any consideration of doubt it will be necessary to be aware of emotional as well as intellectual aspects of the experience.

Attitude Formation

From the psychological point of view, doubt may be viewed as an attitude. Bonner suggests that an attitude is a determining tendency, an anticipatory response, a postural state of readiness. English and English (57, p. 50) show that the word "attitude" came originally from "aptitude" and meant basically a posture of the body suitable for certain action. By extension it came to mean "posture of the mind." The mind is in a state of readiness for action, in a predetermined manner.

Or to change the metaphor, there is a sense in which an attitude may be thought of as a mental sausage machine. No matter what is put into the sausage machine, it all comes out sausage. All of the experiences of life pass through the mental sausage machine in the form of an individual's attitude. Allport (3, p. 810) defines an attitude by saying, "An attitude is a mental and neural state of readiness, organized through experience, exerting a directive or dynamic influence upon the individual's response to all objects and situations with which it is related."

It has been shown that there are a number of elements which go into the building up of an attitude. (1) The integration of numerous specific responses of a similar type. (2) Individuation, differentiation, and segregation—further experiences make the attitude more specific and distinguishes it from allied attitudes. (3) Trauma or a dramatic experience. A single emotional experience may give rise to an attitude even though the traumatic origins are forgotten. (4) Attitudes may be adopted ready-made by imitation of parents, teachers, and so on. (5) Another source of attitude formation would be seen by the psychoanalyst as a direct or indirect reflection of family relationships.

The whole process is complicated by the meddlesome emotions. Attitudes are often associated with emotionalized experiences, which cause them to persist long after the original causes have been forgotten or intellectually denied. This dynamic influence is often all out of proportion to the original precipitating circumstances. Passing time continues the hardening process, and the economy of time and effort brought by certain attitudes fosters fixity of reaction and rigidity of response.

If religious doubt is viewed as an attitude, it complicates rather than simplifies an understanding of the experience. Trying to plumb the depths of doubt, we will make an arbitrary but not necessarily logically consistent division of the areas of thought. We will consider the physiological, sociological, psychological, and pseudo-religious aspects of doubt.

Physiological Aspects of Doubt

Age and doubt.—As the individual grows, development brings changes in one's attitude towards religion. In early childhood religion is uncritical. The child accepts the literal facts of religion and absorbs the ideas presented to him by authority figures. Much of the child's curiosity is concerned with the mysteries of life concerning birth, death, and growth. Explanations by adults are generally made in religious terms. The simple interpretations give him a frame of reference for his developing world view.

Later childhood brings a turn in the religious perspective. Relationships are often fostered in a religious setting where the growing child meets with his friends. He may have an interest in Sunday school lessons, but the organizational framework of the school provides friendships which are more important. Hurlock maintains that skepticism first raises its head at this stage of development. The child is often proud of his capacity to ask his parents and Sunday school teachers embarrassing questions about religion. The little boy who had moved to the South was much concerned about the race question. After being assured by his father that God had made people both white and colored, he proudly asserted that he felt God had made a big mistake by creating some people white and some colored. At this stage the child does not hesitate to argue some of his more obvious points and show that the generally accepted religious ideas are wrong.

Adolescence is the period of religious awakening, and the individual passes through a process of religious revision and evaluation. At about the thirteenth year he begins subjecting his beliefs to a process of systematic criticism. Hurlock (92, p. 305) claims that "the more dogmatically religion was taught to them when they were children, the more skeptical they are likely to be when they are adolescent." Religious doubt seems to follow a predictable pattern in adolescence. Religious forms and duties are the first objects of criticism. Later, the critical spirit shifts towards the facts of religion. The nature of God and man, belief, sin, and the problem of life beyond the grave become the focal point for the doubting process.

In later adolescence doubt is not so intense as it was in the younger days. At college, or away from home with a widened circle of acquaintances, beliefs become more steady, although there will be periodic onslaughts on the citadel of faith. Contact with new and unusual ideas in college is frequently an unsettling experience. Hurlock asserts that an absence of doubt in adolescence is either a sign of a low intellectual level or of a logic-type mind which refuses to reconsider long accepted ideas. Starbuck's (168, p. 232) conclusion was, "Doubt seems to belong to youth as its natural heritage." He concluded that almost all doubts begin between the age of eleven and twenty, with a few scattered through the twenties, and almost none after the thirties.

Allport (5, p. 37) considers the early and middle twenties to be the least religious periods of life. He suggests several reasons. The youth has broken from parental codes. He also feels secure in his life's ambitions, not having yet experienced the rude shocks which come with the realization that earlier goals will not be reached. In the early twenties he has not yet married a wife, who will probably be more religious than he, nor does he feel the responsibility for children and the passing on of the religious heritage. Moreover, he has not developed sufficient perspective to appreciate the sincerity and piety of his parents' attitudes and to accept them as a model. When he does marry, the advent of children and the responsibilities of parenthood may bring a revival of the religious process. However, mixed marriages probably do more to disrupt religious convictions at this stage of life than any other factor.

Attainment of adulthood brings respite from struggle, as religion is rejected or doubts are resolved and a philosophy of life formulated. A strengthening of religion frequently comes with middle age, but attendance at church and participation in its activities may drop off. Religious belief is not characterized by intellectual difficulties; middle-aged people are less dogmatic in their own religious convictions and more tolerant of other people's.

The widely accepted view is that in old age people turn to religion, but studies do not show this is so. "There is no evidence of a large scale turning to religion of people as they grow older" (92, p. 573). Patterns laid down in earlier days are carried on. While people of the lower middle class and upper lower class find social contacts probably the most significant factor in religious affiliation, religious beliefs often take on a stark reality. With the end of life close, many oldsters become very certain of their beliefs.

Doubt and age have a correlation. Paradoxically, the child commencing his religious quest has, in a sense, arrived before he starts. Primitive credulity is the characteristic of childish religion which is uncritical, accepting ready-made concepts of parents. The widening experiences of life lead to an undermining of this primitive credulity. Like the clothes which are changed in style to match one's growth, so the individual's religious concepts are challenged and revised. Doubts begin to assail in later childhood, step up their attack in adolescence, gradually recede in adulthood, and in old age leave one with something akin to, but not the same as, the calmness of faith of his early childhood religion.

Sex.—Starbuck's pioneer investigation showed that whereas 53 per cent of the women in his sample reported doubt, 79 per cent of the men expressed this feeling. Moreover, masculine and feminine doubts were of a different quality. Of the men 73 per cent reported that their doubts came through educational influences, while only 23 per cent of the women reported this factor in their doubts. Starbuck (168, p. 241) concluded that "adolescence is for women primarily a period of storm and stress, while for men it is in the highest sense a period of doubt."

Allport's findings were similar. Whereas 82 per cent of the women students reported feeling a need for religious orientation, the corresponding figure was 76 per cent among nonveteran men and 64 per cent among veterans. Allport (5, p. 37) concluded:

It is common in all studies to find women more interested in religion, however defined. They are more often the church goers, more devout in their personal lives, and more often the family mentors in the matter of religion.

Hurlock similarly reports that girls do not appear to have as much doubt in adolescence as boys, that later adolescence brings a greater falling away from religious convictions amongst boys than girls, and that in early adulthood women are more interested in religion than men.

Moberg (130, p. 396) discusses the fact that the sex ratio, which represents the number of males per hundred females, was 102.5 in 1930 and was 100.7 in 1940. However, the sex ratio of church memberships as reported in the 1936 census was 78.5. Seeking an explanation, Moberg sees a number of factors as operative. A psychological factor is that women, whose primary physiological function is childbearing, have to face more crises in life and need the support which religion can give.

A moral aspect of the question is that the biological facts of masculinity and femininity mean that in sexual experiences the female has more to lose than the male. She may be left literally, as well as metaphorically, to "carry the baby." Although women have come a long way in their struggle for status, there is still an unfortunate "double standard of morality." There is often a tacit acknowledgment that young men can "have their fling," but women must "guard their virtue." Very often, men of doubtful morals will expect high moral standards from their future wives. Many women find encouragement in their religious faith as they stay with their standards of morality. On the other hand, a young man may give loose allegiance to his religion because of the restrictions it places upon him. The whole idea is religiously and ethically wrong, but it must be considered in assessing the place of sex in doubt.

A social aspect of the question is the claim by some that the activities of church life are more appropriate for women than men. Men have more opportunities for social contacts at work, or while commuting, whereas women are more confined to the home and have few outlets for their energies. Moreover, the church has traditionally provided an outlet for the creative energies of women when other institutions were dominated by males.

As improbable as it at first seems, there is considerable evidence for physiological factors in doubt. Both age and sex have a correlation with the quality and the amount of doubt experienced by the individual.

Sociological Aspects of Doubt

It has long been acknowledged that social influences are operative in the experiences of religious conversion. Although questions have arisen, the evidence is strongly in favor of this contention. However, it is not so obvious that sociological factors are operative in doubt. Nevertheless, sociological factors are just as vital for influencing an individual to doubt as they are in guiding him to faith.

The religious tradition in which an individual is reared plays a part in the formation of his attitudes. One investigator reported that his studies of a youth group within his own denomination apparently showed that there was no appreciable evidence of religious doubts. A closer study revealed that his denomination was rigid and literalistic in its religious teachings. Belonging to such a group, the individual will either avoid doubt at any cost or divorce himself from the group. Consequently, the remaining members are free from doubt.

The incidence of doubt is higher among Protestants and Jews than among Roman Catholics. This can be accounted for in terms of the liberty of thought which is given to Protestants and Jews concerning religious beliefs. On the other hand, the Roman Catholic Church, with its highly centralized monolithic organization handing down its dogmatic point of view, limits doubt by the very nature of its institutional life. Strangely enough, the two largest Communist parties outside the Iron Curtain are to be found in Italy and France, both Roman Catholic strongholds. The argument often advanced is that these people find it easy to change from one authoritarian institution to another. Apparently, faith could be placed in a materialistic philosophy just as easily as it could be placed in a religious concept, with the type of institution obviously important in determining the type of belief.

Shortcomings of the church as an institution have given rise to religious doubts in some minds. Religion has been involved in some of the most terrible wars in history and in the upholding of privileges such as in the "divine right of kings." Proof texts from the Bible have been used to prove the inferiority of women or of people with colored skins. Medical and social progress has been blocked by religious bigotry. These past performances repel many who prefer to reject all religion along with the church's mistakes of the past.

Many feel disappointed in the failure of the church to make its influence felt in society. Douglas Hyde, telling of his experience in leaving a church and becoming a Communist, relates that his church would not allow him to paint the house or weed the garden on Sunday but showed no concern about the economic conditions of society. During the years of the great trade depression, a man held an important church position and gave unstintingly of his time and his money. He was also a member of a trade union. As he saw people losing their jobs on every hand, he conceived the idea that the church should be doing something about it. He went to see his minister, and the minister confessed that he didn't know what he could possibly do. Filled with disgust, the man left the church and declared himself an atheist. Strangely enough, in old age he confessed his disappointment with the trade union movement and spoke about missing the church and its fellowship.

For many people the failure of the church members to live by high ethical standards is a cause of doubt. Commenting on the apparent hypocrisy of churchgoers that bothers people, Canon Pastor Pyle says, "That's not surprising. It bothered Jesus, too" (**96**, p. 86).

Doubt may be a status symbol. People get attention from their fellows in devious ways—some by the automobiles they drive, the clothes they wear, the house they live in, while others gain it by parading their doubts. Some writers use the terms "neurotic doubt," "psychological doubt," or "pathological doubt" to describe the attitude. Dr. Frederic F. Flach says this type of doubt can be distinguished from intellectual doubt by its symptoms. It is usually destructive, hostile, and charged with an "I bet you can't prove it" attitude. He concludes that this type of doubt really has little or nothing to do with religion.

Status symbol doubt is seen on college campuses where there are certain students who derive great satisfaction from "shocking" people.

There is often the implication in much of the talk heard on the college campuses that people who do not believe in God are the real intellectuals, whereas those who have a religious faith are of a lesser mold. The ego satisfactions these individuals gain is an indication of the value of doubt as a status symbol.

In Eaton's book, *Freedom of Thought in the Old South*, he tells of the wave of skepticism which spread across the southern colonies, largely as a result of the distribution of Tom Paine's *Age of Reason* and the writings of the French Revolution. A blacksmith with a skeptical turn of mind made an intensive study of Paine's work and other atheistic writings. As the backwoodsmen came into his shop, he expounded his atheistic beliefs and joyfully watched the look of horror spread over the faces of his simple customers.

Word of his atheism spread, and a number of Methodist ministers preached against him. The result was that whenever a Methodist minister came by the blacksmith's shop, the blacksmith would pull him from his horse and proceed to pummel him with his hamlike fists.

On one occasion a very muscular minister came along, responded to the challenge with great gusto, and in the words of Eaton, "beat hell out of him." The result of the encounter was that the blacksmith was converted and became a fervent Christian. The role that this man's self-esteem played in his transformation from belief to skepticism and back to belief again is very obvious.

Akin to the status symbol type of doubting, but separate from it, is scientific doubting. Doubt is a tool of science. If scientists had been prepared to take over generally accepted concepts, few of the great scientific discoveries would have been made. The Danish physicist, Niels Bohr, used to tell his students, "Every sentence I utter must be understood not as an affirmation but as a question." He once defined truth as "something that we can attempt to doubt, and then perhaps, after much exertion, discover that part of the doubt is unjustified" (123, p. 56). Doubt has a large part to play in scientific discovery.

Because of his attitude towards facts, the scientist is often likely to be an agnostic as far as religion is concerned. Consequently, this may lead people to point out that a certain great scientist does not believe in God. One is an intellectual, therefore, if others think he will not believe in God. Prestige is the determinative factor. One writer claims that the word "prestige" comes from a Latin word which means "sleight of hand." Thus, prestige may be "illegitimate."

An expert in science has no more right to speak in an authoritarian way about religion than an expert in religion has the right to dispute the claims of the scientist in his field. As well informed as the scientist may be in his own field, he must have better grounds before he can be an expert in religion and be capable of speaking with such an authoritarian attitude that people will feel compelled to abandon their faith at his behest.

Psychological Factors in Doubt

Traumatic experiences may play a large part in the development of doubt. Psychotherapy has long struggled with the problem of a single traumatic episode which continues to color the total life experience. It is difficult enough when a painful experience is recallable. A woman was an enthusiastic church member, attending all of the services of her church. When she missed church for several weeks in succession, the pastor called on her, and she declared that she was through with religion and would never attend church again. The conversation revealed that the husband of her deceased daughter had decided to remarry and take his small son to live with him. The child had lived with his grandmother, and she could not bear to give him up. Her son-in-law was a deacon in the church. Injured emotionally by the deacon's behavior, she wanted no part in any religious concepts or organizations.

Adjustment is further complicated when an incident is repressed and the traumatic experience is unwittingly relegated to the unconscious and forgotten. The subject is worried by doubt and is maladjusted emotionally, with no possibility of comprehending the cause of his difficulty.

Allport's description of the processes of attitude formation included the accretion of numerous experiences. Freud's name frequently recurs in psychological circles. Many people accept the major tenets of Freud's psychological theory; yet they are overwhelmed by his skepticism. However, an examination of Freud's life helps to show some of the reasons why he may have developed this attitude towards religion. Thorpe (**175**, pp. 513-14) states the case:

Reared in a culture which was rejecting of Jews and which already was building up to the final outbreak of horror which occurred during the Nazi regime, Freud suffered the consequences of being a member of this minority group. His father became a "free thinker" and, it is believed, to a considerable extent dominated his son's life. Much of Freud's early life also was marked by poverty and anxiety. As some of his critics see it, in his struggle to free himself from the grip of such a situation, Freud as far as possible abandoned traditional modes of thought, making psychiatry and science his twin gods. Just as he accused the religionist of engaging in "wishfulfillments," he also presumably was involved in the same mechanism, one which he rationalized with great vigor.

Once again, the process is altogether unconscious. This makes the position of Freud all the more ironical and gives evidence of his fond assertion of the impelling force of man's unconscious motivations.

Doubt may be a manifestation of a revolt against authority. Psychoanalysis emphasizes the experiences of the family setting in determining attitudes. A new possibility of evaluating the Freudian attitude towards religion is opened up. Bishop Pike said:

Twenty years ago, people influenced by Freud ,thought that religion could be explained as a projection of the father image. Today it begins to look more and more as if we can now explain a great deal of disbelief in these very terms. A vast amount of religious rebellion can be traced to a harsh, domineering father. Psychologists are now pretty well convinced that a child's image of God is fashioned by his image of his own father. If this is a negative image, his religious attitude is bound to be negative also (96, p. 89).

The son in revolt against his father may at the same time tend to revolt against his father's God.

It has often been noted that an individual's attitude towards authority has some relationship to his attitude towards God. One writer quoted a revolt in which the revolutionaries cried out, "Down with God!" God apparently represented authority. This is probably the case more frequently in countries with state religions, a particular religion being seen as closely associated with the tyranny of the rulers. During the French Revolution the revolutionaries, not only overthrew their decadent government, but also rejected the closely associated religion. Rationalism became the order of the day. In rejecting authority, God is also rejected.

Rationalization is the strange capacity of the human mind which has been called the "counterfeit of reason." In mental illness a paranoid person can be very intelligent and make excellent use of his reason in all of life except the one isolated area where his paranoid system is involved. The rationalizing person does exactly the same thing and offers a perfectly logical explanation for his conclusions, while overlooking the real reason. Bernard Hart presents an illustrative case:

> One of my patients, a former Sunday School teacher, had become a convinced atheist. He insisted that he had reached this standpoint after a long and careful study of the literature on the subject, and, as a matter of fact, he really had acquired a remarkably wide knowledge of religious apologetics. He discoursed at length upon the evidence of Genesis, marshalling his arguments with considerable skill, and producing a coherent and well-reasoned case. Subsequent psychological analysis, however, revealed the real complex responsible for his atheism; the girl to whom he had been engaged had eloped with the most enthusiastic of his fellow Sunday School teachers. . . . Resentment against his successful rival had expressed itself by a repudiation of the beliefs which had formerly constituted the principal bond between them. The arguments, the study and the quotations were merely an elaborate rationalization (**176**, p. 82).

"The victory of desire over reason" is one definition of rationalization. When an individual finds religion blocking his desire, an easy way out is to question the validity of his religion. An evangelist counseled with a man about becoming a Christian. The inquirer told the preacher that he could not become a Christian because of his inability to understand where Cain got his wife. The preacher sat down and tried to give him a good rational reason for the conservative position with regard to the incident of Cain's wife. Later, the preacher said that as he continued with the discussion, he discovered that it was not Cain's wife that was worrying the man; it was somebody else's wife. At least some doubt has a moral root, and the verbalization of the doubt is but a rationalizing process.

Reaction formation is a defense mechanism of the ego. It may be defined as, "Establishment of a trait or a regular pattern of behavior that is directly opposed to an unconscious trend." The individual acts out at a conscious level the very opposite to the desires which may haunt him. Writers of psychology textbooks sometimes delight in pointing out that religious people offer examples of the mechanism. The person who crusades against loose morals, or the evils of alcohol, is probably trying to cover up his own desire in these areas by taking a position of opposition to them. Allport suggests the application of the principle to those opposed to religion, and it can be seen as an indication of a genuine interest in religion, covered up by an aggressive opposition to it.

One study has revealed that emotion plays a large part in an experience of doubt and that the intellectual aspects of it are often overrated (50). In an examination of the place of intelligence in an experience of religious awakening, a comparison was made of two groups of students. The "high" group had IQs of 125-139, and the "low" group had a range of 83-96. The mean IQ for the "high" group was 129.3, and the mean IQ for the "low" group was 91.6. In answering a series of questions there was a difference of response significant at the one per cent level of confidence. It showed that the "low" group had doubts about the inspiration of the Bible, the divinity of Christ, the existence of God, and the lives of professing Christians. The "high" intelligence group was not significantly concerned about these matters. The same study also showed that the students with low IQs had a more emotionalized experience of religious awakening. The logical conclusion would be that the more emotionalized attitude was the cause of the doubts. In this particular study there was no relationship between intelligence and doubt.

The Pseudo Religion

Gordon Allport refers to a zealous apostle of free thought, of whom it was said that he believed in "No-God" and worshiped him, and of another, that he would believe anything as long as it was not in the Bible. Robert Ingersoll, the atheist, wrote:

I belong to the Great Church which holds the world within its starlit aisles: that claims the great and good of every race and clime; that finds with joy the grain of gold in every creed, and floods with light and love the germs of good in every soul.

Tom Paine rejected the biblical concept of religion; yet he went on to avow his faith in his own peculiar atheistic religion. Aldridge (2, p. 299) states:

Although most people view *The Age of Reason* as a formal attack on religion, Paine maintained that he wrote it specifically to keep the French people from "running headlong into atheism." In a famous letter to Samuel Adams, 1 January 1803, Paine affirmed: "I had the work translated and published in their own language to stop them in that career, and fix them to the first article (as I have before said) of every man's creed who has any creed at all, *I believe in God.*"

Although militantly atheistic in its rejection of all concepts of religion, Marxism has facets which are essentially religious in nature. Douglas Hyde, (**93**, p. 1,326), for many years a Communist himself, comments:

For the Communist, his Communism is a substitute religion. He will hotly deny this, because he is opposed to all religion. Yet, you could only explain the degree of devotion which he gives to his evil cause, his sacrifice, and his total dedication in terms of religion.

Hewlett Johnson, dean of Canterbury, who has done much to help the Communist cause throughout the world, claims that atheistic Communists are religious. He says, "A passionate assertion of atheism no more means that a man is fundamentally irreligious from a Christian point of view" (**98**, p. 314). It may be that Johnson was unconsciously telling us something about the true nature of communism.

Stalin's famous speech at the death of Lenin exemplifies the atheistic religion.

Comrades, we Communists are people of a special cut. We have been cut out of peculiar stuff. . . . There is no loftier title than that of a member of the party, of which Comrade Lenin has been founder and leader. It is not given to everyone to be a member of such a party. It is not given to everyone to endure the hardships and storms that go with the membership of such a party. Sons of the working class, sons of misery and struggle, sons of incredible privation and heroic endeavour, these, above all, ought to be the members of such a party. . . .

In leaving us, Comrade Lenin ordained us to hold high and keep pure the great title of member of the party. We vow to thee, Comrade Lenin, that we shall honourably fulfil this thy commandment. . . .

In leaving us, Comrade Lenin ordained us to guard the unity of our party like the apple of our eye. We vow to thee, Comrade Lenin, that we shall fulfil honourably this thy commandment, too. . . .

In leaving us, Comrade Lenin ordained us to guard and strengthen the dictatorship of the proletariat. We vow to thee, Comrade Lenin, that without sparing our strength we shall honourably fulfil this thy commandment, too. . . .

In leaving us, Comrade Lenin ordained us to strengthen with all our might the alliance of workers and peasants. We vow to thee, Comrade Lenin, that we shall fulfil honourably this thy commandment, too. . . .

In leaving us, Comrade Lenin ordained us to strengthen and broaden

the Union of the Republics. We vow to thee, Comrade Lenin, that we
shall honourably fulfil this thy commandment, too. . . .

In leaving us, Comrade Lenin ordained us to keep faith with the principles of the Communist International. We vow to thee, Comrade Lenin,
that we shall not spare our lives in the endeavour to strengthen and
broaden the alliance of the workers of the whole world—the Communist
International.

Deutscher (46, p. 270) might well comment about the speech, "Its
revolutionary invocations sound like a litany composed for a church
choir."

Communisms's god is history. The Communist sees forces moving
inexorably onward within the world. He envisages himself as working
with these forces and helping to bring to pass the irresistible laws of
history. Communism's scriptures are the inspired writings of Marx,
Engels, Lenin, and Stalin. The church is the Communist party, idealized and seen as the means of leading the masses in bringing history's
purposes to pass. Communists have their conversion experiences, and
their literature is replete with the stories of agonizing conversions to
communism. Communism's hereafter is the glorious paradise, only
vaguely defined but which comes into existence on the earth after
the ultimate and final withering away of the state. And so the new
philosophy, with its aim of eliminating religious ideas, itself becomes
psuedo religion.

It has frequently been charged that religion is an overemotion-
alized process, which is the product of ego frustration or the manifestation of an escape mechanism. However, those who are opposed to
religious belief cannot have it all their own way. If there are emotional
factors involved in faith, there are certainly also emotional factors
which are involved in unbelief. Paul E. Johnson (100, p. 183)
well states it: "Atheism is, by every test, as much a belief as theism,
and is evidently quite as incapable of escaping the waves of emotion
that beat upon beliefs."

Involvement

As far back as 1928, Uren, after examining the whole field of
psychology of religion but particularly as it had been developed in
the American scene, made some pungent comments in his book *Recent Religious Psychology*. One of his major criticisms was of psychologists' tendency to stand aside and look at religious experience.

Uren charged that writers who have never experienced religion have little right to evaluate it. He ridiculed their idea of objectivity, made on the basis that they were able to stand off and examine religion, free from any entanglements with it. Existential thinkers, too, have raised their voices against this much-vaunted objectivity. They claim that a great deal of this is pompous fraud and say that every belief tells us something about the believer. There can be no pure objectivity.

Elton Trueblood has emphasized that in our Christian faith we must sail between two dangerous reefs. On the left he sees the danger of dogmatic negativity, in which all sorts of sweeping denials are made. On the other hand, there is the danger of an easy belief, which lies in just accepting traditional ideas. Between these two there is a middle course that can be taken as we seek to know religious experience at its best.

In the development of a person's religious concepts there is often a thesis of belief met by an antithesis of doubt. From the clash of belief and unbelief there frequently comes the synthesis of a new and more substantial faith. As we test beliefs, examine them, and seek to know, a process of clarification takes place so that our faith is more mature than it ever was before. Most would agree with Gordon Allport (5, p. 73) when he says: "We may say then that the mature, religious sentiment is ordinarily fashioned in the workshop of doubt." Paul Johnson states it very clearly when he says that sturdy faith welcomes doubt as democracy welcomes freedom of speech, as judicial bodies welcome minority opinions, and as a scientist welcomes revolutionary discoveries.

In scientific studies the ideal is for the investigator to be detached and completely objective as he makes his evaluations of the situation. Trueblood points out that it is relatively easy to be detached and objective on the question as to whether Pluto is a planet, or the satellite of a planet, because this does not affect our personal lives. But when we become concerned about things that have to do with our personal lives, it is increasingly difficult for us to be detached or objective. Trueblood does not feel that we can trust the judgment of people whose approach to the subject of religion is purely abstract or historical. We do not trust the scientist who spurns the laboratory, or the musician who never performs. Can we, then, accept the judgment of the scholar when he has never himself experienced religion? The

important thing is involvement. An individual must be involved in a
vital religious experience, and this involvement is essential if he is
to make a true evaluation of religion.

Faith always has an element of risk within it. Kierkegaard emphasizes this when he says, "Fear and trembling signifies that a God
exists" (**162**, p. 6). In one of his essays F. W. Boreham emphasized
that every man had something of the skeptic within him. There are
moments when a man struggles with his faith. He told the story of Dr.
Wescott visiting Bishop Lee. Bishop Lee said to the visiting Dr. Wescott, "People say the Lord's Prayer or the Sermon on the Mount contain the sum of the gospel, but for me it is in simpler terms— 'Fear
not, only believe.'" The dying bishop thought for a moment, then
was frightened by the frailty of his faith and said, "Only believe, only
believe. Ah, Wescott, mark the *only*." Tears filled his eyes and he said,
"Lord, I believe; help thou my unbelief."

14

Conversion

The first full-length book on the study of the psychological aspects of religion was Starbuck's *The Psychology of Religion*. Criticism of it has often centered on its preoccupation with the subject of conversion. But it was a characteristic of early writing. Edward's pioneering studies focused on religious experience; G. Stanley Hall, George Albert Coe, and William James all gave a large portion of their writings to dealing with the subject. Conversion experiences were dramatic, and the sudden change of the course of a life, often with unusual emotional manifestations, presented itself as a phenomenon representing aspects of both religion and psychology. These called for the attention of the investigators of psychology of religion.

Of more recent days, there has come an unfortunate swing away from the study. While books on psychology of religion may grudgingly give a chapter to conversion, the psychologist shuns it like the plague. Walter Houston Clark (**34**, p. 188) says, "It is quite obvious that the latter [conversion] is regarded as a sort of psychological slum, to be avoided by any really respectable scholar." Clark takes psychologists to task and indicates that experiences of sudden change, with apparent reversals in personality patterns, offer an excellent field for study. He is correct. The strange changes in the personality of the newly won Marxist, the brainwashing processes of the Communists with their captives, the abrupt changes in life's course which are periodically seen—all emphasize the necessity of understanding the experience.

Clinical psychologists have been compelled to come to terms with conversion as a mental mechanism. They have used the word to describe the process whereby the emotional conflict is "converted" into a physical manifestation. The different usage of the word by clinical psychologists highlights the difficulties of defining the troublesome word. Elmer T. Clark divides the conversion experience and employs the phrase "religious awakening" to describe the individual's entry into a religious experience, reserving the word "conversion" for the more radical and emotionalized experience of a change from irreligion to religion. But definitions have often been broad and inclusive. Coe (36, p. 152) writing in 1900 showed that there were at least six ways in which the word could be used in that day:

"Conversion" is used in at least six senses: (1) a voluntary turning about or change of attitude toward God; this is the New Testament sense; (2) the renunciation of one religion and the beginning of adherence (doctrinal, ethical, or institutional) to another; similarly, a change from one branch of religion to another (as Roman, Greek, or Protestant Christianity); (3) individual salvation according to the evangelical "plan of salvation"—repentance, faith, forgiveness, regeneration, sometimes with assurance; (4) becoming consciously or voluntarily religious, as distinguished from mere conformity to the religious ways of one's family or other group; (5) Christian quality of life as contrasted with an earlier, non-Christian quality—a "really converted" man, for instance; (6) any abrupt transfer, particularly a very rapid transfer, from one standpoint and mode of life to another, especially from what the subject recognizes as a lower to what he recognizes as a higher life.

The type of religious group to which the individual belongs will probably influence his view of conversion. Amongst Protestants, Moberg (130, pp. 422-423) sees three major conversion patterns. The liturgical churches, exemplified by the Lutheran and Episcopalian, emphasize confirmation, for which there is a period of preparation and a study of Christian doctrine, and in which it is claimed that the subject accepts Christ as Saviour and Lord. There is no stress upon emotion or drastic change in the process.

The second pattern of religious awakening is seen in the groups that once strongly emphasized the revival meeting but now have largely given up the practice. This group would embrace Methodists, Congregationalists, and Presbyterians. Moberg would also include some Baptists. New members are prepared in special classes, and there is a strong trend toward the confirmation pattern.

The younger sect-type churches emphasize the older revival pattern. Commitment to Christ with an emotional upheaval is looked for, and it is anticipated that there will be a sharp transition from being "lost" to being "saved."

With this variety of backgrounds, it will be seen that a definition will not be easy to arrive at. Any attempt at defining the word "conversion" must be both elastic and comprehensive.

Probably the most widely quoted definition is that of William James. James (**97**, p. 189) says that conversion is "the process, gradual or sudden, by which a self hitherto divided, and consciously wrong inferior and unhappy, becomes unified and consciously right superior and happy." James makes a characteristically heavy emphasis on emotion. The way an individual feels gives an indication of the validity of the experience.

The turning aspect of conversion was the main emphasis of G. Stanley Hall who defined it as "a natural, normal, universal, and necessary process at a stage when life pivots over from an autocentric to a hetrocentric basis" (**32**, p. 35). However, it all sounds much too inevitable and smooth, with no mention of a possible suddenness nor the amount of emotion accompanying the experience.

A happy compromise, in which the best of both James and Hall have been retained, comes from Walter Houston Clark. Clark (**34**, p. 191) says that conversion is

that type of spiritual growth or development which involves an appreciable change of direction concerning religious ideas and behaviour. Most clearly and typically it denotes an emotional episode of illuminating suddenness, which may be deep or superficial, though it may also come about by a more gradual process.

Clark has made the emphasis on suddenness without excluding development, effective change, and the possibility of an emotional accompaniment of varying intensity.

A Physiological Theory of Conversion

Possibly the most startling theory of religious conversion in recent days is that of William W. Sargant, presented in his book, *The Battle for the Mind*, with the subtitle, "A Physiology of Conversion and Brainwashing." The writing would be more aptly titled *The Battle for the Brain*, for Sargant sees man from a mechanistic, physiological point of view. In the foreword of his book, Sargant clarifies his position by saying that he is not concerned with man's eternal soul, which is the province of the theologian, nor even with the mind in the broadest sense, which is the province of the philosopher, but with the brain and nervous system, which man shares with the dog and other animals.

Sargant is a materialist of the first order, joining the behaviourists in seeing man as a machine. The brain secretes thought just as the liver secretes bile, and the subject of religious conversion is best approached with a study of the brain. The pioneer work of Pavlov with dogs laid the foundation for Sargant's work in investigating confessions under duress, brainwashing, and religious conversion. Sargant (158, 39) says:

> The possible relevance of these experiments to sudden religious and political conversion should be obvious even to the most skeptical: Pavlov has shown by repeated and repeatable experiment just how a dog, like a man, can be conditioned to hate what it previously loved, and love what it previously hated. Similarly, one set of behavior patterns in man can be temporarily replaced by another that altogether contradicts it; not by persuasive indoctrination alone, but also by imposing intolerable strains on a normally functioning brain.

Pavlov placed dogs in laboratories where they were fed and at the same time given a stimulus, such as a buzzer or flashing light. A tube was inserted in the dog's mouth so that the amount of its salivation could be checked. Later, the stimulus was given without the food, and the dog reacted physiologically as if it had ingested food. It was thus said to have been "conditioned."

One incident of singular importance took place in 1924 when Pavlov's laboratory in Leningrad was flooded. The dogs had been conditioned and a set of responses developed within them. On the day of the flood, the water rose gradually until the terror-stricken animals were swimming frantically to keep their heads above water. At the last moment, an attendant rushed in and pulled the dogs down through the water and out of their cage doors to safety. It was afterwards discovered, when the dogs were tested, that implanted conditioning processes had disappeared.

Pavlov came to call this response "transmarginal inhibition." He saw it as a mechanism whereby the brain protected itself to avoid the damage which might come from stress. He found that there were four ways in which transmarginal inhibition could be induced. (1) If the intensity of the conditioning signal was increased, as when an electric current was applied to the leg of an animal and intensified until it became too great for the dog's system, the dog broke down. (2) The time between the giving of the signal and the arrival of the food could be increased. Conditioned to expect the food in a given time, the dog's brain revolted against prolonged waiting. (3) Signals given to the dogs could be confused. The dog might be given positive and negative signals in rapid succession, and the resulting confusion would upset the dog's stability. (4) If the dog's physical functionings were tampered with, it would easily succumb.

From Pavlov's work and his own observations, Sargant deduces what he calls the "physiological principles" which lead to a breakdown or dramatic change in the behavior patterns in both humans and animals. (1) The prolongation of a state of tension and expectation could affect brain function and lead to transmarginal inhibition. (2) Confusion of stimuli lead to difficulties in adjustment. (3) Physical debilitation could be effective when everything else has failed.

From this materialistic and purely physiological basis, Sargant proceeds to make varied applications. Reared in a Methodist church, he tells of a wartime visit to his father's home. Thinking of the application of Pavlovian principles to men suffering with battle stress, he chanced to pick up John Wesley's *Journal*. Reading of the revival meetings of that day, he saw a parallel with the emotional excitement of the battle stressed soldiers. In his chapter on "Religious Conversion," Sargant proves to his own satisfaction that the Wesleys, Charles through his hymn writing and John through his preaching, created emotional tensions within the individual, and the resulting confusion led to a conversion experience.

It might be noted, incidentally, that Sargant speaks of John Wesley as if the preacher equated "conversion" with "sanctification." He refers to a statement of Wesley's that sanctification must be sudden to be effective and then goes on to discuss the matter as if this were a reference to conversion. In reality, in Wesley's teaching conversion and sanctification are different experiences. Conversion means justification before God through faith in Christ, while sanctification is an experience which results in holiness of life. Teaching about sanctification experiences cannot be validly applied to conversion.

Three main areas of experience discussed by Sargant are brainwashing by the Communists, the eliciting of confessions of prisoners, and religious conversions. In Pavlov's experiments, as in any scientific investigation, control was a basic element. The dogs were in harness, kept in a room from which all outside stimuli had been excluded, thus making the laboratory environment a controlled situation. In Communist brainwashing methods, the victims are confined and kept under constant observation. Police practices in eliciting confessions restrict the subjects so that their total environment is decided by their interrogators. But where is this element of control in a religious environment? Even in great evangelistic meetings, the individual comes of his own free will and can leave whenever he wishes. In fact, in most enlightened countries the constitution specifically gives the individual freedom of religious choice. The analogy with a Pavlovian experiment is obviously far stretched and fails at the point of control.

Sargant (**158**, p. 13) makes one important admission:

I do not discuss some types of purely intellectual conversion, but only those physical or psychological stimuli, rather than intellectual arguments, which seem to help to produce conversion by causing alterations in the subject's brain function. Hence the term "physiology" in the title.

But there are intellectual conversions, and many conversions take place in churches today where the service is correct, dignified, and precise, with very few emotional overtones. Despite Sargant's claim that in Billy Graham's meetings there is a strong emotional impact, an unbiased observer cannot help but wonder at the calm, deliberate way in which Graham gives his invitations, with no exhortation or pleading. It is almost as if he says, "I have stated the case, what will you do about it?"

Later in the chapter in the discussion of the place of intelligence in conversion, it will be seen that, amongst children at any rate, there is strong evidence for a relationship between intelligence and conversion. The inquiring mind, demanding an answer to life's problems, is a factor in a conversion experience.

Anticipating the protests that "men are not like dogs," Sargant (**158**, p. 26) gives the humorous but not very satisfactory answer, "indeed they are not. Dogs at least do not experiment with man." Sargant answers his own argument. It is because dogs do not have the capacity to experiment with men that many psychologists are turning from animal experimentation as a means of studying human reactions. Experiments with animals might be of value for the student of the nervous system, or certain physiological responses, but the student of personality finds little help coming from animal experimentation.

Sargant's casual reading of John Wesley's *Journal* caused religious conversion to finish up in strange company. McKenzie comments,

Whether the author realized it or not, the linking of Wesley's preaching and the practices of beating on drums, chanting, dancing, shaking, and handling poisonous snakes, pursued by some religious cults in order to induce "religious" experience or conversion, with Pavlov's conclusions from his experiments, gave the impression that the whole thing was just a "rape of the mind" (122, p. 4)

Sargant's wedding of religious conversion with Pavlovian conditioning might well merit Johnson's celebrated comment about another matter. "It is like a dog walking on its hind legs. It is not done well. But you are surprised to find it done at all" (24, I, 266).

However, as bad as the situation is, all is not debit. Sargant (158, p. 27) says,

The conclusion reached is that simple physiological mechanisms of conversion do exist, and that we therefore still have much to learn from a study of brain function about matters that have hitherto been claimed as the province of psychology or metaphysics. The politico-religious struggle for the mind of man may well be won by whoever becomes most conversant with the normal and abnormal functions of the brain, and is readiest to make use of the knowledge gained.

Sargant seems to finally say that a conversion experience is part of the physiological nature of man. He may be unwittingly saying what another said when he stated, "Thou hast made us for thyself and we are restless until we find rest in thee."

Psychological Aspects of Conversion

The factors of tension and conflict, so prominent in Sargant's speculation, point to a psychological rather than a physiological basis for conversion experiences. Clark (34, p. 202) comments, "We must, then, regard religious conversion psychologically considered, as a special case of a wider psychological variety." Personality's systems, the unregulated urges, the value system, and the ego are in a constant state of tension. The unregulated urges, the primitive strivings of personality, exist only for their own pleasure-seeking, and even Freud saw this "id" as fundamentally selfish.

At the other extreme is the value system, built up by the experiences and teachings of years and by incorporating the "you ought" and "thou shalt not" principles. Between the unregulated urges and the value system stands the ego, or self, which must make its decisions in consideration of the drives of the unregulated urges, the demands of the value system, and the reality of the total life situation. The solution may only come with the upset in the balance of power of the systems of personality. The upheaval and consequent reorientation by the self may represent a psychological aspect of conversion.

Experiences which bear a close resemblance to a religious conversion are to be seen in nonreligious areas of life. A crisis is faced, a new pathway is agonizingly chosen, and life is altogether different, with turmoil calmed. Alcoholics Anonymous is probably one of the best examples of the possibility of a totally changed life pattern. Alcoholics have been the despair of professionals, who acknowledge that alcoholism is an illness but have been highly unsuccessful in its treatment. Alcoholics Anonymous has had outstanding success with a technique which calls for a quasi-religious experience. At the heart of the Alcoholics Anonymous plan is its twelve steps which are:

1. We admitted we were powerless over alcohol—that our lives had become unmanageable.
2. Came to believe that a Power greater than ourselves could restore us to sanity.
3. Made a decision to turn our will and our lives over to the care of God as we understood Him.
4. Made a searching and fearless moral inventory of ourselves.
5. Admitted to God, to ourselves, and to another human being, the exact nature of our wrongs.
6. Were entirely ready to have God remove all these defects of character.
7. Humbly asked Him to remove our shortcomings.
8. Made a list of all persons we had harmed, and became willing to make amends to them all.
9. Made direct amends to such people wherever possible, except when to do so would injure them or others.
10. Continued to take personal inventory and when we were wrong, promptly admitted it.
11. Sought through prayer and meditation to improve our conscious contact with God as we understood Him, praying only for knowledge of His will for us and the power to carry that out.
12. Having had a spiritual awakening as the result of these steps, we tried to carry this message to alcoholics, and to practice these principles in all our affairs.

The steps contain within them aspects of an evangelical conversion experience. The honest acknowledgment of failure, confession of shortcomings, the recognition of a higher power, and the sense of mission and obligation to carry the message are all factors found in a religious crisis. It must be acknowledged that the "higher power" is only "seen through a glass darkly," and that the subjective individual aspects are much more in evidence than the objective deity.

From the halfway house of Alcoholics Anonymous, with its vaguely defined "higher power," it is a big step to move to atheistic philosophy and discover conversion experiences. Marxism is basically atheistic both in philosophy and practice. Religion is viewed as an outdated bourgeois superstition used by the capitalists to enslave the workers, and one of Marxism's objectives is the elimination of all religious concepts. Yet, within this atheistic system, individuals have experiences with all the characteristics of a religious conversion.

Harry Chang, a Shanghai-born Chinese, was a Roman Catholic. He resisted the Communist regime and was loyal to his religion, but his brother-in-law, a member of the Communist party, worked on him until he began to think that the Communists were right and that religion was just the opium of the people. At last in his mind he reached the place where he felt that he should join the party and become a Communist. He describes his experience:

> I became a little happier. An odd feeling I had never had before came over me. I thought I was a new man. I myself had been liberated. At least I had rid myself of the evil influences of capitalistic society. This thing had created a new meaning in life for me, I told myself. I had some goal in life to achieve. I knew this was not just a natural phenomenon, but an international affair. I now felt that I had to do my best for the liberation of the entire human race (91, p. 81).

A new feeling of happiness, with its sense of release from guilt, a new life opening up with the sense of being part of a great, ongoing movement, and a new goal to strive for are frequently found portions of a religious conversion.

The Russian, Victor Kravchenko, tells of meeting Comrade Lazarev while working in a coal mine. Comrade Lazarev was a party official and took an interest in him, inviting him to his room. While the younger man was there he spoke to him about joining the party. The talk has all the marks of the effort of a fervent "personal worker" in evangelical circles. In fact, Kravchenko says he had been "pressured" by other party members before this. After the conversation, he decided to join the party. Kravchenko (**112,** p. 38) tells of his feelings:

> Now life had for me an urgency, a purpose, a new and thrilling dimension of dedication to a cause. I was one of the *elite,* chosen by History to lead my country and the whole world out of darkness into the socialist light. This sounds pretentious, I know, yet that is how we talked and felt. There might be cynicism and self-seeking among some of the grown-up Communists, but not in our circle of ardent novitiates.

Like the Calvinist coming to believe in his all-powerful God, so the Communist novitiate has a strange sense of election. He sees himself predestined by history. Dedication is here, too, and the sense of mission so often found in the fervent religious conversion.

Quoting from a statement by a Communist who had recently joined the party, Eells recounts a case of conversion. Educated in England and the United States, the subject was formerly dean of Ginling College, and at the time he was serving as a professor in the institution. After speaking of his former experience, Eells (**55,** p. 206) states:

> Now I have received the revelation of truth. To say it in a word, I have been converted, and so my attitude toward my past mistakes and toward the objective world has been entirely changed. My conversion was gradual and painful . . . after several days of mental struggle I began to realize my past mistakes. . . . The hideous appearance of imperialist cultural aggression stood out plain before me.

The light of revelation had dawned; past sins became obvious; soul struggle had led to a new light.

Richard L. Walker tells of a group of Chinese passing through a process of indoctrination. Following a period of hard physical labor, they were given intensive indoctrination, and the unpromising candidates were eliminated. After about six months of training came the crises and breakdowns:

> The crisis usually starts with hysteria and sobbing at night, which go on during the small group meeting the next day and are immediately discussed. . . . The crisis usually comes about the same time for all the members of a small group. Apparently the breakdown of one of the members launches a chain reaction. (**158,** p. 168).

Walker reports that one participant claimed that about one-fifth of the trainees broke down completely. Along with this went the process called by the Chinese "tail-cutting," as associations with old friends, society, and values were broken. Following the change, new values became more firmly implanted.

Up to the period of crisis, most of the Communist jargon was relatively meaningless. It was just a new language to be memorized, played with, and rearranged in patterns. Now he begins to find that it does have some pertinence to his problem. . . . In place of his feeling of guilt he is now fired with the conviction that he must publicize his newly found security and help others find peace of mind through service to the Organization (158, p. 168).

The experience bears a close resemblance to a religious conversion, in which the convert finds that verses of the Bible and material taught through the years in Sunday school take on a new and significant meaning following his conversion.

When the opposite situation comes to pass in the decision to leave communism, at least one writer sees it in terms of what might be called a "counter conversion." So Whittaker Chambers (30, p. 16) states:

One thing most ex-Communists could agree upon: they broke because they wanted to be free. They do not all mean the same thing by "free." Freedom is a need of the soul, and nothing else. It is in striving toward God that the soul strives continually after a condition of freedom. God alone is the inciter and guarantor of freedom. He is the only guarantor. External freedom is only an aspect of interior freedom. Political freedom, as the Western world has known it, is only a political reading of the Bible. Religion and freedom are indivisible. Without freedom the soul dies. Without the soul there is no justification for freedom. Necessity is the only ultimate justification known to the mind. Hence every sincere break with Communism is a religious experience, though the Communists fail to identify its true nature, though he failed to go to the end of the experience.

Chambers sees the move to communism as filling the vacuum in the individual's life. Religion is what he really needs if an adequate reorientation is to take place.

Evaluating a conversion experience psychologically, it is possible to draw a number of conclusions:

1. It has been said that just about the time liberal theologians convinced us that there was no such thing as hell, psychologists and psychiatrists brought us the knowledge of the hells of psychosis and neurosis. The thought might be extended to include conversion, which has been denied as an old-fashioned emotional experience not to be looked for in an enlightened twentieth-century culture. Meanwhile, modern day miracles are taking place as alcoholics, despaired of by medicine, are rehabilitated through an experience akin to conversion. Also, an unscrupulous, new political philosophy is indoctrinating and changing the life patterns of many of its followers through similar experiences.

2. Ferm (62, p. 194) claims that the common denominator in all conversion experiences is a surrender to an ideal and says, "Either the surrender of the self to the ideal occurs or no conversion can take place." The position is opposite to that of Sargant, who accounts for the experience in subjective terms. Most psychological conversions involve some objective ideal of value.

3. It must be frankly acknowledged that conflict is an integral part of a conversion experience. Sargant is correct in his assumption that conflict generally precedes a dramatic conversion experience, but his physiological explanation is inadequate. Although Sargant wants no part in considering a "mind," the concept offers better possibilities. The unconscious carries on its dynamic activity. Material committed to it is worked on, and from the process of incubation there comes a moment in time when it is ready to break into consciousness, and the event takes place.

4. Human personality is such that men and women have a capacity for a conversion experience. Here is the heart of the conflict with Sargant, who places police confessions, brainwashing, and religious conversions on the same level. It is not so much that the methods used are similar but rather that the subjects all have personalities with common functionings. The individual may have a religious or some other kind of conversion, and the framework within which the experience takes place will make the difference. Even Sargant (158, p. 118) acknowledges the possibility:

The proof of the pudding lies in the eating. Wesley changed the religious and social life of England for the better, with such methods in a modified and socially acceptable form. In other hands and countries they have been used for sinister purposes.

From the religious perspective, we could say that man has the capacity for conversion experience, and if he does not find it in truth, he may find it in error. The moment the church turns its back on religious conversion experiences, it leaves a vacuum to be filled by unworthy substitutes.

Faced with the problems of Christian distinctives in conversion, Ferm observes three distinguishing marks of what he calls the "evangelical crisis." He sees a *uniformity* of faith within evangelical conversions, in that they bear a close resemblance to each other. Another factor noted by Ferm is the *sense of sin*. In non-Christian conversions there is little said about sin, whereas the heart of the evangelical crisis lies in the discovery by the individual that his is an offense against God. The third distinctive is the *permanence* of the evangelical crisis. In the more subjective experiences there are frequent lapses. Ferm (**62**, p. 198) comments: "In this quality of permanence the evangelical crisis conversion has a distinctiveness not found in purely psychological stimulus type of religious emotion, because it has objectivity as well as subjectivity." A volume about the experiences of Communists who fell by the way has the appropriate title, *The God That Failed*. The difficulty was that there was no God. The whole experience was purely subjective. However, Ferm's reasoning is not altogether convincing.

The Processes of a Religious Conversion

What happens in a religious conversion experience? Because it is highly individualistic, any generalization will have many exceptions, but there is a sequence of events in the experience of the convert. Formulations of the steps of the experience vary all the way from Starbuck's three stages of unrest, crisis, and peace, to the more recent writing of Ferm (**62**, p. 183), who says the steps are:

First, an event or circumstance disrupts the established pattern of thought. Second, the individual is confronted with certain claims or demands. Third, he grasps the core of the gospel. Fourth, the moment of crisis occurs. Fifth, certain results follow.

A happy synthesis of the most frequently accepted ideas would see the stages as (1) a period of unrest, (2) the conversion crisis, (3) a sense of peace, release and inner harmony, and (4) a concrete expression of the experience. As each of these stages is examined, the

results of research carried on with the students at Southwestern Baptist
Theological Seminary will be woven into the discussion.

A Period of Unrest and the Conversion Experience

Before any change in personality takes place, there must be a certain
amount of "psychological distress." In his "characteristic steps in the
therapeutic process," Rogers (**156**, p. 31) places the fact that "the individual comes for help" at the head of the list. The individual has
become conscious of his need and has accepted responsibility for
himself. In counseling circles it is acknowledged that children sent by
parents, or husbands talked into coming by wives, have a poor prognosis for counseling. Until the awareness of need dawns, little can be
done to help. Alcoholics Anonymous insist that the alcoholic must be
dissatisfied with himself and seek help before he can gain benefit from
the organization.

William James (**97**, pp. 127-165) designated the initial period of
a conversion experience as "soul sickness." Elmer T. Clark (**32**, p.
38) called it a "period of storm and stress." Ferm (**62**, p. 183) would
gather at least two of his steps under this heading: "an event or circumstance disrupts the established pattern of thought" and "the
individual is faced with certain claims or demands." The causes of
the unrest may not be clearly perceived by the person involved.
The older type of theology spoke of the experience as "conviction

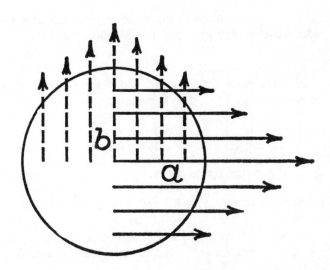

of sin," and it is sometimes referred to as a sense of unworthiness and incompleteness.

Starbuck's (168, p. 159) interpretation of conviction is illustrated in the figure above, which shows (a) as the way old habits, associations tastes, and ideas carry along the current of life. Lines going in the direction (b) are the beginning of a possible better life, finer associations, and a glimpse into the larger spiritual world. The even flow of life is disturbed. The person is pulled in two directions, and there is conflict between the possible better self and the habitual self, thus giving rise to a feeling of incompleteness. Ambivalent feelings cause discomfort within the individual, and recognition of the alternative possibilities leads to a clarification of choices.

Students of the dialectic speak about the "dialectic leap." No change is smooth and even, and one of the laws of the dialectic is "the transformation of quantity into quality and vice versa." Water is used to illustrate.With the application of heat it warms until 100° centigrade is reached and a qualitative change takes place as it becomes steam. Reduction of temperature to 0° centigrade brings a

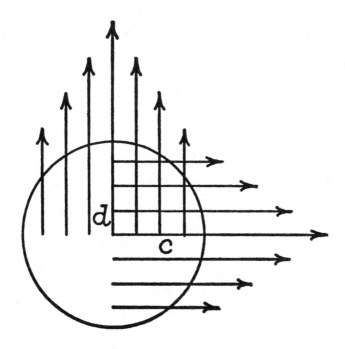

change from water to ice. In each instance the nodal point is reached, and the qualitative change ensues.

In conversion the condition of unrest leads to a nodal point. Starbuck (**168**, pp. 159-160) described it by referring to his diagram illustrating crisis in conversion shown above. In this, (c) is the habitual self striving with all its might to preserve its self-consistency, and (d) is the divine urge which has become irresistible. This is seen as the critical point which finally culminates in the surrender of the will. Earlier it was noted that Ferm sees this surrender of self to an ideal as the universal psychological likeness of all conversion experiences. He dogmatically declares, "Either the surrender of self to the ideal occurs or no conversion takes place." The climactic experiences of a group of students at Southwestern Seminary are seen in the list below of items checked as "very important." In the perception of religious awakening, the most frequently used description was "a yielding, a self-surrender" (**50**, p. 35).

Perception of Religious Awakening	Per Cent
A yielding, a self-surrender	86
Having a consciousness of God's nearness	82
Accepting forgiveness	71
Making a public confession	70
A determination to live a new life	64
Joining the church	50
A gradual growing experience which took place at no specific time	44

Emotion engendered during the period of conflict may flood forth, and this aspect often concerns critics of the "evangelical crisis," who deplore the excessive emotionalism. But the expression of emotion is frequently an integral part of psychotherapy. Catharsis, or the purging of the emotion, is almost inevitable in successful therapy. In some counseling centers the prominently displayed box of Kleenex tissues gives evidence of the frequency of emotional manifestations. Even a critic like Sargant finally comes to the place of saying that there will be no Protestant revival like that of Wesley while preachers appeal mainly to intelligence and reason, without seeing the power of strong emotions for disrupting old emotional patterns and implanting new ones. If an emotional upheaval is a part of psychotherapy and clears the way for new emotional health, it is small wonder that there should be emotional expression in a life-changing conversion experience.

Carl Rogers (**156**, pp. 207-10) sees insight as involving the perception of relationships, the acceptance of self, and the element of choice. Applying the description to a conversion experience, it could be said that the conversion crisis is the moment of religious insight. The subject comprehends a wrong relationship with God and his fellowmen; he drops his defenses, accepts the biblical evaluation of himself as a sinner, and then makes the deliberate choice of Christ and the Christian way of life.

A Sense of Peace, Release, and Inner Harmony

After the storm comes the calm. The decision made with difficulty may still leave some questionings and apprehensions, but the pre-

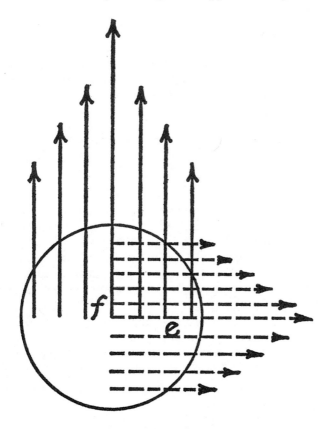

dominant feeling is of oneness with God, of sins forgiven and problems solved, of relaxation and sense of harmony. Starbuck (**168,** pp. 159-60) portrays the experience in his diagram illustrating the new life as seen above.

Only a vestige of the old life, (e), is left. The new life, (f), is now the real self. The feelings following the experience of religious awakening checked by Southwestern Seminary students are seen to be similar to those enunciated by Starbuck, with happiness, peace, and release checked as "very important" (**50,** p. 37).

Feelings Following Religious Awakening	Per Cent
Happiness	90
Peace	82
Relief	67
Calmness	52

Ferm reports that in his inquiry 90 per cent of the respondents indicated that a sense of joy and release followed their crisis in conversion. Nevertheless, the vestige of the old life does remain. Like a ghost, it will periodically return to haunt the convert and maybe to fill him with loathing.

A Concrete Expression of the Experience

Walter Houston Clark claims that the success of the itinerant John Wesley was seen, not only in his zealous preaching, but also in his genius in organizing Methodist societies with an ironclad spiritual discipline. Included in the discipline were rules for rising at five in the morning for prayers and preaching. The expression of the experience helped to confirm it. Among Baptists, the emphasis on believer's baptism is that an individual makes a vital, life-changing decision and is then baptized, making a confession of his faith, Baptism becomes an outward manifestation of the inward experience, with all the psychological value of confession.

Clark (**34,** p. 195) feels that the expression stage may sometimes precede the conversion crisis. When Wesley was striving for faith and wondering if he should preach, he was told, "Preach faith until you have it, and then because you have faith, you will preach faith." In Alcoholics Anonymous, the new member is told that he must rely on a power higher than himself for strength. If he protests that he does not have such a power, the answer is given that he must behave as if there were a higher power. Baptist history illustrates the point. The first Baptist church in Philadelphia was organized at Pennepak. In 1688 a young man named Elias Keach came to the community. He was the son of Benjamin Keach, an outstanding Baptist minister of London, England. However, he himself was not a Christian. Needing food and clothing, he accepted an invitation to preach at the Pennepak Baptist Church. Doubtless familiar with his father's sermons, he launched boldly into his message. While addressing the congregation, the enormity of his offense dawned upon him. He fell on his knees and confessed his hoax to the church. They led him to Christ, and he became the first pastor of the Pennepak church. Experiences such as these leading to a conversion are probably an example of autosuggestion at its best.

Elements of a Conversion Experience

Assuming that there is a similarity in the mechanics of conversion, as far as the individual is concerned, we are still confronted with the problems of motivating factors in the experience. As in other areas of life, there are multiple causations. The age at which conversion takes place has been a constant subject of discussion. Is it just an experience for impressionable children, or do adults go through it also? The level of intelligence has seldom been thought worthy of discussion by writers on the subject. This presents a new aspect which must be considered.

Institutions involved in religious education prepare the individual for life-changing decisions, and new guidelines for religious education programs could come from investigations concerning which factors have been the most effective in fostering conversion experiences. Personality is affected in conversion, and the influence of one personality on another is an appropriate subject for discussion. Which personalities are seen by the converts as influential? The perennial question of whether a conversion is a gradual or sudden experience must also be faced and some conclusion reached.

Age of Conversion

In the early studies of psychology of religion, where so much attention was focused on conversion, the relationship between adolescence and conversion was considered a revolutionary discovery. Clark (34, p. 207) says,

The first great student of the psychology of adolescence, G. Stanley Hall, was much ridiculed in 1881 when in a public lecture in Boston he pointed out that this (adolescence) was the most characteristic age for conversion. Since then the researches of many students have confirmed this judgment.

Starbuck's early investigations found a close relationship between puberty and conversion, with the typical conversion age for males being 16.4 years and for girls, 14.8 years. The two-year difference in the onset of puberty between boys and girls appears to strengthen the case of Starbuck for a puberty-conversion relationship.

The correlation of adolescence and conversion is now widely accepted, but of recent days some dissenting voices have been heard. Ferm has attacked the view that adolescence is the time for conversion on two grounds. He sees a basic error in research technique. Questionnaires on conversion have been filled out mainly by college students, because it is easier to get information from them. It will naturally follow that most college students could not have experienced conversion in adulthood, and so the sample is not adequate for drawing conclusions about conversion age. Ferm contends that if a survey were made in maturer years, the age level of conversion would have been raised.

A second line of evidence provided by Ferm is from a survey of three churches where the average ages of conversion were 43, 46, and 41 years respectively. Of Billy Graham's British campaign, Ferm (62, p. 218) says, "The average age of conversion for Billy Graham's British campaign was in the middle twenties, while that of his Scottish campaign was at least fifteen years higher than that." Ferm is convinced that the current revival movement is characterized by conversions at a higher age than formerly.

A problem of methodology concerns the use of the "average" as a small number of people with conversions later in life can pull up the average. A survey of adult leaders in the Southern Baptist Convention showed the average age of conversion to be 13.2 years for women and 15.3 years for men. But the age when most conversions took place was found to be 12 years, which was quite different from the average. Similar studies carried on at Southwestern Seminary showed a much higher average conversion age, but the large proportion of men who had decided to study for the ministry later in life tended to inflate the average. However, most investigators seem to feel that the age of conversion is going down. Paul E. Johnson's (**100**, p. 127) tabulation of a series of studies on the age of conversion is seen below.

Studies	Date	Number of Cases	Average Age
Starbuck	1899	1,265	16.4
Coe	1900	1,784	16.4
Hall	1904	4,054	16.6
Athearn	1922	6,194	14.6
Clark	1929	2,174	12.7

A study among Baptist ministers in West Kentucky showed that about half the persons baptized in their churches were between the ages of six and twelve. Observations by professional workers in Southern Baptist churches lead them to believe that most conversions take place in the 10 to 11 year age bracket. Rather unfortunately, it is difficult to get a confirmation of this from well-validated studies.

A somewhat unexpected correlation with age is the intensity of the experience. Elmer T. Clark reported that the more radical experiences are taking place at age seventeen, and in this he agreed with the findings of both Starbuck and Hall. When religion was a gradual developing experience, the awakening came at about twelve years of age. Johnson feels that if the process were interrupted or resisted at the twelve-year level, it might be deferred for five years and require a more emotionalized crisis to overcome obstructions. The later the experience the more drastic it is likely to be.

Intelligence

Is intelligence a factor in conversion? Sargant's controversial book casually brushed off intellectual aspects of conversion as not worthy of consideration. Unfortunately for those who would seek to answer Sargant, very little research has been done into the place of intelligence in conversion. It may be that our preoccupation with other areas has caused us to overlook a factor of vital importance.

Considering the role of intelligence in religious awakening, some of the best leads are found in the investigations of gifted children. Speaking of these, Charles F. Kemp (**107**, p. 76) says:

Several studies have shown that gifted children show a greater degree of interest in religion than do others and that this interest appears much earlier. The gifted child is quite likely to have an intense curiosity about the meaning of the world, about the purpose of life and the reason for things.

In support of his statement, Kemp quotes Hollingsworth (**86**, p. 6) whose view is that religious questions are not so much associated with puberty as with mental age, and that when a child reaches a mental age of about twelve, religious questions arise. She says, "The higher the IQ the earlier does the pressing need for an explanation of the universe occur; the sooner the demand for a concept of the origin and destiny of self appear." If these conclusions can be verified, the widely accepted thesis of Starbuck may have to be reconsidered.

One study was carried out with a group of students in an effort to discover the relationship of intelligence and religious awakening (**50**). A total of 196 students were given the Otis Quick Scoring Mental Abilities Test. Also they filled out a detailed questionnaire on their experiences of religious awakening. From the 196 students there were chosen the 25 with IQ's of 125 or higher and the 25 whose IQ's were 96 or under on the Otis Test. The two groups were then compared.

A difference showed up in the age of conversion. The group with the highest intelligence had an experience of religious awakening 1.7 years earlier than the lower intelligence group. This may serve to confirm Hollingsworth's assertion that in this instance at least, mental age was probably more important than puberty in religious awakening.

An examination of the items on the questionnaire which were significantly different at the 1 per cent and 5 per cent levels of confidence revealed a number of interesting facts. One, which might have been anticipated, was that the respondents with lower intelligence gave evidence of a more emotionalized conversion experience than the high intelligence group. Apparently, the lower intelligence group lives more on the emotional rather than the rational level. Nevertheless, the correlation of high intelligence and rationality is not inevitable, and psychotherapists' offices are frequently inhabited by individuals whose intellectual capacity would be well above average. Another indication not so much to be anticipated was associated with doubt. It might have been expected that the group with the higher intelligence would have more doubts than the others. However, the reverse was true, with the low intelligence group indicating more concern about doubt than the high intelligence group. A logical conclusion would be that the doubts may have been a part of the more emotionalized experience of the lower intelligence group rather than a part of the reasoning processes leading to faith.

Altogether, the study was breaking new ground. Sweeping generalizations should not be made from the findings, but future investigators will have to give a larger place to considering intelligence as a factor in conversion. Along with the psychological and physiological, there must be a place for intellectual aspects.

Institutions Involved in Conversion

Institutions and organizations are an integral part of the ongoing Christian enterprise, and they play their part in the developing religious education program. Most people who are converted have some background of religious education which helps to prepare them for the experience. Ferm reports that his investigations show that 60 per cent of the people claiming a conversion experience had clear Bible teaching prior to their conversion. The responses of students surveyed at Southwestern Seminary are seen below in the list of educational agencies checked as "very important."

Agency	Per Cent
Sunday school	58
Church worship service	58
Home	46

Sunday school and the church worship service were seen as equally important in an experience of religious awakening, but this perception must be evaluated in consideration of Southern Baptist tradition. A constant evangelistic emphasis, not only in periodic revival meetings, but also in the calls for professions of faith in most church worship services, stresses an open confession of faith at a church gathering. Even if a religious decision is made at home or in a Sunday school class, it is still expected that the subject will "come forward" during the invitation at the church service. Baptism follows just as also does joining the church.

In many Southern Baptist churches the three experiences of "a profession of faith," "being baptized," and "becoming a church member" are often subsumed under the expression "joining the church." Other Baptist groups separate the steps more widely and avoid the confusion and misunderstanding which are latent in the procedures of many Southern Baptist churches. It might be noted that this "instant evangelism" has come under fire in Samuel Southard's *Pastoral Evangelism* (164).

In biblical times, the home was the great institution in religious education. When Moses was rehearsing the great truths of God, he spoke of the technique which was to be used in teaching them:

These words, which I command thee this day, shall be in thine heart: and thou shalt teach them diligently unto thy children, and shalt talk of them when thou sittest in thine house, and when thou walkest by the way, and when thou liest down, and when thou risest up (Deut. 6:6-7).

In more modern times the home has remained the basic institution in religious education. Among the respondents to Ferm's questionnaire, 80 per cent who reported a conversion experience said that they had a good, religious background. This confirmed Clark's (34, p. 228) statement, "If it were practical, the best single piece of advice we could give one seeking a sound experience of religious faith would be, 'See that you are born into a genuinely religious family.' " While this might be the ideal, the Southwestern studies showed that it was not often attained. In the comparison of the influences of church, Sunday school, and home, the home came third. The religious home, with Bible reading, family prayers, and religious instruction, has become the exception rather than the rule. The modern family is adept at delegating its responsibilities to other institutions in society, and nowhere is this more so than in the religious training of children. Consequently, the church will have to take up the slack left by inadequate religious education in the home.

Influential Personalities

The child's developing value system is built, in a large measure, by the surrounding adults with whom he identifies and from whom he seeks approval. Prominent among these are his parents and teachers.

The child's image of God is often shaped in the image of respected adult figures. Consequently, the individuals seen by the convert as influential in his experience of coming into contact with God make an appropriate but often neglected subject for study.

The Southwestern Seminary study indicated the influential figures in a conversion experience. Listed below are persons checked by the students as being "very important" in the experience of religious awakening.

Person	Per Cent
Mother	64
Minister	48
Father	44
Sunday school teacher	28

Of the group surveyed, 64 per cent indicated that their mother was "very important" in the experience of religious awakening. Mother is obviously still the most potent religious force of the family. The somewhat startling revelation is the place of father as an influential figure. If Freudian speculation about God being a father image is correct, it might be expected that father would have headed the list.

However, other factors enter to complicate the picture. Fathers are notoriously less religious than mothers, and the example of religious living is not so often set. A mounting divorce rate may also be a factor. Custody of the children is generally given to the mother, and the children are thus left without a father figure in their life. The *Social Security Bulletin* reported that as of January, 1962, there were 2,120,000 fatherless children under 18 years of age in the United States. In these children's lives, fatherly influence will be negligible unless there are surrogate parents. However, there are pretty good reasons to believe that historically mother has frequently been the family guide in religion. Jerry McCauley, who spent so much time in running a mission in the slums of a great city, once said, "Far be it from me to limit the grace of God, but I never yet knew a man to be permanently reclaimed who did not have a godly mother."

The place of the minister says something, with 48 per cent classifying him as "very important" in an experience of religious awakening. Being the spiritual leader, it might be expected that he would be a prominent influence in a religious experience, but his ranking above father may be an indication that he fills the father role in some children's lives. Roman Catholic and high church Anglican priests are referred to as "Father." In the British Commonwealth armies, chaplains of all faiths are referred to as "Padre," the Spanish word for father.

The minister's place in the experience may come from his prominence in the church worship services, but most pastors are conscious of the attachment which many children have to them. The minister frequently becomes a spiritual father for many children. Like Paul, who could refer to Timothy, the son of a non-Christian, as his "son in the faith," pastors have many children in the faith whose spiritual decisions are made under their guidance.

A puzzling feature of the Southwestern survey is the relative lack of importance of the Sunday school teacher. Southern Baptists lay great emphasis on religious education. Sunday school classes are usually small and divided by sex, with men teaching boys and women teaching girls. The fond anticipation has been that children would identify with teachers who would lead them to a religious experience. However, Southern Baptists have not encouraged enduring ties between teachers and pupils. They object to a Sunday school class becoming a "little church," and annual promotions are a fixed custom in most Southern Baptist churches. The promotion means ties between teachers and pupils do not develop to great strength and are annually broken.

Gradual or Sudden?

Among those accepting the validity of religious conversion, there still remains the thorny question of gradualness or suddenness. Clark's (34, p. 191) definition envisages the possibility of either aspect being predominant. "Most clearly and typically it denotes an emotional episode of illuminating suddenness, which may be deep or superficial, though it may also come about by a more gradual process." Advocates of the essentially dramatic type of conversion frequently overlook aspects of gradualness.

The oft-quoted example of a sudden conversion is the experience of Saul of Tarsus on the Damascus road, but Jung (176a, pp. 189-190) sees elements of gradualness in the event.

Although the moment of a conversion seems sometimes quite sudden and unexpected, yet we know from repeated experience that such a

fundamental occurrence always has a long period of unconscious incubation. It is only when the preparation is complete, that is to say, when the
individual is ready to be converted, that the new view breaks forth with
great emotion. St. Paul had already been a Christian for a long time, but
unconsciously; hence his fanatical resistance to the Christians, because
fanaticism exists chiefly in individuals who are compensating for secret
doubts.

A further complication of the simple reference to Paul's conversion
on the Damascus road comes from establishing just when Paul's conversion took place. Writing from a conservative theological viewpoint,
Ferm (**62**, p. 97) says:

Students of Paul's life find it difficult to point accurately to the exact
moment of his conversion. No doubt various occurrences contributed,
but the real crisis seems to have come not on the road to Damascus, but
rather in the house of Judas, on Straight Street, when Ananias put his
hand upon him that he might receive his sight (Acts 9:17); it was then
that the light came, it was then also that Paul arose, was baptized, and
identified himself with Christ and the believers in Christ.

Moreover, most Bible students agree that the conversion of Paul at
least had its beginnings at the stoning of Stephen, when "the witnesses
laid down their clothes at a young man's feet, whose name was Saul"
(Acts 7:58). The chain of events was probably put in motion in
preparation for the culmination of the conversion experience.

On the other hand, it does not seem as if there were ever a smooth,
even development of life, with never a jolt to upset its onward move.
The optimism of the early twentieth century, with the hope of the
peaceful evolution of a new and equitable society, was shattered by
the crisis and wars which followed. As Fritz Kunkell says, "Human
life, then, appears as an unending chain of crises" (**48**, p. 150). The
crisis may not be catastrophic but life's contradictions are faced, the
alternatives evaluated, and the decision made.

A happy compromise is that the two ideas of dramatic suddenness
and gradual evolution may be two sides of the same coin. In some
experiences of religious awakening, the element of suddenness is most
apparent, while in others that of gradualness is uppermost. One of the
most frequently used categorizations of conversion experiences sees
three types: (1) the *definite crisis*, involving a crisis experience; (2)
the *emotional stimulus*, wherein the upheaval is slight or absent but

the individual is able to designate some event which served to spark the experience; and (3) the *gradual awakening,* which involves no specific event.

Ferm's investigation showed that 55 per cent of his respondents had a definite crisis experience. The Southwestern study revealed that 44 per cent of the subjects described their conversion as a gradual, growing experience, which is the more remarkable because of the conservative theological atmosphere in which they were reared, with the consequent expectation of dramatic conversion experiences. Ferm has an explanation for all this. He claims that children often have difficulty in evaluating a religious experience and cannot report the experience for what it actually was. However, honest evaluation indicates a drop in the number of dramatic conversions and, as far as Southern Baptists are concerned, it is probably the outcome of the heavy emphasis on religious education.

Summary

Conversion, the earliest subject of study in the psychology of religion, is still a fertile field for investigation. A definition of terms presents difficulty, and any acceptable effort must include the idea of turning, the possibility of suddenness without the exclusion of gradualness, and the probability of emotional reactions.

Theories of conversion include Sargant's radical enunciation of a physiological basis and the widely accepted psychological formulations. Each of these theorizings helps in understanding conversion as a possible experience in all normal personalities. Turning specifically to religious conversion, both the processes and the elements of the experience provide guidelines for the educational activities of the church. Psychological investigation, far from abolishing conversion (in at least some aspects), confirms the warning of the one who said, "Except ye be converted . . . ye shall not enter into the kingdom of heaven" (Matt. 18:3).

15

Christian Vocation

In our discussion of the definitions of religion, the aspects of inwardness, individuality, and solitariness were stressed. Once man has had his inward and solitary experience, there should come a sense of mission which motivates him to live out his experience and declare it to his fellowmen. There is generally a relationship between the two, so that the intensity of the experience determines the enthusiasm with which the subject becomes involved in his faith. In terms of our underlying thesis it could be said that he not only finds his own soul but feels a compulsion to nurture it, not only in contemplation, but also in service.

Johnson (100, p. 253) claims that a sense of vocation comes from a right relationship with God.

The sense of vocation arises when a person's basic relationships give a new depth of meaning to his occupation. An occupation is any activity to keep one busy or occupied in space and time, as the root meaning of the word indicates. A vocation, however, is literally a calling which signifies address and response. To have a vocation is to feel called to do a work and to accept that call.

But how can an individual know just what his calling is? The complexity of the problem and the issues involved will emerge as the chapter progresses. Attention will be focused on the problems of the call to the ministry, the mixture of the motives in responding to the call, the layman's calling, and personality characteristics of successful vocational religious workers.

There are many psychological elements which go into the making up of the "call of God." Even if we limit the discussion to the call to the ministry, it is still complex and confusing. Among Southern Baptists there are two entirely contradictory concepts about the call to the mission field (**43**, I, 224). At either end of the continuum there stands an extremist group. One of these maintains that all are expected to go to the foreign mission field unless there is some hindrance to prevent them from going. The other idea is that one must not go unless he feels a strong individual compulsion to do so. To have these two contradictory ideas successively presented can be quite a traumatic experience for the young mission volunteer.

Some have simplified the idea of the call. One of these is John Oliver Nelson who says, "To be called of God is to be confronted with a life situation where God is needed, and to realize that you must help meet the need." In this definition there are three parts: (1) The call is from God. (2) The call is to meet a definite need. (3) It results from a feeling of compulsion or conviction on the part of the person who is being called.

Niebuhr, Williams, and Gustafson (**139**, p. 64) point out the complexity of the call to the ministry by showing that it really involves a series of calls:

(1) the *call to be a Christian,* which is variously described as the call to discipleship of Jesus Christ. . . ; (2) *the secret call,* namely, that inner persuasion or experience whereby a person feels himself directly summoned or invited by God to take up the work of the ministry; (3) *the providential call* . . . which comes through the equipment of a person with the talents necessary for the exercise of the office and through the divine guidance of his life by all its circumstances; (4) the *ecclesiastical call,* that is, the summons and invitation extended to a man by some community or institution of the Church to engage in the work of the ministry.

The secret, providential, and ecclesiastical calls present some of the most puzzling aspects of the whole process and necessitate further consideration.

The Ecclesiastical Call

The ecclesiastical framework of a given church often provides the setting for the call. However, ecclesiastical structures vary and provide for differing types of experiences. Four examples from divergent groups will illustrate the complexity of the situation, even if they do not elucidate the problem.

A call to preach among the Anabaptists was sudden, dramatic, and undertaken with alacrity:

A peasant, Hans Ber of Alten-Erlangen, rose from his bed one night and began to put on his clothes. "Whither goest thou?" asked his wife. "I know not, God knoweth," was his answer. She entreated him to stay, with the words: "What evil have I done thee? Stay here and help me nourish my little children." "Dear wife," he replied, "harry me not with the things of time. God bless thee. I will from hence, that I may learn the will of the Lord" (17, p. 34).

The call was clear and apart from any ecclesiastical apparatus. Though not often as drastic as this illustration, somewhat similar experiences are still heard of to this day.

In the spiritual pilgrimage of Martin Luther, his call to the pastoral office came through the instrumentality of his superior:

Staupitz . . . cast about for some effective cure for this tormented spirit. . . . Plainly argument and consolation did no good. Some other way must be found. One day under the pear tree in the garden of the Augustinian cloister—Luther always treasured that pear tree—the vicar informed Brother Martin that he should study for his doctor's degree, that he should undertake preaching and assume the chair of Bible at the university. Luther gasped, stammered out fifteen reasons why he could do nothing of the sort. The sum of it all was that so much work would kill him. "Quite all right," said Staupitz. "God has plenty of work for clever men to do in heaven."

Luther might well gasp, for the proposal of Staupitz was audacious if not reckless. A young man on the verge of a nervous collapse over religious problems was to be commissioned as a teacher, preacher, and counselor to sick souls. Staupitz was practically saying, "Physician, cure thyself by curing others." He must have felt that Luther was fundamentally sound and that if he was entrusted with the cure of souls he would be disposed for their sakes to turn from threats to promises, and some of the grace which he would claim for them might fall also to himself (13, p. 45).

As Hudson (88, p. 37) shows, it was not the call of a congregation but a church. Staupitz was Luther's ecclesiastical superior.

In the Reformed church, John Calvin's call to the ministry was through a human voice. Calvin was traveling from Italy to Strassburg, where he intended to settle down and spend his life in quiet study. An incident in his journey changed his life's course. He tells of the experience:

As the most direct route to Strassburg, to which I then intended to retire, was blocked by the wars, I had resolved to pass quickly by Geneva, without staying longer than a single night in that city. . . . A person

(Louis du Tillet) who has now returned to the Papists discovered me and made me known to others. Upon this Farel, who burned with an extraordinary zeal to advance the Gospel, immediately strained every nerve to detain me. After having learnt that my heart was set upon devoting myself to private studies, for which I wished to keep myself free from other pursuits, and finding that he gained nothing by entreaties, he proceeded to utter an imprecation, that God would curse my retirement and the tranquility of the studies which I sought, if I should withdraw and refuse assistance when the necessity was so urgent. By this imprecation I was so stricken with terror that I desisted from the journey which I had undertaken (**120**, II, 101-2).

Almost as famous in the same stream of tradition was John Knox, who went through a similar experience. The castle preacher, John Rough, singling him out in the congregation, charged him, "In the name of God and of his son Jesus Christ, and in the name of these that presently call you by my mouth, I charge you, that ye refuse not this holy vocation. (**185**a, pp. 189-90).

The emphasis of Baptists on the congregation and the autonomy of the local church does not prevent a similar experience, with the church being the mouthpiece. George W. Truett tells of his experience:

From the time of my conversion on, everywhere I went, godly men and women would pluck me aside and say, "Oughtn't you to be preaching?"

I was ambitious to be a lawyer from my earliest recollection; and therefore had that big battle to fight. All my plans pointed toward the calling of the lawyer. And with me, it was a great battle to yield that. I was perfectly willing to talk for Christ, but not from a pulpit.

I went West—to Texas, where father and the rest of the family had gone. Very soon I was chosen to be superintendent of the Baptist Sunday School at Whitewright, Texas. I often conducted services, making it a point always to stand out in front of the pulpit, feeling myself utterly unfit to be in a pulpit. I was still ambitious to be a lawyer.

We had there, in the village church, the old Saturday meeting. On a certain Saturday in 1890, the attendance was enormous. I thought within myself, "This is singular: here is a house full of people on Saturday."

And when they got through with all the rest of the church conference, at the close of the minister's sermon, the oldest deacon, then quite frail in health, rose up and began to talk deliberately and very solemnly. I thought, "What a remarkable talk he is making—perhaps he thinks it is his last talk." Presently, I became disturbed by it. He said to the church in conference:

"There is such a thing as a church duty when the whole church must act. There is such a thing as an individual duty, when the individual, detached from every other individual, must face duty for himself; but it is my deep conviction, as it is yours—for we have talked much one with another—that this church has a church duty to perform, and that we have waited late and long to get about it. I move, therefore, that this church call a presbytery to ordain Brother George W. Truett to the full work of the gospel ministry."

It was promptly seconded and I immediately got the floor and implored them to desist. I said, "You have me appalled; you simply have me appalled!" And then one after another talked, and the tears ran down their cheeks and they said, "Brother George, we have a deep conviction that you ought to be preaching." Again I appealed to them and said, "Wait six months . . .!" And they said, "We won't wait six hours. We are called to do this thing now and we are going ahead with it. We are moved by a deep conviction that it is the will of God. We dare not wait. We must follow our convictions."

There I was, against a whole church, against a church profoundly moved. There was not a dry eye in the house—one of the supremely solemn hours in a church's life. I was thrown into the stream, and just had to swim (95, pp. 47-49).

Truett himself throughout his life continually emphasized the individual's personal call, but the role of other people in it was of great significance in his own experience.

If a vocation involves a call having address and response, the process of address is variously conceived by groups of Christians in differing traditions. To hear the authentic voice amid the babble of sounds of groups, ecclesiastical personalities, and inward drives and urges will require sincerity, simplicity of faith, and dedication of purpose.

Influential Personalities in the Call

Studies in the experiences of people who feel that God has called them into the ministry reveal that in this area, as in any other in life, great decisions are influenced by other people. In each of four studies by Southard, (163), Crawley, (42), Felton, (61), and Draughon (52), there is essential agreement upon the ranking of these influences.

The minister is the most important single person. Felton discovered that 34 per cent of his subjects had been influenced by their pastor. Of Southard's respondents, 27 per cent mentioned talking with their pastor before a definite decision to enter a church-related vocation.

Draughon's study showed that 54.7 per cent had received help from the pastor at the time of their call.

Similarly, as was the case in the conversion study reported in chapter 14, mother was the next highly rated person in the experience of the call. Felton discovered that 17.4 per cent of his respondents had indicated that mother was influential. Southard's study showed 20 per cent of those answering the call as indicating that mother was important in helping with the decision.

Father limped in as a poor third in the responses. Of Felton's respondents, 11.2 per cent listed father as influential. Twelve per cent of those surveyed by Southard listed father. Once again, this might have been anticipated, as father was also third in terms of influence in the conversion study.

The role of the Sunday school teacher presents a puzzling aspect of the process. In the Felton study 5 per cent indicated that the Sunday school teacher was influential. Of Southard's respondents, 3 per cent, and in Draughon's study, 3.9 per cent referred to the Sunday school teacher's influence in the call.

Even though the call is secret, there is generally some human instrumentality involved. Churches beset with the problem of declining numbers of candidates for the ministry might well give consideration to the personalities involved and how they can be better prepared for their role in these important decisions. Fathers certainly need to be considered, and the church might have to ask itself just what it is doing about preparing the men of its ranks for their responsibility as fathers. It is certain that the Sunday school situation demands some attention. In the previously mentioned conversion experience the Sunday school teacher did not exercise very much influence. It may be that we will have to spend more time in majoring on the quality of the work of our Sunday school teachers.

Motivations in the Response to the Call

Not only is address in the call difficult to comprehend, but response is often more than Isaiah's simple, "Here am I, send me." The general procedure now is for the newly called recruit to seek training in a seminary. It might be anticipated that within the seminary's walls there would be found outstanding Christians, with peace of mind and a clear sense of calling as they prepare themselves for a position of leadership. But if each individual were questioned, an amazing variety of experiences would be discovered. As with other areas of life, there is a variety of motives involved.

In the book, *The Advancement of Theological Education,* Niebuhr, Williams, and Gustafson (**138**) report the results of an intensive visitation of seminary campuses, during which a close study was made of personality patterns of students preparing for the ministry. While reporting these personality types, they warn us that the patterns are not static, and theological students, of all people, are in a constant state of change. However, after acknowledging the risks involved, the investigators formulated ten types of personality patterns to which Robert C. Leslie (**117**, p. 118) has given designations.

1. *Coerced.*—There is the student who is in the seminary because someone else thought he would make a good minister. Maybe a minister, a fond parent, or people within his own church. This individual is often worried and harried by a lack of certainty about his calling.

2. *Disturbed.*—A man may be suffering from deep wounds within himself. He thus seeks a theological education to heal his own disturbed mind and spirit. Some people have feelings of guilt and conceive that this guilt can only be expiated by giving a life of service to God. The obvious difficulty is that though there may be therapy within the seminary fellowship, the theological seminary is not in existence for the primary purpose of supplying psychotherapy. It should be noted that Niebuhr, Williams, and Gustafson maintain that there is no evidence that seminaries have more maladjusted personalities among their student bodies than do other educational institutions.

3. *Manipulating.*—The student who functions well in interpersonal relationships may be drawn toward the ministry. He may have been a successful salesman or have worked in some other kindred occupation. He comes to feel that greater prestige would accrue to him from the position of church leadership. If he is just a careerist, the manipulation of people may have a particular attraction for him. His church life may, or may not, give him the opportunity for exercising his manipulative power.

4. *Resistant.*—A person may have prematurely tasted the fruits of success within church life as a boy evangelist, dynamic youth leader, or a student movement executive. He comes to the seminary because everybody insists that a seminary training is necessary. He is not sure that he ought to be there but comes simply to fulfil the

pro forma requirements of ministerial status. He often finds it difficult to fit into seminary life, having a sneaking suspicion that he knows much more than the theoretically minded professor. The future pathway is likely to be rocky if he does not learn to make adjustments that go with the hard and realistic grind of the ministry.

5. *Sheltered.*—The man who decided for the ministry at an early age and who enjoyed the protection of the preministerial group in college will sometimes find his way to the seminary. He may have the right vocabulary but has feelings of uncertainty about launching into the rigorous experience of church life. Niebuhr and his associates quote a historian as saying, "We need ministers who have a hardheaded realism." This type of student may feel somewhat disappointed in life at the seminary. The future for him is far from bright.

6. *Zealous.*—A zealous spirit characterizes the student who has found the message of the gospel and its saving power. Within him there burns an intense desire to share the good news with the world. The student very often discovers in the course of his studies that he has oversimplified the issues of life and the message of the gospel. He has to come to the situation where he becomes aware of the totality of the gospel message. He will constantly face the temptation to be critical of his fellow students, especially those who are further along the way but seem to lack the zeal and enthusiasm which he knows to characterize his own life. He is always open to the temptation of embracing theological positions uncritically and may pass through several swings in his theological orientation.

7. *Skeptical.*—Religion and theology present themselves as objective intellectual problems to a searching mind, and for a student the theological school seems to be the place to pursue these problems. These sort of people very often become the "theological eggheads," who despise all practical concepts and live only in terms of "bull sessions." In these sessions they have an answer for every argument, but when they become a part of the church life they often find that people are not interested in their intellectual concepts. The down-to-earth life of the ministry may be something of a bitter disappointment for them.

8. *Humanitarian.*—An experience of a tragically disorganized society often leads a student to study for the ministry. He sees the church as the institution out of which will flow the healing processes for the social evils of our time. The student is often disappointed by

the indifference of the church to social problems and in his disillusionment leaves the ministry to study one of the areas of the social sciences.

9. *Searching.*—Frequently found in the present generation is the man seeking for a faith adequate to bring order into the intellectual and moral confusions that have characterized his previous personal and academic experience. He is frequently uncertain about the workings within the church, although he has a certain loyalty to it.

10. *Maturing.*—Fortunately, there is the rare student of mature faith and judgment, who lives in the knowledge that it is God who saves and justifies. The student is seeking to become an adequate servant for his Lord and will faithfully represent him in his work in the ministry.

Behavior of any type has multiple causations. This is particularly true of a decision to respond to a call of the ministry. In his investigation among theological students, Southard said that most of them had taken from one to three years to make their decision to enter a church vocation. He further found that with the majority of them this decision was made only after much inner struggle. Niebuhr, Williams, and Gustafson's categorizations give ample evidence of this turmoil.

Problems of the Ministry

The problems faced in the theological school pale into insignificance as the minister takes up his work within the church. An article in a national magazine, "Why I Quit the Ministry," revealed the shock and disillusionment the young minister faces with the down-to-earth problems of church life. Stolz (**169**, p. 231) has characterized "the vocational neuroses of the ministry." He concludes:

1. *Egocentricity through pampering.*—As soon as a young man in the church announces that he feels called to the ministry, there is a good possibility that he will find himself set apart and noted as a person who is particularly pious. Later, he may get special tuition rates at college, free education at the seminary, and the adulations of kind ladies in his congregation. The result may be that he will become dependent, always expecting people to help him and becoming very sensitive to any form of criticism.

2. *The number and character of his masters.*—The church is a voluntary organization and frequently has highly individualistic mem-

bers within its ranks. There are often groups within the church who represent particular points of view and feel that the minister should fit in with their group's plans. It has been said, "The democratic leader is always on trial," and the minister discovers the reality of that statement as he tries to weld the diverse personalities into a cohesive group.

3. *Competition with members of his own profession.*—There is a strong spirit of competition in church life. Churches are measured against each other in size of plant, money in the budget, number of baptisms, members in Sunday school, and many other ways. The young minister is often frustrated with this competition. He may feel that his church is older or younger, in a poorer situation, or has had a more checkered history than another more successful church. Consequently, he builds a strong resentment to the denominational structure which encourages such competition. But he is often dependent upon these leaders for recommendation to other churches, and so he has to repress his hostility.

4. *Temptation to indolence.*—The minister does not have a clock to punch. Very often, he is given a membership in a country club or some other social group. If he doesn't learn to discipline himself, he may get to the place where he just keeps up an impressive front and does very little real work.

5. *Economic stringency.*—The minister has worked at getting through college, then attended a seminary. When, at last, he gets his position in a church he may receive a very ordinary salary. He often has unseen benefits, but these are not obvious in his salary check. He is always tempted to compare himself with the doctor or the lawyer who did about the same amount of preparatory work but is so much better paid.

6. *Exposure of self and family to social scrutiny and criticism.*— The minister and his family live in a glass house, and their affairs are open to the congregation's inspection. In some church situations they know how much salary he earns and many details of his life which are normally man's own personal secret. His children are expected to live by higher standards than most of the other children in the congregation. The situation is liable to breed a smoldering resentment about the unfairness of the life of the ministry.

As in any other types of work, there are two sides to the work of the ministry. In its public aspect it provides attention and adulation and sincere affection from many people. On the other hand, there are few callings in which an individual has to put up with so much pettiness and littleness of spirit. Jeremiah, the weeping prophet, is frequently the personification of the inner anxiety with which the pastor must cope.

The Successful Church Leader

What type of person does best in this difficult situation? In an effort to discover the personality characteristics of the successful church leader, a study was made in the School of Religious Education at Southwestern Seminary (51).

A group of 323 students participated in a program of field work which involved working in church situations under supervision. From this number were chosen the thirty best students who were classified as "superior" and the twenty whose field work was of low quality and who were classified as "poor." Three tests—the Minnesota Multiphasic Personality Inventory, the Bernreuter Personality Inventory, and the Strong Vocational Interest Blank—were taken by each of the students. An item analysis was made to discover the way in which each of the 1,091 questions had been aswered. By statistical analysis, items answered in a significantly different manner by the two groups were ascertained. Examination and categorization of the items revealed the following personality traits.

Suggestibility.—The poor students were apparently more suggestible than the superior. Working with Roman Catholic seminarians, William C. Bier utilized the M.M.P.I, and following a simple tallying procedure he found that the poorly adjusted students had a proneness to consistently mark items "true." Bier suggested that this was generally a tendency with less well-adjusted personalities. In the Southwestern study the same trend was noted. The students who did poorly in their church work more frequently checked items as true, while the superior students appeared to discriminate more carefully, checking a larger number of items as false. Apparently the religious "yes man" is not a success, and it could be that he lacks the definiteness needed for adequate leadership.

Self-confidence.—Lack of self-confidence characterized the poor group. Their responses showed a strong emotional overtone. They felt disappointments keenly, harbored a sense of being misunderstood, and were much worried about moods. Their attitude of uncertainty was shown by the stated necessity of having to rewrite letters before mailing them. On the other hand, the superior group manifested a feeling of self-confidence. They checked that they liked being the first to wear new fashions, enjoyed taking responsibility, delighted in developing plans, felt sure of themselves, and took pleasure in starting activities within the group. The factors all had to do with ego-strength, apparently as important in leadership in church work as in other areas of life.

Sociability.—Sociability was another characteristic of the superior group of students. Their preference ran to parties and socials, interviewing prospects and selling, living in the city and enjoying amusements where there was a crowd of people. They were "joiners," stating that they belonged to a number of societies and felt drawn toward politics. On the M.M.P.I. they had a high "M-F," or Masculine-Feminity score. While this scale has been seen to indicate homosexuality, it has been more recently considered to be a measure of the willingness to mix with people of the opposite sex.

By way of contrast, the poor group showed a tendency to withdraw from group activities. At parties they liked to sit by themselves or just be with one person; they avoided crowds wherever possible, often had feelings of loneliness, had few intimate friends, and their feelings were easily hurt. It is almost axiomatic that a leader who influences and leads a group must have a love of people, and a willingness to be with them.

Emotionalized attitudes.—In their emotionalized attitudes another difference showed up. The poor students indicated a proneness to excessive emotionality. Their responses denoted anxiety about money and business, swings between pleasant and unpleasant moods, and a frequently experienced state of excitement. Their feelings were easily hurt, and they worried much about their mistakes. In contrast, the superior group revealed a more rational and objective attitude in their relationships. They were not usually self-conscious, and they were able to meet emergencies quickly. They enjoyed reading editorials in the newspaper and showed their objectivity by indicating that they were reticent in confidential and semiconfidential affairs.

Creativity.—The attitudes of the members of the two groups toward their work were different. The superior group looked for opportunities for promotion, liked freedom in working out their own method of doing a job, enjoyed teaching others, and were mainly concerned about work which was interesting, even though the remuneration was not high. With the poor group the emphasis was upon tangible returns and more closely delineated tasks, work involving few details, which was steady and permanent, with regular hours. The joy of work is vital in vocation. Work should bring its own reward even apart from salary.

Compulsiveness.—The personality trait which stood out clearest in the responses of the two groups was a bent toward pathological compulsiveness, seen in the poor group. Compulsiveness has been defined as "an irresistible inner force compelling the performance of an act without, or even against, the will of the individual performing the act." The poor group told of periodic urges to do something harmful and shocking, and how that on occasions they felt like picking a fist fight with someone. They also stated that an unimportant thought sometimes went through their minds for days. There was no indication of this same pathological compulsiveness among the superior group.

A certain amount of compulsiveness can be an asset to a person involved in administration, but strangely enough this compulsiveness of the poor group did not carry over into the detail of their work. The poor group told of preferring work with few details. On the other hand, the superior students showed a readiness to plan and to keep up with their work. They evinced a liking for studying and reading about things at which they worked, preferred to be always on time with their work, and enjoyed writing reports. They said that they planned their work in detail and looked for opportunities to use their knowledge and experience. Any sort of administrative work calls for detail. Capacity to plan and look ahead has already been seen as a mark of maturity, and here the carry-over of personality maturity is clearly seen.

Family background.—Family background becomes obvious in the responses of the superior and poor groups. The tests did not contain many questions about family backgrounds, but the superior group indicated that in their homes they at least had the ordinary necessities of life. By way of contrast the poor group felt that they were deprived and said that they were not sure that they had the ordinary necessities of life in their homes. There were some things which their families had done that frightened them.

Rigidity of parental attitudes was shown by the statement that their mother or father made them obey when they thought it was unreasonable. This very rigidity may have had something to do with the fact that as children they had engaged in petty thievery. Obviously, the family background of the poor students left much to be desired, and it seems as if there was a carry-over into their positions of church leadership.

A picture of the superior church leader begins to emerge. He comes from a family background which provides the necessities of life and has a reasonable amount of flexibility. He has strongly held convictions, is confident about his ability, and enjoys being a leader. He is a good mixer, delighting in other people's company, but has a certain detachment and objectivity. He likes to be challenged, enjoys work for its own reward, and seeks freedom of action. Along with this there is a certain compulsion which makes him pay attention to detail and anticipate the future.

The Layman's Calling

If the religious vocation or call is viewed as the peculiar property of the professional, one of the most dynamic aspects of Reformation teaching is lost. Bainton's life of Luther shows that before Luther's day the monks in the monastery had a vocation. Superior Christians were invited to observe the counsels of perfection, while ordinary Christians were simply to fulfil the commandments of Christianity. Luther rejected this notion of vocation as Bainton (13, p. 156) shows: "There is no special religious vocation," declared Luther, "since the call of God comes to each man at the common tasks."

Our expression "vocational guidance" comes directly from Luther who claimed that God also works at a common vocation. God works as a tailor who makes the deer a coat that will last a thousand years. God is the butler who sets forth a feast for the sparrows and spends more on them annually than the total revenues of the king of France. Luther emphasized that God has no hands but our hands, and no feet but our feet. He defended the lowly tasks: "The lowlier the task the better. The milkmaid and the carter of manure are doing a work more pleasing to God than the psalm singing of a Carthusian"(13, p. 181).

Max Weber's essay, *The Protestant Ethic and the Spirit of Capitalism*, drew many of its conclusions from the Reformation concept of vocation or calling, and resultant attitude towards work. The "spirit of capitalism" was a spirit of dedication and commitment to work. Although capitalism is self-perpetuating, there was an original impulse which set it in motion. Two main elements stood out in the original motivations. One was the Reformation emphasis that work was not a penalty for sin but a worthwhile activity in its own right. The second element was the puritanical conviction that personal indulgence was to be avoided. Each wave of revival brought new motivations to work at self-denial. Wesley stated it, "Religion must necessarily produce both industry and frugality." The natural result of these two factors was the accumulation of wealth, thus the spirit of capitalism was the unintended by-product of the Reformation.

The frontier movement played a large part in the development of religion in America. With the spread of the frontier, as the population moved across the new country, a distinctive type of religion evolved. Frontier religion emphasized the individual who was seen as sovereign. Herberg (**82,** p. 160) notes, "Even more repugnant than theology, liturgy, and institutional order was any separation between clergy and laity, particularly such as is involved in an educated and specially placed ministry." Thus the frontier movement with its elevation of the layman left its impress upon Baptist, Methodist, Campbellite, and similar groups.

Laymen have played a large part in the growth of religious education. Summing up the difference between modern religious education and that of ancient and medieval schools, Benson (**18,** p. 119) suggests three differentiating principles: (1) It is a laymen's movement. (2) It is a Sunday enterprise. (3) It is organized. The latter two grow obviously out of the work of the layman. Sunday was the only time he had for his work, and he used the organizing skills acquired in the business world as a part of his religious expression. Laymen have shown themselves particularly adept at organization. Not only the local Sunday school organizations but the great national Sunday school conventions, to a large measure, were dependent upon laymen. Strangely enough, there was opposition from the ecclesiastical authorities of that day, and many ministers thundered out their denunciation of the developing religious education movement.

Southern Baptists have probably utilized religious education more than any other denomination, and with the development of this religious education program has come their period of greatest growth. The confusion of the roles of layman and minister has been dramatized in the case of many Southern Baptist professional religious education workers. They have been trained in the seminary and are giving all their life to professional religious work as leaders in the field of religious education; yet they are frequently called laymen.

Johnson points out that in secular work a man who serves his fellows may be set apart from them so that they are "laymen" in contrast to him. A physician comes to church to worship; he is a layman with reference to the minister. But when the minister is a patient in the hospital, he is a layman with reference to the physician. Johnson (**100**, p. 257) comments: "There is a juxtaposition among the professions implying that they are all engaged in a common service to mankind." This would prompt the question as to whether the minister who sits in a Southern Baptist officers and teachers' meeting is a layman in relation to the minister of education, who in this setting is functioning in a position of leadership.

A church was noted for the exceptionally fine way in which the ushering was done. The obvious organization, the precision of movement, and anticipation of every aspect of the church service from beginning to end revealed some organizing genius behind it all. Later the chairman of the ushers was commended, and he replied, "I feel that God has called me to be an usher in the church." The thought was somewhat overwhelming at first, but why not?

The layman does have a vocation or calling. This sense of vocation has affected the economics of life as well as its spiritual values. Laymen conscious of their vocation have made notable contributions to the life of the church, and often in the face of ecclesiastical opposition.

A vocational call is at the same time one of the most ennobling and frustrating aspects of Christian experience. To many work is an irksome necessity to be faced with fortitude and endured. But the ancient writer had enunciated a view of work which brought God into the workaday world: "Hate not laborious work, neither husbandry, which the most High hath ordained (Eccles. 7:15, *Apocrypha*). Industry was commended: "Go to the ant, thou sluggard; consider her ways, and be wise" (Prov. 6:6).

In the New Testament, Jesus called people to discipleship and service, and in the Acts of the Apostles missionaries were separated for a special ministry. As simple as it sounds in New Testament terms, a modern day servant of God has great difficulty in discerning the "call." One of the most puzzling aspects is to know from whence comes the voice that bids him, "Go work today in my vineyard." Without, within, or both? Does it come from heaven, the lips of another person, or an ecclesiastical body? And what of motives? Can an unworthy motive be transformed into a positive and ennobling drive? All of these and a thousand other questions tantalize and frustrate the man who would serve God with his whole life.

Despite Paul's certainty of his calling to missionary service, there were times when he turned to tentmaking to earn his daily bread. A vocation is a "calling," and whatever a Christian does, whether it be as professional leader in a church or worker in industry, it should be done unto the Lord.

> Jesus calls us o'er the tumult
> Of our life's wild, restless sea;
> Day by day His sweet voice soundeth,
> Saying, "Christian, follow me!"

Epilogue

At the beginning we started out as eyewitnesses to one of the great searches of history. It was, as we noted, "psychology in search of a soul." Many areas were explored, and we often wandered off into bypaths. It has frequently been a frustrating experience. But there were rewarding interludes along the way. Psychology and religion are not really as widely separated as is sometimes imagined, and there were moments of rapprochement.

However, psychology and religion do not have to smother each other. There was a time when a powerful church could make a scientist retract his words and swallow over his convictions. The sincerely religious person would never want to see this situation again. Psychology as the youngest of the sciences must be free to investigate, hammer at some of our cherished ideas, and theorize boldly.

Standing off and viewing it in perspective, it seems that religion has become very hospitable to the insights of psychology. The introduction of personality tests for candidates for the ministry, the research into the motivations of decisions for the ministry, the larger number of courses in counseling being offered in the seminaries, and the rapid development of clinical pastoral training have all meant that the church leader of tomorrow will at least be familiar with the psychological formulations concerning personality development.

But the scientific spirit of psychology must also put its own house in order. Having overthrown the rigid censorship of religion, it must not now itself institute a new inquisition, feeling that it has a monopoly on truth and trying to bind religion hand and foot. Religion has a special contribution to make in the areas of values, motivations, and the higher aspirations of the individual. If psychology will pay more attention to religion, seeking to *get* as well as to *give*, it might well be that psychology will find its soul.

Bibliography

1. ABRAHAMSEN, DAVID. *Who Are the Guilty?* New York: Grove Press, 1958.
2. ALDRIDGE, ALFRED OWEN. *Man of Reason: The Life of Thomas Paine,* New York: J. B. Lippincott Co., 1959.
3. ALLPORT, GORDON W. "Attitudes," *Handbook of Social Psychology,* ed. C. A. MURCHISON. Worcester, Mass.: Clark University Press, 1935.
4. ———. *Becoming.* New Haven: Yale University Press, 1955.
5. ———. *The Individual and His Religion.* New York: The Macmillan Co., 1950.
6. ———. *The Nature of Prejudice.* Cambridge: Addison-Wesley Publishing Co., 1954.
7. ———. *Pattern and Growth in Personality.* New York: Holt, Rinehart & Winston, 1961.
8. ———. *Personality and Social Encounter.* Boston: Beacon Press, 1960.
9. ———. *Personality: A Psychological Interpretation.* New York: Henry Holt & Co., 1937.
10. ———. *The Use of Personal Documents in Psychological Science.* New York: Social Science Research Council, 1942.
11. ALMOND, GABRIEL A. *The Appeals of Communism.* Princeton: Princeton University Press, 1954.
12. ARMSTRONG, FRANK ALEXANDER. *Idea-Tracking.* New York: Criterion Books, 1960.
13. BAINTON, ROLAND H. *Here I Stand.* New York: The New American Library of World Literature, 1950.
14. BAKHAREV, A. N. *I. V. Michurin.* Moscow: Foreign Languages Publishing House, 1954.
15. BANKS, LOUIS A. "The Preaching Needed in Revivals," *How*

to Promote and Conduct a Successful Revival, ed. R. A. TORREY. New York: Fleming H. Revell Co., 1901.

16. BAUGHMAN, E. EARL, and WELSH, GEORGE SCHLAGER. *Personality: A Behavioral Science.* Englewood Cliffs, N. J.: Prentice-Hall, 1962.

17. BAX, E. B. *The Rise and Fall of the Anabaptists.* New York: The Macmillan Co., 1903.

18. BENSON, CLARENCE H. *History of Christian Education.* Chicago: Moody Press, 1943.

19. BLANTON, SMILEY. *Love or Perish.* New York: Simon & Schuster, 1956.

20. BOGGS, WADE H., JR. *Faith Healing and the Christian Faith.* Richmond: John Knox Press, 1956.

21. BOISEN, ANTON T. *The Exploration of the Inner World.* New York: Willett, Clark & Co., 1936.

22. ————. *Religion in Crisis and Custom.* New York: Harper & Bros., 1955.

23. BONNER, HUBERT. *Psychology of Personality.* New York: The Ronald Press, 1961.

24. BOSWELL, JAMES. *Life of Dr. Johnson.* 2 vols. New York: E. P. Dutton & Co., n.d.

25. BOWERS, MARGARETTA K., and GLASNER, SAMUEL. "Auto-Hypnotic Aspects of the Jewish Cabbalistic Concept of Kavanah," *International Journal of Clinical and Experimental Hypnosis,* (January, 1958).

26. BRADEN, CHARLES S. "Study of Spiritual Healing in the Churches," *Pastoral Psychology,* V (May, 1954).

27. BRYAN, WILLIAM J., JR. *Religious Aspects of Hypnosis.* Springfield, Ill.: Charles C. Thomas, 1962.

28. BURTON, ARTHUR, and HARRIS, ROBERT E. (eds.). *Case Histories in Clinical and Abnormal Psychology.* New York: Harper & Bros., 1947.

29. CARRINGTON, W. L. *Psychology, Religion, and Human Need.* Great Neck, N.Y.: Channel Press, 1957.

30. CHAMBERS, WHITTAKER. *Witness.* New York: Random House, 1952.

31. CHAPLIN, J. P. *The Unconscious.* New York: Ballantine Books, 1960.

32. CLARK, ELMER T. *The Psychology of Religious Awakening.* New York: The Macmillan Co., 1929.

33. CLARK, ROBERT A. *Six Talks on Jung's Psychology.* Pittsburg: The Boxwood Press, 1953.
34. CLARK, WALTER HOUSTON. *The Psychology of Religion.* New York: The Macmillan Co., 1958.
35. CLARKE, ARTHUR C. "The Gulf Stream," *Holiday,* Vol. 29 (June, 1961).
36. COE, GEORGE ALBERT. *The Psychology of Religion.* Chicago: The University of Chicago Press, 1916.
37. COLEMAN, JAMES C. *Abnormal Psychology and Modern Life.* Chicago: Scott, Foresman & Co., 1956.
38. ————. *Personality Dynamics and Effective Behavior.* Chicago: Scott, Foresman & Co., 1960.
39. COUÉ, EMILE, AND BROOKS, C. HARRY. *Better and Better Every Day.* London: Unwin Books, n.d.
40. COVILLE, WALTER J., COSTELLO, TIMOTHY W., and ROUKE, FABIAN L. *Abnormal Psychology.* New York: Barnes & Noble, 1960.
41. CRAGO, T. HOWARD. *The Story of F. W. Boreham.* London: Marshall, Morgan & Scott, 1961.
42. CRAWLEY, J. WINSTON. "The Call to Foreign Missions Among Southern Baptists, 1845-1945." Unpublished Th.D. thesis, Southern Baptist Theological Seminary, 1947.
43. ————. "Call to Foreign Mission Service," *Encyclopedia of Southern Baptists.* 2 vols. Nashville: Broadman Press, 1958.
44. CUDDON, ERIC. *Hypnosis, Its Meaning and Practice.* London: C. Bell & Sons, 1957.
45. DEKOSTER, LESTER. *Communism and Christian Faith.* Grand Rapids: William B. Eerdman's Publishing Co., 1962.
46. DEUTSCHER, ISAAC. *Stalin: A Political Biography.* New York: Random House, 1960.
47. DEWAR, LINDSAY. *The Holy Spirit and Modern Thought.* New York: Harper & Bros., 1960.
48. DONIGER, SIMON (ed.). *Religion and Human Behavior.* New York: Association Press, 1954.
49. DRAKEFORD, JOHN W. *Counseling for Church Leaders.* Nashville: Broadman Press, 1961.
50. ————. "Intelligence As a Factor in Religious Awakening." Unpublished Th.M. thesis, Brite Divinity School, Texas Christian University, 1959.

51. _____. "Selected Personality Scales Related to Success in Religious Education." Unpublished M.A. thesis, Texas Christian University, 1958.
52. DRAUGHON, WALTER D., JR. "Psychological Aspects of the Call to Church-Related Vocations." Unpublished D.R.E. thesis, Southwestern Baptist Theological Seminary, 1960.
53. DUVALL, EVELYN MILLIS, and HILL, REUBEN L. *When You Marry.* rev. ed. New York: Association Press, 1962.
54. DUVALL, SYLVANUS M. *Men, Women and Morals.* New York: Association Press, 1952.
55. EELLS, WALTER C. *Communism in Education in Asia, Africa and the Far Pacific.* Washington, D.C.: American Council on Education, 1954.
56. ELLICOTT, CHARLES JOHN. *Commentary on the Whole Bible.* 8 vols. Grand Rapids: Zondervan Publishing House, 1954.
57. ENGLISH, HORACE B., and ENGLISH, AVA CHAMPNEY. *A Comprehensive Dictionary of Psychological and Psychoanalytical Terms.* New York: Longmans, Green & Co., 1958.
58. ERICKSON, MILTON H., et al. *The Practical Application of Medical and Dental Hypnosis.* New York: The Julian Press, 1961.
59. ESTABROOKS, G. H. *Hypnotism.* rev. ed. New York: E. P. Dutton & Co., 1943.
60. FAY, JAY WHARTON. *American Psychology Before William James.* New Brunswick, N.J.: Rutgers University Press, 1939.
61. FELTON, RALPH A. *New Ministers.* Madison, N.J.: Drew Theological Seminary, 1949.
62. FERM, ROBERT O. *The Psychology of Christian Conversion.* Westwood, N.J.: Fleming H. Revell Co., 1959.
63. FISHER, MARGUERITE J. *Communist Doctrine and the Free World.* Syracuse: Syracuse University Press, 1952.
64. FOSDICK, HARRY EMERSON. *Great Voices of the Reformation.* New York: Random House, 1952.
65. FRANKL, VIKTOR E. *The Doctor and the Soul.* New York: Alfred A. Knopf, 1955.
66. FREUD, SIGMUND. *The Future of an Illusion.* New York: Doubleday & Co., 1957.
67. _____. *A General Introduction to Psychoanalysis.* New York: Permabooks, 1953.

68. ———. *On Creativity and the Unconscious.* New York: Harper & Bros., 1958.
69. ———. *Totem and Taboo.* New York: Random House, 1946.
70. FROMM, ERIC. *The Art of Loving.* New York: Harper & Row, 1962.
71. ———. *Psychoanalysis and Religion.* New York: Yale University Press, 1950.
72. GAYLE, R. FINLEY, JR. "Conflict Between Psychiatry and Religion," *Pastoral Psychology,* (November, 1956).
73. GERBER, ISRAEL JOSHUA. *The Psychology of the Suffering Mind.* New York: J. David Co., 1951.
74. GILL, MERTON M., and BRENMAN, MARGARET. *Hypnosis and Related States.* New York: International Universities Press, 1959.
75. GLUECK, SHELDON, and GLUECK, ELEANOR. *Predicting Delinquency and Crime.* Cambridge: Harvard University Press, 1959.
76. GURIN, GERALD, VEROFF, JOSEPH, and FELD, SHEILA. *Americans View Their Mental Health.* New York: Basic Books, 1960.
77. HADFIELD, J. A. "The Psychology of Power," *The Spirit,* ed. B. H. STREETER. New York: The Macmillan Co., 1919.
78. HALL, CALVIN S. *Psychology.* Cleveland: Howard Allen, 1960.
79. ———, and LINDZEY, GARDNER. *Theories of Personality.* New York: John Wiley & Sons, 1957.
80. HARDING, M. ESTHER. *Journey into Self.* New York: Longmans, Green & Co., 1956.
81. HAVIGHURST, ROBERT J. *Developmental Tasks and Education.* 2d ed. New York: Longmans, Green & Co., 1952.
82. HERBERG, WILL. *Protestant-Catholic-Jew.* Garden City, N.Y.: Doubleday & Co., 1960.
83. HILL, RALPH NADING. *The Doctors Who Conquered Yellow Fever.* New York: Random House, 1957.
84. HILLWAY, TYRUS. *Introduction to Research.* Boston: Houghton Mifflin Co., 1956.
85. HOFMANN, HANS (ed.). *The Ministry and Mental Health.* New York: Association Press, 1960.
86. HOLLINGSWORTH, LETA A. *Children Above 180 IQ.* New York: World Book Co., 1942.

87. HOOVER, J. EDGAR. *Masters of Deceit*. New York: Holt, Rinehart & Winston, 1958.

88. HUDSON, WINTHROP S. "The Protestant Concept of Motivation for the Ministry," *Conference on Motivation for the Ministry*, comp. SAMUEL SOUTHARD. Louisville: Southern Baptist Theological Seminary, 1959.

89. HULL, CLARK L. *Hypnosis and Suggestibility*. New York: Appleton-Century-Crofts, 1933.

90. HUNT, MORTON M. *The Natural History of Love*. New York: Grove Press, 1959.

91. HUNTER, EDWARD. *Brain-Washing in Red China: The Calculated Destruction of Men's Minds*. New York: The Vanguard Press, 1951.

92. HURLOCK, ELIZABETH B. *Developmental Psychology*. 2d ed. New York: McGraw-Hill Book Co., 1959.

93. HYDE, DOUGLAS. "The Communist Mind," *Vital Speeches*, (July 21, 1955).

94. IKIN, A. GRAHAM. *Religion and Psychotherapy*. London: Rylee, 1948.

95. JAMES, POWHATAN W. *George W. Truett*. rev. ed. Nashville: Broadman Press, 1945.

96. JAMES, T. F. "The Agony of Religious Doubt," *Cosmopolitan*, Vol. 147 (December, 1959).

97. JAMES, WILLIAM. *The Varieties of Religious Experience*. New York: Longmans, Green & Co., 1928.

98. JOHNSON, HEWLETT. *The Soviet Power*. New York: International Publishers, 1941.

99. JOHNSON, PAUL E. *Personality and Religion*. New York: Abingdon Press, 1957.

100. _____. *Psychology of Religion*. rev. ed. Nashville: Abingdon Press, 1959.

101. JONES, ERNEST. *The Life and Work of Sigmund Freud*. 3 vols. New York: Basic Books, 1953.

102. JOSEPH, HELEN HAIRMAN. "The Mask," *Saturday Review*, (August 13,1932).

103. JUNG, C. G. *Modern Man in Search of a Soul*. New York: Harcourt, Brace & Co., 1933.

104. _____. *Psychology and Religion*. New Haven: Yale University Press, 1938.

105. KALTENBORN, H. V. *Fifty Fabulous Years.* New York: G. P. Putnam's Sons, 1950.
106. KELLY, AMY. *Eleanor of Aquitaine and the Four Kings.* New York: Random House, 1957.
107. KEMP, CHARLES F. *The Church: the Gifted and the Retarded Child.* St. Louis: The Bethany Press, 1957.
108. ————. *Physicians of the Soul.* New York: The Macmillan Co., 1947.
109. KINNAIRD, CLARK (ed.). *A Treasury of Damon Runyan.* New York: The Modern Library, 1958.
110. KLUCKHOHN, C., and MURRAY, H. A. (eds.). *Personality in Nature, Society, and Culture.* rev. ed. New York: Alfred A. Knopf, 1953.
111. ————, *et al.* "Values and Value Orientations in a Theory of Action," *Toward a General Theory of Action,* eds. TALCOTT PARSONS and EDWARD A. SHILS. Cambridge: Harvard University Press, 1951.
112. KRAVCHENKO, VICTOR. *I Chose Freedom.* New York: Charles Scribner's Sons, 1946.
113. LEBON, GUSTAVE. *Crowd: A Study of the Popular Mind.* London: T. Fisher Unwin, 1897.
114. LECRON, LESLIE M. (ed.). *Experimental Hypnosis.* New York: The Macmillan Co., 1952.
115. LEDERER, HENRY D. "How the Sick View Their World," *Pastoral Psychology,* VIII (May, 1957).
116. LENSKI, GERHARD. *The Religious Factor.* Garden City, N.Y.: Doubleday & Co., 1963.
117. LESLIE, ROBERT C. "A Discussion of Gotthard Booth's Article and Paper," *Conference on Motivation for the Ministry,* comp. SAMUEL SOUTHARD. Louisville: Southern Baptist Theological Seminary, 1959.
118. LIGON, ERNEST M. *Dimensions of Character.* New York: The Macmillan Co., 1956.
119. LINDNER, ROBERT M. *Rebel Without a Cause.* New York: Grove Press, 1956.
120. LINDSAY, THOMAS M. *A History of the Reformation.* 2 vols. Edinburgh: T. & T. Clark, 1907.
121. LINK, HENRY C. *The Return to Religion.* New York: The Macmillan Co., 1936.

122. LLOYD-JONES, D. MARTIN. *Conversions: Psychological and Spiritual.* Chicago: Inter-Varsity Press, 1959.
123. "A Man of the Century," *Time,* LXXX (November 30, 1962).
124. MARCUSE, F. L. *Hypnosis: Fact and Fiction.* Baltimore: Penquin Books, 1951.
125. MARX, KARL. *The Communist Manifesto.* Chicago: Henry Regnery Co., 1954.
126. MASLOW, A. H. *Motivation and Personality.* New York: Harper & Bros., 1954.
127. MAYER, WILLIAM E. "Why Did Many G.I. Captives Cave In?" *U.S. News and World Report,* XI, (February 24, 1956).
128. MENNINGER, KARL, and MENNINGER, JEANETTA L. *Love Against Hate.* New York: Harcourt, Brace & Co., 1942.
129. MILLER, PERRY. *Jonathan Edwards.* New York: William Sloane Associates, 1949.
130. MOBERG, DAVID O. *The Church As a Social Institution.* Englewood Cliffs, N.J.: Prentice-Hall, 1962.
131. MONTAGU, M. F. ASHLEY. *The Direction of Human Development.* New York: Harper & Bros., 1955.
132. MOWRER, O. HOBART. *The Crisis in Psychiatry and Religion.* Princeton: D. Van Nostrand Co., 1961.
133. MUDD, EMILY H., *et al.* (eds.). *Marriage Counseling: A Casebook.* New York: Association Press, 1958.
134. MUNN, NORMAN LESLIE. *Psychology.* New York: Houghton Mifflin Co., 1946.
135. MURDOCK, WALTER. *Selected Essays.* Sydney, Australia: Angus & Robertson, 1956.
136. MURPHY, G. *Personality: A Biosocial Approach to Origins and Structure.* New York: Harper & Bros. 1947.
137. NIEBUHR, H. RICHARD. *The Social Sources of Denominationalism.* Hamden, Conn.: The Shoe String Press, 1954.
138. _____, WILLIAMS, DANIEL DAY, and GUSTAFSON, JAMES M. *The Advancement of Theological Education.* New York: Harper & Bros., 1957.
139. _____. *The Purpose of the Church and Its Ministry.* New York: Harper & Bros., 1956.
140. NYGREN, ANDERS. *Agape and Eros.* Philadelphia: The Westminster Press, 1953.
141. OATES, WAYNE E. *The Religious Dimensions of Personality.* New York: Association Press, 1957.

142. ———. *Religious Factors in Mental Illness.* New York: Association Press, 1955.
143. OVERSTREET, H. A. *The Mature Mind.* New York: W. W. Norton & Co., 1949.
144. PACKARD, VANCE. *The Hidden Persuaders.* New York: David McKay Co., 1957.
145. PARKER, WILLIAM R., and ST. JOHNS, ELAINE. *Prayer Can Change Your Life.* Englewood Cliffs, N.J.: Prentice-Hall, 1957.
146. "People," *Time,* LXXVI (November 7, 1960).
147. POLGAR, FRANZ J. *The Story of a Hypnotist.* New York: Hermitage House, 1951.
148. POPENOE, PAUL. *If Your Daughter Pets.* Hollywood: American Institute of Family Relations, 1938.
149. PROGOFF, IRA. *The Death and Rebirth of Psychology.* New York: The Julian Press, 1956.
150. "Quiet Healers," *Time,* LXXX (September 28, 1962).
151. REED, JOHN. *Ten Days That Shook the World,* ed. BERTRAM D. WOLFE. New York: Random House, 1960.
152. REIK, THEODOR. *Of Love and Lust.* New York: Grove Press, 1959.
153. RENNIE, THOMAS A. C., and WOODWARD, LUTHER E. *Mental Health in Modern Society.* Cambridge: Harvard University Press, 1946.
154. RIDENOUR, NINA. *Mental Health in the United States: A Fifty-Year History.* Cambridge: Harvard University Press, 1961.
155. ROBBINS, JHAN, and ROBBINS, JUNE. "The Strange Facts About Faith Healing," *Redbook,* (July, 1960).
155a. ROGERS, CARL R. *Client-Centered Therapy.* Boston: Houghton Mifflin Co., 1951.
156. ———. *Counseling and Psychotherapy.* Boston: Houghton Mifflin Co., 1942.
157. ROGERS, HENRY. *The Works of Jonathan Edwards.* 2 vols. London: F. Westley & A. H. Davis, 1835.
158. SARGANT, WILLIAM W. *Battle for the Mind.* Garden City, N.Y.: Doubleday & Co., 1957.
159. SCHWARTZSCHILD, LEOPOLD. *Karl Marx: The Red Prussian.* New York: Grossett & Dunlap, 1947.
160. SHAFFER, LAURANCE FREDERIC, and SHOBEN, EDWARD JOSEPH,

JR. *The Psychology of Adjustment.* 2d ed. Boston: Houghton Mifflin Co., 1956.

161. SHELDON, W. H., STEVENS, S. S., and TUCKER, W. B. *The Varieties of Human Physique.* New York: Harper & Bros., 1940.

162. SHINN, ROGER L. *The Existentialist Posture.* New York: Association Press, 1959.

163. SOUTHARD, SAMUEL, JR. "The Counseling of Candidates for Church Vocations." Unpublished Th.D. thesis, Southern Baptist Theological Seminary, 1953.

164. _____. *Pastoral Evangelism.* Nashville: Broadman Press, 1962.

165. SOUTHEY, ROBERT. *The Life of Wesley and the Rise and Progress of Methodism.* London: Oxford University Press, 1925.

166. "Space," *Time,* LXXIX (March 2, 1962).

167. STACEY, CHALMERS L., and DEMARTINO, MANFRED F. *Understanding Human Motivation.* Cleveland: Howard Allen, 1958.

168. STARBUCK, EDWIN DILLER. *The Psychology of Religion.* London: Walter Scott, 1901.

169. STOLZ, KARL R. *The Church and Psychotherapy.* New York: Abingdon-Cokesbury Press, 1943.

170. _____. *The Psychology of Religious Living.* Nashville: Cokesbury Press, 1937.

171. STONE, IRVING. *The Agony and the Ecstasy.* Garden City, N.Y.: Doubleday & Co., 1961.

172. STRANG, RUTH. *The Role of the Teacher in Personnel Work.* rev. ed. New York: Columbia University Bureau of Publications, 1946.

173. STRECKER, EDWARD A. *Their Mothers' Sons.* New York: J. B. Lippincott Co., 1946.

174. THOMPSON, MORTON. *The Cry and the Covenant.* New York: New American Library, 1960.

175. THORPE, LOUIS P. *The Psychology of Mental Health.* 2d ed. New York: Ronald Press, 1960.

176. THOULESS, ROBERT H. *An Introduction to the Psychology of Religion.* New York: Cambridge University Press, 1923.

176a. _____. *The Psychology of Religion.* New York: Cambridge University Press, 1961.

177. TILLICH, PAUL J. "The Impact of Psychotherapy on Theological

Thought," *Bulletin, Academy of Religion and Mental Health* (1960).

178. TROTSKY, LEON. *Stalin.* New York: Harper & Bros., 1941.

179. UREN, A. RUDOLPH. *Recent Religious Psychology.* New York: Charles Scribner's Sons, 1928.

179a. VAUGHAN, WAYLAND F. *Social Psychology.* New York: Odyssey Press, 1948.

180. VINCENT, CLARK E. *Unmarried Mothers.* New York: Free Press of Glencoe, 1961.

181. WALKER, DONALD E. "Carl Rogers and the Nature of Man," *Journal of Counseling Psychology,* (Summer, 1956).

182. WATSON, J. B. *Behaviorism.* New York: W. W. Norton & Co., 1925.

183. WEATHERHEAD, LESLIE D. *Prescription for Anxiety.* New York: Abingdon Press, 1956.

184. ———. *Psychology, Religion, and Healing.* New York: Abingdon-Cokesbury Press, 1951.

185. WEITZENHOFFER, ANDRE M. *General Techniques of Hypnotism.* New York: Grune & Stratton, 1957.

185a. WILLIAMSON, WILLIAM CROFT (ed.). *John Knox's History of the Reformation in Scotland.* London: Thomas Nelson & Sons, 1949.

186. WILLIAMSON, WILLIAM P. "Relationship of Christian Faith to Health," *The Journal of the Omaha Midwest Clinical Society,* Vol. 22 (March, 1961).

187. WITTKOFSKI, JOSEPH. *The Pastoral Use of Hypnotic Technique.* New York: The Macmillan Co., 1961.

188. WOLBERG, LEWIS R. *Medical Hypnosis.* 2 vols. New York: Grune & Stratton, 1948, 1949.

189. YOUNG, RICHARD K., and MEIBURG, ALBERT L. *Spiritual Therapy.* New York: Harper & Bros., 1960.

Acknowledgments

Quotations from the following items in the numbered bibliography were used by permission of the publisher or author: 7, 16, 35, 39, 93, 96, 100, 102, 127, 155, 160, 177, 179. The quotation from item number 35 was reprinted by permission of the author and the author's agent, Scott Meredith Literary Agency, Inc.

Acknowledgment is also made to Hodder & Stoughton Ltd. for permission to use "The Psychologist" by G. A. Studdert-Kennedy, and to Anna Russell for permission to use her "Psychiatric Folk Song."

Index